A Theology of Mission

Challenges and Opportunities in Northeast Asia

Gaylan Kent Mathiesen

Lutheran University Press
Minneapolis, Minnesota

A Theology of Mission
Challenges and Opportunities in Northeast Asia
Gaylan Kent Mathiesen

Copyright © 2006 by Gaylan Kent Mathiesen. All rights reserved.
Published by Lutheran University Press, an imprint of 1517 Media.

Library of Congress Cataloging-in-Publication Data

Mathiesen, Gaylan Kent.
  A theology of mission : challenges and opportunities in Northeast Asia / Gaylan Kent Mathiesen.
      p. cm.
  Includes bibliographical references.
  ISBN-13: 978-1-932688-26-9 (alk. paper)
  ISBN-10: 1-932688-26-9 (alk. paper)
  eISBN: 978-1-942304-38-8
  1. Missions—Theory. 2. Missions—Asia. 3. Asia—Religion. 4. Christianity—Asia. 5. Buddhism—Asia. I. Title.
  BV2063.M39 2007
  266.0095—dc22
                                              2007027333

Table of Contents

List Of Abbreviations 4

Preface 5

1. Introduction: A Theological Foundation 7
   Missio Dei 9
   Ecclesia Dei 27
   Regnum Dei 34

2. Rooting the Message in Culture: Models of Contextualization 47

3. Buddhism as a Missions Movement in Northeast Asia 69
   Buddhism in Korea 88
   Buddhism in Japan 98
   Chapter Summary 109

4. Early Christian Missions in Northeast Asia 111
   The Jesuits: Accommodation 125
   The Protestants: Gospel of Power 152
   Chapter Summary 172

5. Conclusion 174

Works Cited 191
Endnotes 197
Acknowledgements 223

List of Abbreviations

AC	Augsburg Confession
Ap	Apology of the Augsburg Confession
BC	Book of Concord
BCC	The Buddhist Conquest of China: The Spread and Adaptation of Buddhism in Early Medieval China
BIC	Buddhism in China: A Historical Survey
CBC	Confucius, the Buddha, and Christ: A History of the Gospel in Chinese
CT	Contextualization of Theology: An Evangelical Assessment
CTB	The Chinese Transformation of Buddhism
EBCK	Early Buddhism and Christianity in Korea: A Study in the Emplantation of Religion
GCK	Gospel, Church, and Kingdom: Comparative Studies in World Mission Theology
HCA I	A History of Christianity in Asia, Volume I: Beginnings to 1500
HCA II	A History of Christianity in Asia, Volume II: 1500-1900
HCM	A History of Christian Missions
HJB	A History of Japanese Buddhism
LC	Large Catechism
MW	Mission on the Way: Issues in Mission Theology
OUJR	On Understanding Japanese Religion
PPK	Protestant Pioneers in Korea
RIC	Religion in China
RW	Religions of the World
SA	Smalcald Articles
TM	Transforming Mission: Paradigm Shifts in Theology of Mission
TPG	Theology of the Pain of God

Preface

Chapter 1 presents a theology of mission utilizing a triad of *missio Dei*, *ecclesia Dei* and *regnum Dei*. It incorporates Old and New Testament texts, and an examination of mission practice in the Early Church, Reformation and post-Reformation periods up to the present day. Mission work of *ecclesia Dei* must find its grounding and source in *missio Dei*, with its goal located in *regnum Dei*. Chapter 2 explores various theories of contextualization, while asking how *ecclesia Dei* should respond to and collaborate with *missio Dei*. Certain terms have become critical in guiding missiological praxis, such as: contextualization, indigenization, enculturation, inculturation and incarnation. Chapter 2 defines these terms, discussing their theological underpinnings while examining the ecclesial and theological location of these diverse approaches.

Chapters 3 and 4 cover Buddhism and Christianity as missions movements in China, Korea and Japan, and examines the challenges and opportunities for each.

CHAPTER ONE

A Theological Foundation

The missionary movement of which we are a part has its source in the Triune God Himself.
International Missionary Council, Willingen, July 1952[1]

In spite of a great outlay of human and material resources over the centuries, why have we still not seen greater receptivity to the gospel in Northeast Asia? The other imported religion of major significance, *viz*, Buddhism, has created a home there, while Christianity, with few exceptions,[2] is still the alien stranger standing outside the gate. In my own personal ministry among the people of Japan, this conundrum presented itself as much more than an academic exercise. It has long been, and still is, a troubling question that lies behind ecclesiological and theological praxis throughout the region for both pastors and missionaries. As those called to proclaim the gospel in Northeast Asia ponder the role of the Church in *missio Dei*, they face a seemingly impregnable wall of a culture that is highly resistant to their message.

This first chapter will initially tackle this problem by employing the following theological categories: *missio Dei, ecclesia Dei,* and *regnum Dei*. Our exploration will very briefly lay out the salient elements of the biblical, doctrinal and theological interpretation which undergirds the triad. We will then move quickly through early Church history, and afterward examine a bit more closely how the Reformers interpreted and acted upon this triad. After establishing such a foundation, we will look critically into the content of the current debate. It is my contention that an understanding of this triad is vital for any serious consideration of mission—past, present or future.[3] Where does mission originate? What is its goal? What is God's intent for the Church in the realization of this goal? As God comes into the world in love, what does His coming look like? Where does one find God's presence and how does one discern and build upon that presence? These are all-important questions for any articulation of mission, and these questions will serve as the foci for our exploration.

Working from this theological underpinning, the remainder of the investigation will move on to examine the religio-historical context of Northeast Asia. John M. L. Young wrote that by 800 AD, there were more Christians east of Damascus than west.[4] Unfortunately, Young does not cite his evidence for this statement. A. Mingana, who did major work in the twentieth century on the history of the Church of the East, and is one of the sources that appears in Young's woirk, says of this time and period,

> We cannot attempt here to give even a rough estimate of the number of Christians who in ancient times inhabited the zone extending from about the center of modern Persia as far as the end of the continent of Asia, and with the sources at our disposal such an estimate would be well nigh impossible, but there seems to be no exaggeration in asserting that there were Christians scattered in almost all the innumerable districts of this immense territory, and that they were in rather considerable strength in some specified towns or localities.[5]

By the year 1000, the Nestorians had moved through central Asia into China, parts of India, Thailand, and Burma. Nestorian Christianity was dominant between the Caspian Sea and the borders of China. Ruth Tucker says that that twelve million were associated with this church, spread out through two hundred and fifty dioceses. She writes, "Their influence continued to grow, and by the thirteenth century it is estimated that there were no less than twenty-seven metropolitan patriarchs and two hundred bishops under them in China and surrounding areas."[6] David Barrett adds that this represented 24% of all Christians in the world at that time, and over 6% of the population of Asia.[7]

The Church in this region has a rich and interesting history, and yet has repeatedly found herself on the verge of extinction. What important lessons does this remarkable context hold for the krugma?[8] In pursuit of an answer to this question, our investigation will take in a broad sweep of Northeast Asia but it will then narrow our specific attention to the context of Japan, since that is the primary focus of this thesis and the framework of my own personal experience.

Our use of a triadic model follows the pattern of several such models that have surfaced over the years. According to James A. Scherer, Martin Luther employed such a triad consisting of Word, Church, and Believer.[9] Karl Barth in his work, *Church and State*, wrote of the heavenly *polis* reflecting its light to the earthly *polis* via the earthly *ecclesia*.[10] Charles Van Engen also constructs his theology around a similar model consisting of sacred text, missional community, and contextual community.[11] Thus, the expression of mission through means of a theological triad is nothing new or novel. Van Engen cites over twenty other scholars of mission since 1960 who have done something similar.[12]

It is my goal, through utilizing such a model, to build a biblical paradigm for addressing contemporary questions regarding mission. This paradigm will place the ground and the consummation of mission squarely with God himself (*missio Dei*), giving validity to the essential role of the Church (*ecclesia Dei*), the Body of Christ, as His chief instrument. These two aspects (*missio Dei* and *ecclesia Dei*) will then link to the divine goal of the fullness of God's Kingdom reign (*regnum Dei*), which will in turn inform our thinking in regards to the "how" of mission in the present. Although it may seem that the triad calls for a linear movement, it will soon become apparent that these separate parts function in a sort of horizontal co-dependency. Just as the equal but different aspects of the Trinity resist subordination, so these different aspects of *missio Dei*, *ecclesia Dei* and *regnum Dei* resist subordination.[13] Consequently, the importance for *ecclesia Dei* in the triad rests in the "of God" aspect of "Church of God." God is intimately involved in this whole process. He invites us—the beloved bride of Christ—to follow alongside and join Him in drawing the world to Himself. In this way, the entire activity of God takes on an incarnational quality, first in His own incarnation, and then in His involving us, His children, in His mission.

Missio Dei

In debating the role of the Church in mission in light of *missio Dei*, many have proposed that mission is not something that the Church undertakes, like an "add-on;" rather, it is mission that constitutes the Church.[14] The intent of such a statement is to remove the Church as the *ground and source* of mission, and instead to root mission back in the Trinity. A portion of the task in this book will be to demonstrate that the best solution to the problem of defining the role of the Church in God's mission is not to be found in an "either/or" approach to the problem; the solution is found, rather, in the "both/and" approach. That is, while the *missio Dei* concept rightly places the ground and source of mission in the Trinity, this need not, and in truth *does not* render the Church in any way unnecessary or irrelevant to the task. While the statement "mission constitutes the Church" may be true, the very fact implies that the Church properly responds to *missio Dei* by living out the gospel before a watching world in both presence and proclamation. God's divine calling for the Church is to image Him before the world; indeed this task is, in large part, the Church's very *raison d'etre*. Consequently, not to undertake mission indicates a clear act of disobedience to this calling. In light of this reality, I will treat mission as an all encompassing doctrine which gives meaning to, and which is inseparable from, ecclesiology. As Georg F. Vicedom wrote, "...the Bible in its totality ascribes only one intention to God: to save mankind."[15] Mission, then, is not an added function of the Church, but rather, the fundamental work of God in revealing His love and mercy to the world through the Church.[16] Aram I affirms this conviction, and adds that mission is an expression of God's very nature, revealing His plan for the world. "...first, mission is not the church's 'mandate' but God's 'initiative'—it belongs to God, it is *missio Dei*. Moreover, mission is not *one of the functions* of the Church—it is the *esse*, and *the* action of the Church by which the Church becomes fully and authentically itself."[17] Here again, there is a danger of being forced into an "either/or" paradigm, except that Aram I is correct in so far as the authority for mission rests not in the Church, but in the One who calls the Church into mission. His statement is true precisely because the Church is called of God to collaborate with Him in reconciling the world to Himself, toward the ultimate goal of "Thy Kingdom come, Thy will be done." In this light, even the nurture and care of God's flock on earth takes on a mission perspective to that end. Alleviation of poverty, racial reconciliation, issues of political power and economics are all swept up in the *missio Dei* calling, and are laid upon the Church *as God's agent in the world*, that all might have the opportunity to enter into the fullness of God's Kingdom. While saying this, we must keep in mind that the mission and the Kingdom, though related, are not the same. Although mission will take into account the whole person in the above social emphases, the intended outcome is to resolve the alienation between humanity and God, evidenced in repentance (metanoia) and conversion of the whole person—a turning to God.[18]

One immediately encounters this picture of God's initiative in mission in the creation story of Genesis. After Adam and Eve assert their own will apart from God's stated will for them, the Creator comes upon them while walking in His garden and calls to them, "Adam, where are you?" The question is not an inquiry into Adam's whereabouts in time and space. Instead, it appears to be a question for Adam's sake; and the question's purpose is to cause Adam and Eve to acknowledge their now alienated condition. Humanity has fallen out of sync with their God, with His universe, and with each other (cf. Gen. 2:25 with 3:7-8). The Creator God becomes the Seeking God, as He actively takes the initiative in winning back His now estranged creation. Unlike the "Divine Clockmaker" of Deism who has wound the clock and left the universe to itself, the God of the Bible personally engages His human creation. The Transcendent becomes Immanent. The Seeking God comes to His first couple not with a plan of destruction, but with a saving message, the *protoevangelium*.[19] In Gen. 3:15, God makes a promise that there will be a future encounter, where the offspring of the woman will triumph over the offspring of the serpent—a prophetic statement of a plan by which God will remedy the fall of His creation and defeat evil. Good and evil in this story is not dualistic; righteousness will surely win out over evil. This promise resulted from an encounter between Eve and a serpent, "more crafty than any of the wild animals the LORD God made." However, there is more going on here than an innocent but astute animal having a theological discussion with the woman. It would seem that Satan has wrapped himself in the serpent in order to deceive and entice God's couple into disobedience. God addresses the serpent saying that He will, "put enmity between you and the woman, and between your offspring and hers; he will crush your head, and you will strike his heel." Here is the first indication of *missio Dei*. God immediately puts His plan into effect, whereby He promises that the defeat of the offspring of the serpent-tempter will come through the "seed" of the woman. How strange to speak of the "seed" of a woman, a term that is normally reserved for the male species. And yet we know that there is One who descended from this woman's offspring, whose conception came about apart from any human male. The plan of God is reflected in the manner Genesis 3:15 continues, "he will crush your head." The New Testament Gospels bear witness to this, as God the Father sends God the Son by the work of God the Holy Spirit through the flesh of a woman—the incarnation of God. The writer to the Hebrews said, "Since the children have flesh and blood, he too shared in their humanity so that by his death he might destroy him who holds the power of death—and free those who all their life were held in slavery by their fear of death" (Heb 2:15).

There is a fascinating movement in this process within the Triune God, whereby in essence *God sends Himself* to earth through the incarnation—Father God sending God the Son as God the Holy Spirit quickens the seed of the woman and empowers her offspring, Jesus, who in the process has set aside His own powers through the *kenosis* (Phil 2:6-8). All the persons of the Trinity are proactively involved in this process of divine sending and coming. The baptism of Jesus dramatically illustrates this activity for us when the voice of God the Father speaks from heaven, and God the Spirit descends as a dove to rest upon God the Son in a sort of anointing/commissioning for His earthly mission. Clearly, the Triune God took the initiative in revealing His plan for winning back His rebellious creation.

This divine plan, first glimpsed in Genesis 3:15, develops further in God's spoken covenant and is repeated to Abram (to become Abraham) in Genesis chapters 12, 15 and 17. The seed of Abraham will be blessed and the seed of Abraham will in turn bless "all the peoples on earth" (12:3). God's choice of Abraham is a divine and gracious choosing, but it is also a choosing with a specific purpose and intent. Utilizing the covenant form, God chooses Abraham and his seed *out from* the nations, but He also chooses them as a witness or light *to* the nations.[20] The "*to*" element consists of the duty of Abraham and his descendants to give loving service *to* God and their neighbors. This is, moreover, not any choosing of a privileged elite based on any merit in themselves. On the contrary, He is purposely choosing them *despite* their composition. God made it clear He was choosing a small, obstinate, stubborn and rebellious people (Deut. 7:7; Ezek. 2:4-5) through whom He would display His power and glory. One can see this revealed in the graciously patient *process* that God applied to Abraham, evident, in Abraham's early act of going to Egypt and prostituting his own wife in order to save himself from harm, an act that even the "pagan" Pharaoh condemned (Gen. 12:10-20). Throughout all time, this same God is working His process of *missio Dei* through very weak and fallible human instruments.

In this peculiar manner, God is engaging His world through His chosen people. The writings and the prophets refer back to this promise and plan of God. The Psalmist wrote, for example, "Declare his glory among the nations, make his deeds known to all peoples" (Ps. 96:3). Through the prophet Isaiah God extended to Israel His call to be His instrument to bless the Gentiles (Isa. 42:6 49:6)." For example, "It is too small a thing for you," says the Lord, "to restore the tribes of Jacob and to gather Israel..." Instead, God's plan is, "I will make you a light to the Gentiles (Isa. 49:6)." This tells us that the grace extended to Israel by God was indeed a gift given; they did not earn it. Neither was it something to which they alone were to lay claim as only a private possession.[21] This point of claim becomes an important part of the discussion in C. S. Song's work, *The Compassionate God*.[22] Israel was to be God's conduit to the world, a vessel through which He manifested His glory to all peoples, a role now performed by the Church—the spiritual sons and daughters of Abraham (Rom. 9:8).

However, in spite of the ravages of sinful human nature and frailty, God accomplishes His purposes. The Old Testament is replete with examples of God reaching out to the nations through His weak human vessels. We have Melchizedek, Ruth, Rahab, Naaman, Uriah and many others who were drawn into the gathering of God's chosen people. An intriguing example of this is that of Naaman in II Kgs. 5. One cannot help but wonder what went through the minds of early Hebrews as they heard the first verse of that chapter read, where the writer gave an account of how the Lord gave victory *to Aram* (Syria) over Samaria through Naaman, commander of the Aramean forces. Even today, the alert reader must wonder, "What is God up to here?"

The rest of the account is equally riveting; on one of the border raids, a young Hebrew girl is taken captive and given to Naaman's wife as a servant. Through the mouth of this young girl (who is not named in the text) via his wife, Naaman learns that a prophet in Samaria can cure his skin disease. The story then quickly unfolds as God brings Naaman down to meet the prophet. We soon find Naaman healed not only in body but also in heart. First, God restores his skin to that of a young boy (this statement parallels in structure the reference to the Hebrew girl). Naaman then makes the remarkable monotheistic confession that he now knows that "there is no God in all the world except in Israel (II Kgs. 5:15)." This is a remarkable conversion.

What follows is intriguing as Naaman asks for bags of soil to bring back to Damascus (Is the purpose in this to build an altar for worship? Gerhard von Rad does not think so.[23] Nonetheless, the idea of God being tied to the land of Israel, at least in regards to being worshiped, has validity and is supported by others.)²⁴ Elisha then finds himself confronting a classic missiological problem as Naaman asks for Yahweh's mercy, worried that upon his return, his king may force him to bow before the idol of Rimmon. Rather than giving Naaman a catechetical lesson on the first commandment, Elisha entrusts Naaman to God and gives the blessing of peace (*sha-lōm*) to this representative of the enemy of Israel. The following scene of Gehazi greedily running after Naaman's chariot further underscores the significance of this. Our English translation has Naaman asking Gehazi, "Is everything all right (5:21)?" However, the Hebrew wording has Naaman asking if the *sha-lōm* (peace) is still in force (*vaiy-yō-mer hᵃsha-lōm-* "He said, 'Is there peace?'"). Richard Nelson comments in *Interpretation*, "Gehazi appears out of nowhere to serve as a foil to Naaman's conversion. He is faithless and greedy whereas Naaman is faithfully generous...Naaman's question whether the "shalom" is still in force (v.21) and Gehazi's insistence that it is...actually is in itself a sign that shalom has been broken!"²⁵ Because Gehazi has disturbed this God-given "peace," the Lord now passes the leprosy of Naaman on to Gehazi. The lesson from this passage appears to be twofold: (1) let humans beware of interfering with *missio Dei*, and (2) Gehazi's greed for personal benefit from an act of God's grace resulted in his losing even what he first had. One can see immediately a parallel with the parable of the talents, as the master said to the servant who buried his talent, "Whoever does not have, even what he has will be taken from him. And throw that wicked servant outside, into the darkness, where there will be weeping and gnashing of teeth."

This passage in II Kings 5 becomes especially interesting when connected to the startling reference that Jesus makes to it in Luke 4. In this passage, Jesus is in the synagogue instructing the Jews, and He has just read an account of his divine calling from Isaiah 61. Through the prophecy of Isaiah, He announces that He has come to bind the brokenhearted, to open the eyes of the blind, to comfort the prisoner and to proclaim the year of the Lord's Jubilee.²⁶ After this, Jesus refers to a foreign widow whom God fed, when others in Israel were starving. He follows this with a reference to the healing of the leper Naaman, the Syrian, when other lepers in Israel were not healed. The effect was immediate: His listeners wanted to kill Jesus on the spot. Jesus had openly challenged their claim that *missio Dei* exclusively included Israel. To the contrary, Jesus would teach Israel that they were to *embrace* the nations rather than *despise* them.

There is a dramatic "breaking out" of the *Missio Dei* in the New Testament. What has been a mostly passive and centripetal role for Israel in the Old Testament is increasingly becoming centrifugal in Jesus and those who follow him.[27] There is an interesting dialectical movement here, as Jesus is very particular in some of His statements to the disciples. For example, "Go only to the house of Israel." Then we later read of Jesus being agreeable to entering into the homes of Gentiles, ministering in "Galilee of the Gentiles" and so on. He will heal Jairus' daughter in secret, but for the woman on the periphery of society who had the issue of blood, He heals her openly in public.[28] This action "on the periphery" is a theme that frequently appears in the writing of Kosuke Koyama,[29] illustrating what Koyama calls the "crucified mind," the giving of self to those who usually fall through the cracks of society.[30]

The book of Acts is even more forceful in this "breaking out" of the *missio Dei*. On the day of Pentecost, those from all the surrounding regions are hearing the gospel in their own language. God is speaking through his servants, and these visitors from afar are hearing Him in their own tongue. It is an unusual display that some observers can only attribute to alcohol—a charge that the disciples reject by referring them to the prophet Joel in his prophecy of the last days. These initial members of the Early Church are to wait for the outpouring of the Holy Spirit, and they are to go into the entire world with the gospel—both in Jerusalem, and in Judea (E-1), to Samaria (E-2) and to the uttermost parts of the earth (E-3).[31] The nations *will* be blessed through Abraham's seed. Since this is the purpose and will of God, it will *certainly* happen. It is God's mission, grounded, rooted and acted out from within Himself, and through His chosen means: the Church. There is no allowance for the early Christians in Jerusalem to keep the kerygma to themselves; in fact, through a persecution of believers in Acts 8, all except the apostles were scattered, and as they went about, these relocated believers, "preached the word wherever they went (Acts 8:4)." Here is the priesthood of believers in active response to *missio Dei*, the saving activity of God revealed in his *missio*, or "sending."

The early Church, which was very Jewish in nature, is then compelled to undergo a type of conversion. Are the Gentiles to be included in the gracious activity of God? If so, how is the Church to deal with this? Do the Gentiles have to keep the Law of Moses, or not? Just how is God going to incorporate them into Israel? Bosch made the assertion that we do not see a foundation for mission in the Old Testament. He further accused those who see such a foundation as being "miners" in search of "gold nuggets." He saw no indication in the Old Testament of God sending out a missionary cross culturally, even in Jonah, since Jonah went not with good news but with judgment, condemnation, and no desire to see Nineveh spared.[32] If we limit our understanding of mission to the traditional view of preachers going to distant places, perhaps we do not have "mission" in the Old Testament. Paradoxically, at the same time, Bosch called the God of the Old Testament a "missionary par excellence."[33] In much of what Bosch writes about this, he may be correct, as far as he goes, but he is also inadequate. Since he is selective in what he sees as mission in the Old Testament, one could even consider his method a bit Marcionite. We must look in the Old Testament not for cross-cultural preachers, but for *the saving activity of God*. The evidences in the Old Testament for *missio Dei* are more than a few sparse "nuggets." What we have is a lode of gold that runs all through the Scriptures. It widens and becomes only more glorious in the New Testament. The important thing is to view mission through the lens of the *activity of God*, rather than viewing it as strictly human enterprise. There is much in the Old Testament that can inform theology from the standpoint of mission. The Old Testament patriarchs, for example, can say much about how to live among people of other faiths.[34] The people of God amongst many peoples of gods produce the dynamic that drives the unfolding drama.

Roland Allen supports the continuity of the Old Testament with the New Testament by citing the synagogue preaching of Paul. Commenting specifically on Paul's sermon at Thessalonica, Allen writes,

> The sermon is divided into three parts by dramatic appeals to the attention of his hearers. In the first, St Paul builds upon the past history of the Jewish race and shows that his Gospel is rooted there, that in his message there is no casting away of the things familiar, no denial of the truth of the old revelation made to the Fathers; but rather that the whole history of Israel is the divinely ordered preparation for the new revelation in the Messiah.[35]

As we approach the New Testament, God's expression of *missio Dei* also undergoes some transformation, and this is another place where Bosch shows his inadequacy. Bosch, and Paul Bowers as well, see the Church in much the same way as they view Israel in regards to mission.[36] They view the

Church as only a passive agent in the process (reminiscent of the classical Calvinist extension theology, or limited atonement, that has informed Protestant activity in the past, often resulting in a lack of mission initiative[37]). According to them, while Paul and others are out planting churches and proclaiming the good news, the role of the Church is simply to be winsome. The Church is to evidence a transformed lifestyle before a watching world in order to enhance, and not hinder, the gospel proclamation by Paul and others with similar special calling. Bosch is clear that the vocation of the average Christian is not proclamation, but only lifestyle evangelism.[38] Only the specially called, gifted, and equipped are to have an active role in declaring the saving gospel. The Church as a whole is not moving outward, but is in a receiving position—receiving those whom the select few have won over. This is, again, a largely centripetal, rather than centrifugal movement, more reminiscent of Old Testament Israel than what we commonly attribute to the New Testament Church.

P. T. O'Brien counters Bosch's position in the following manner: Paul certainly exemplifies an unusual missionary approach in his scope and method. O'Brien acknowledges that few will have a ministry of outreach on the level of the Apostle Paul. Moreover, he agrees that Paul indeed makes very little reference to the Church doing proactive outreach to unbelieving neighbors. One might ask, is this because the Church was doing so well in outreach that there was no need for Paul to comment on their participation in mission? Though Michael Green and others make this argument, O'Brien believes this is not the likely reason. We should not be looking for any calling of the Church to a mimicking of Paul's *overt methods*, but instead we should, and do, find a calling to his deep appreciation for what Jesus did for us on the cross, and his *passion (like that of God's heart) for reaching the lost*. In fact, Paul is very clear in calling the church to "imitate" him (e.g. I Cor. 11:1).[39] O'Brien maintains that when Paul calls for imitation, it is always in the context of his passion for winning the lost, "that they may be saved." The salvation of others is of primary importance to Paul, as he calls the Church to participate fully in the *missio Dei*.[40] If the Church is passionate in its zeal for the glory of Jesus Christ, and carries a burden of heart for the lost, then indeed there will be no need to exhort the Church to go out and bear bold witness to the gospel. Instead, such a witness will be an expected and natural outcome of a Pauline, or better yet, Christlike passion for this lost world. In other words, O'Brien is saying that far from calling the Church to a *passive* involvement in *missio Dei*, Paul is exhorting the believers to imitate him in his *passion* for reaching the lost. Method is secondary to passion. If the passion is there, there will be no need to exhort anyone to a particular method. Perhaps it is confusion on this very issue that has propelled one wing of the Church today to a listless passivity in regards to mission, and the other wing to an obsession with method. Both wings are missing Paul's point: viewing lost sheep with the passion of the Good Shepherd, resulting in the whole Church actively engaged in witness.

O'Brien brings up another aspect that has even greater import to our discussion. When speaking of the advance of gospel outreach, Paul does not root this advance in the actions of humans or even in the Church; instead, he speaks of the "advance of the gospel" implying that the gospel moves forward *in its own power*. Accordingly, rather than saying that the *Church* is advancing; Paul says that it is the *gospel* that is advancing. This, says O'Brien, could be another reason why Paul is not often speaking in terms that would give the Church high visibility in this process.[41] In making this point, O'Brien does not play down the role of the Church, but instead exalts the glory of the gospel of Jesus Christ. This same gospel is "the power of God unto salvation to everyone who believes... (Rom. 1:16)."

Bosch and Bowers are missing the thrust of Paul's letters in seeing him argue for the chuch to be passive about evangelism and missiom. On the contrary, says O'Brien, Paul calls the Church to *greater passion* for mission and offers himself as a model for such passion. At the same time, Paul does not root the power of the gospel in the Church, but roots it back into the message of *missio Dei* itself: the good news of salvation in the One who has been sent, the person of Jesus Christ. *Missio Dei* informs Paul's theology, which in turn produces his passion for ministry. Thus, as Paul calls the Church to greater passion for the spread of the gospel, he gives the gospel—not the Church—the limelight.

As we reach the close of the New Testament, there is yet another vivid depiction of all aspects of mission being, firstly, God's own mission. In exile on the isle of Patmos, John is the recipient of a glorious vision. John is a man whom the world has battered; the emperor is severely persecuting the church, and John sees a God-given vision of a victorious and glorious Christ. What is the purpose of this vision? It is because God wants John to know who truly reigns, and who is moving world events to a specific *telos*. Essentially, in spite of the Church's sufferings, and all apparent evidence to the contrary, God reigns. The tree of life first appears in Genesis, and it does not appear again until chapter 22 of Revelation. What God started in the Garden, He will finish in the Holy City in the *eschaton*. The contents of Revelation also serve to remind us that God's plan of salvation for the world, or *missio Dei*, is steadily moving along a divinely orchestrated timeline, and that God's people will continue to have a role in the working out of history to its culmination.

Though the first coming of Christ at that time did not bring the anticipated end of the age, it was nonetheless a "Day of the Lord" kind of event, in that God came to us in Jesus Christ. Jürgen Moltmann calls the coming of Jesus an eschatological event because Christ's coming ushered in a major change in how God's people will relate to Him. Moltmann explains, saying, "the central place of the Torah in late Jewish apocalyptic is thus taken by the person and the cross of Christ. The place of life in the law is taken by fellowship with Christ in the following of the crucified one. The place of the self-preservation of the righteous from the world is taken by the mission of the believer to the world...the universal future of the lordship of the crucified Christ over all is spotlighted in the Easter appearances."[42]

Though the expectancy of the end was present in the people of God at that time, the perception that the Early Church was obsessed with this "awaiting at the end" (*Naherwartung*) is likely an exaggerated one.[43] Nevertheless, the forward-looking expectancy of the early Church played a significant role then, and now, in our view of mission.[44] There is still, after 2,000 years, a sense of urgency in God's people that the world must be prepared for Christ's immanent return. ("Marana tha." I Cor. 16:22b)

This brings us to another significant thought in the doctrine of *missio Dei*: mission is future-oriented. (Moltmann expresses this forward-looking movement vividly in his *Theology of Hope*.) *Missio Dei*, rather than rooting itself backward in a past creation, is forward-looking to the new and coming creation. Just as a sapling does not cause one to contemplate the seed, but rather the sapling's future as a shade tree, so the Church of Jesus Christ points to the fullness of the Kingdom of God still to come. The future element was strong not only in the New Testament Church, but in the Early Church Fathers as well. Consider, for example, the letter written to the Church of Rome by Ignatius as he journeyed to his martyrdom. "Not the wide bounds of earth nor the kingdoms of this world will avail me anything. I would rather die and get to Jesus Christ than reign over the ends of the earth. That is whom I am looking for—the One who died for us. That is whom I want—the One who rose for us...I do not want to live anymore on a human plane."[45] Whereas we are now experiencing the "already" of God's reign, we look forward to the culmination of the "not yet."[46] The Bible speaks of a present experience of salvation and God's Kingdom, and nevertheless makes it clear that this experience is not yet complete. According to Romans 8, for example, the fullness of salvation for the physical body is still future. "But if Christ is in you, your body is dead because of sin, yet your spirit is alive because of righteousness. And if the Spirit of him who raised Christ from the dead is living in you, he who raised Christ from the dead will also give life to your mortal bodies through his Spirit who lives in you...we ourselves, who have the firstfruits of the Spirit, groan inwardly as we wait eagerly for our adoption as sons, the redemption of our bodies (Rom. 8:10, 11, 24)." Our "earthly tent" groans in waiting for the fullness of things yet to come. This hope of the promises of the Kingdom of God is a motivating factor for the life and mission of the Church. For Charles Van Engen, the close association of the Church with the Kingdom of God contributes a dynamism that propels the Church forward, from the already to the not yet. In discussing this concept, Van Engen is careful to move the focus of mission away from "human effort," but at the same time, he sees the Church as having an important role in *missio Dei*. Referring to this emerging Church, Van Engen writes,

> It can never be more fully complete than it is as the one holy catholic and apostolic people of God. Yet the Church is called to grow toward greater fullness in its nature. In this dialectic tension between what is and what is to become, the Church's position in the Kingdom infuses it with a unique quality to emerge as the mysterious creation of God, created not by human effort, but by Jesus Christ through the operation of the Spirit...The Church, like a seed, already contains within itself the generative power necessary to become the plant of which it is seed.[47]

Karl Barth made a point of the future orientation of *missio Dei*, asking if the New Testament anywhere shows any interest in this present world as God's creation, except with regards to the fact that its very grounding, existence, and restoration is found in the person and work of Jesus Christ. Precisely because of this fact, should we not direct our hope forward, to that coming age of the reign of Christ, rather than thinking backward, and abstractly, about creation and how God bonds us to himself through it?[48] The question then becomes not where has God *been*, but rather where is He *going*, and where is He leading us? Essentially, the *telos* informs how one should offer oneself to *missio Dei*. What will the future bring in the economy of God's salvation plan? How does *ecclesia Dei* figure in to that plan?

Justin Martyr's (A.D. 110-165) answer to this question was to establish a connection between Christianity and Greek philosophy. Employing the vocabulary of the Stoic, Justin saw God working in the world through the *logos spermatikos*, or seminal *Logos*. Justin aligned himself with philosophy, seeing in it a great God-given tool.[49] Though he may not have been directing his writings to the people outside of the church, he was in fact developing a self-expression of his own view on mission.[50] He could see the *Logos* at work in Socrates, Plato and Aristotle. In his thinking, all who came before the time of Christ—as far as they aligned themselves with truth—were participating in the *Logos*. The Church councils would later judge Justin's views regarding the doctrine of the person of Christ as inadequate, but he played an important role in developing an inclusive apologetic.[51] Clement of Alexandria and Irenaeus, among others, would follow in that vein, and today we can see seeds of thought from these men resurfacing in contemporary theologians.[52] The contribution of Origen would include an interesting eschatology that even would allow for the redemption of the devil and his demons.

Augustine brought a particularity and individuality to this discussion. Until the fifth century, the "*extra ecclesiam nulla salus*" phrase found in Origen, Cyprian, and others had been employed primarily in reference to those who were led away from the one true Church through heresy or schism. Church leadership applied it increasingly to those who never were a part of the Church after the fifth century. In practice, the leaders of the Church saw the fulfillment of the Great Commission as a responsibility only within their realms, and they judged those who were outside and had never heard the gospel as stubborn, resistant and deserving of hell.

As we come to the time of the Reformation, there is still a territorial mentality regarding the work of *missio Dei*. James A. Scherer comments as follows in the *Evangelical Dictionary of World Missions*:

> A highly restricted view of mission prevailed during the

period of Lutheran orthodoxy (1580-1675). Lutheran rulers were obligated to evangelize their non-Christian subjects (Jews, Muslims, pagans), but any wider applicability of the GREAT COMMISSION was in effect denied. The Lutheran theological faculty at Wittenberg in 1651 maintained that Lutherans had no obligation to send missionaries beyond their territories to convert the heathen, as Jesuits and other Catholics had done. A Lutheran layman, Justinian Welz (1621-68), who proposed a new Protestant society for sending missionaries overseas, was condemned as a heretic.[53]

Yet, it is important to note with Scherer that Luther also believed and taught that every baptized believer was responsible to preach the gospel; as long as there are those who are not yet saved, it is the responsibility of every believer to proclaim the gospel in word and deed.[54]

Johannes Verkuyl has defined mission as, "the study of the salvation activities of the Father, Son and Holy Spirit throughout the world geared toward bringing the kingdom of God into existence."[55] Gisbertus Voetius, a Calvinist, was perhaps the first to use the concept of *missio Dei* in the way that we understand it today. He also advocated the preaching of the gospel to the "Gentiles" and used the doctrine of mission in a very broad sense, which included the renewal of lukewarm churches, the healing of factions etc., as well as the need to bring the good news to those who had not yet heard.[56]

In the seventeenth century, Protestant expression of the Church in Europe settled into a doctrinal and formalistic orthodoxy. Ruth Tucker refers to a "cold formalism" in this period.[57] James J. Scherer describes how the proclamation of the gospel "gave way to dogmatic hair splitting and ecclesiastical retrenchment. In the period of Orthodoxy, Lutheranism erected formidable dogmatic barriers to mission work by evangelical churches."[58] What mattered now was getting one's doctrine straight, and establishing the Lutheran claim to be a truly apostolic church. Again, quoting Scherer:

> On the one hand, Luther's theocentric emphasis was maintained: mission *is* the work of the triune God. On the other hand, Orthodoxy now affirmed much more dogmatically than Luther had that mission is *not* the task of human agents except in the closely controlled circumstances where the *ius*

reformandi applied, viz., that evangelical princes are responsible for evangelizing their non-Christian subjects. Under the privilege known as *cuius regio, eius religio*, each ruler had the right to determine the religious allegiance of his subjects. In accordance with this proviso, Lutheran princes—especially from Sweden and Denmark—carried out territorial missions in their overseas possessions, sending chaplains to preach the gospel to both Christians and non-Christians.

Under this territorial policy, however, missionary responsibility ceased when one went beyond the territories ruled by an evangelical prince, whether at home or abroad.[59]

Mission lagged for several hundred years, and when the Catholic apologist Robert Bellarmine accused the Protestants of not being the Church, the Lutherans countered the charge with the statement that the Great Commission was meant for the apostles, who had already fulfilled it.[60] This belief would continue to hamper mission for some time, but the Lutheran Pietist movement would, in some measure, overcome this hindrance. Philip Jakob Spener (1635-1705) and August Hermann Francke (1663-1727) taught a renewed Christianity, with an emphasis on a personal relationship with Christ and a rejuvenated vigor for mission.[61] These Pietists reaffirmed the Great Commission. One important outcome of this movement for world evangelization was the Danish-Halle Mission, under which Bartholomaeus Ziegenbalg and Henry Plütschau became the first Lutheran missionaries, arriving in Tranquebar, India in 1706.

The Moravian Brethren was another group influenced by the Pietists at Halle. In a very short time, Moravian missionaries were at work on every continent as this new fringe movement responded to *missio Dei* under the leadership of Count Nicholaus von Zinzendorf. The proportion of missionaries to lay people among the Moravians was 1:60, while it was 1:5000 in Protestantism as a whole.[62] This expression of mission under Zinzendorf was unique in a couple of other ways as well—firstly, Moravian piety was not the kind of piety that preached only to the "soul" of humanity; and secondly, it was self supporting. Bosch gives support to this view in his book, *Transforming Mission*, as follows:

> Early Pietists were not only interested in people's souls. In 1701, Francke defined the goal of the renewal movement as the

'concrete improvement of all walks of life, in Germany, Europe, in all parts of the world' (quoted in Genshichen 1975a:156—my translation). Ziegenbalg declared that the *Dienst der Seelen* ("service of souls") and the *Dienst des Leibes* ("service of the body") were interdependent and that no ministry to souls could remain without an 'exterior' side...Neither did this remain at the level of talking. In Germany, Francke and other pietists were involved extensively in "home missions", ministering to the destitute and deprived people of Halle and environs and founding a school for the poor, an orphanage, a hospital, a widows' home and other institutions. [63]

Moravian missionaries were entrepreneurial; consequently, they did not place a great burden upon the Church to support them. Moreover, their mission was unique in that Zinzendorf brought renewed prominence to the word oikumene, working to involve various expressions of the Church in an ecumenical effort to reach the world with the gospel. The Moravian church was a classic example of doing mission through a truly Church-wide emphasis. The ecumenical emphasis got its start in missions.

James A. Scherer is critical of the Pietist movement, casting it in terms of a reductionist and elitist approach to mission. In a section on strengths and weaknesses of this movement, his words on its weaknesses are far more numerous than his words on its strengths.

> In making mission work the special concern of spiritually regenerated groups and individuals, rather than the task of the entire church, pietists contributed to a divorce between church and mission which still formally exists in many European regional churches. Even in those churches where mission has been "integrated into the life of the church," mission work is generally seen as the cause of special interest groups. Pietism activated many laypersons in mission, but it did not establish a genuine universal priesthood based on Baptism.[64]

Scherer is certainly correct that mission must be more than the concern of a few spiritual elitists. However, Pietism was a response to both a territorial approach to mission and what some perceived to be a cold and lifeless orthodoxy in the Church. As the Roman Catholic Robert Bellarmine had already correctly pointed out, the Reformation was grossly deficient in its response to mission.[65] A Protestant structure of mission—based upon a priesthood of believers—under a State Church employment of baptism as the sole criterion for this priesthood was not, in fact, responding to *missio Dei*. As demonstrated above, it was precisely the Pietist movement that reaffirmed the urgency of a Church-wide response to the Great Commission. Moreover, the Moravian emphasis in mission shied away from any attempt to organize believers into churches at all, a reaction that Bosch attributes to orthodoxy's insistence on a link between church and state with the result, "that everybody in a given territory would, at least nominally, have to be regarded as Christians."[66] Pietism was not strong theologically, and the Pietists did not do mission perfectly, but they powerfully demonstrated a whole-hearted dedication to *missio Dei*. Says Bosch, "Surely, this was Protestantism's 'answer' to the very best there was in Catholic monasticism."[67] That is, to say the least, an unusual compliment to a Pietistic Lutheran phenomenon.

The seventeenth century Evangelical Awakening mirrored the influence of the Moravians. They were instrumental in John Wesley's own conversion as he encountered the spiritual calm of the Moravians in a storm at sea on a trip to North America. Upon landing, a Moravian leader asked Wesley what he thought of Jesus. When Wesley replied, "I know he is the Savior of the world," the Moravian leader replied, "Yes, but do you know that he has saved *you*?" Here was a kind of Christianity Wesley heretofore had not known. Though Wesley had gone to America to work with the Native Americans, his time was consumed with ministering to the colonists who had little appreciation for his Methodist ways. Thus, he sailed back to England a defeated man. Wesley's understanding of personal faith, however, was to take a leap upon his return to England. He heard Luther's preface to the book of Romans read publicly at a Moravian prayer meeting at Aldersgate. At that moment, Wesley personally appropriated what he had been preaching publicly.

With the coming of the eighteenth century Enlightenment, the Church would again begin a process of adjustment and change. Interestingly, the Reformation had been instrumental in sowing the seeds of the Enlightenment. As Luther moved soteriology from "outside *the Church* there is no salvation" to "outside of *Christ* there is no salvation," he was calling for the liberation of the gospel from *any one* cultural tradition. The spokespersons for the Enlightenment then called for the liberation of truth from *any* tradition *at all*. The result was the opening of the door to relativism, and truth was "democratized with a vengeance."[68] Increased individualism and openness to other religions and cultures followed. The West would experience a grand optimism in human ability and endeavor, especially by the time of the French Revolution. There was, of course, some good fruit to be harvested here as well, and yet the impact of this new openness to a sourceless truth had a major effect on the thinking of the Church and, consequently, on missions for some time to come. This departure from a central standard for truth is all the more evident in today's postmodern culture where even empirical scientific method has been dethroned as the final arbiter of truth.

Colonialism and the French and Industrial Revolutions followed the Enlightenment. These three movements also affected mission in a substantial way. The upside is that the age of discovery awakened the Church to the great "unfinished task" that would later become a central theme in the world conference on mission at Edinburgh in 1910 and the recruiting work of John R. Mott.[69] The downside was that mission—incorporating the growing optimism of the day—would become closely aligned with the colonialism of Europe and the imperialism of North America. Compounding this problem was the vision of the perceived opportunity to plant a theocracy—the Kingdom of God—in North America.

With the dawn of the nineteenth century, we enter the "Golden Era" or the "Great Century of Mission," a time in which mission became very *ecclesio*-centered. *Missio Dei* and the coming of *regnum Dei* were both grounded in the "Church being sent" and the "Church emerging." During this period, as the Church availed itself of the colonial umbrella (often the best or only way to get to these places), optimism for the coming consummation of the Kingdom of God was ever increasing.

However, with the coming of two world wars in the twentieth century, we see a crashing of Enlightenment optimism, and the Western Church reels from this loss of confidence. Whereas mission had been closely associated with the power of the colonial West, that power now dwindles, and the umbrella of Western power is no longer available to protect the Church from the many indigenous freedom movements that surface. According to people like Leslie Newbigin and James Scherer, these developments, along with a persistent trend toward secularism, resulted in a *"crisis of faith*, spirit, and theological conviction in the Western world."[70] Scherer comments further, "The Christian West in our day, in contrast to the spiritual climate of a century earlier, appears to have been gripped by a loss of *nerve* which may conceal an even more serious loss of *faith*—some would even speak of massive 'apostasy.'"[71] The Church takes on a more self questioning role, losing its confidence over time. The *ecclesio*-centric pattern would soon find itself in deep trouble. This leads us to the next part of our discussion: the role of the Church in God's mission. In this next section, we will look at the contemporary part of mission history, and we will further integrate the three categories we are discussing.

Ecclesia Dei

Scholars have proposed a number of views of the Church over the centuries. Although the Church is only in seed or germ form in the Old Testament—a foreshadowing—there has been vigorous debate as to whether the Church is a sharp break from Israel of the past or whether it is a continuation of it. To what degree is it like Israel or different? Is *ecclesia Dei* to be equated with *regnum Dei*? How does *ecclesia Dei* play out in *missio Dei*? Again, the questions here are too many for any complete treatment in the scope of this work, but we will at least touch on these. As Kähler said, "Mission is the mother of the church."[72] This is true because *missio Dei*—by its very nature—is first rooted in the Sending God. This will be our focus here. (Now, one may also argue that the Church is the mother of mission, since mission activities flow out of the Church, but this is true only in the sense that the Church is a *channel* of *missio Dei*, which *pre-existed ecclesia Dei*. To illustrate, we could compare this to Mary giving birth to Jesus. It can be said that Mary is the *Theotokos*, the "mother of God." However, the Godhead *predates* Mary; Mary is not the mother of the *Godhead*. Rather, she is a *temporal* servant of the Incarnation of the eternal God on earth. In the same way, *ecclesia Dei* exists as a *temporal* creation of God to serve as a channel for *missio Dei*.)

So how does *ecclesia Dei* fit into the continuum of God's mission? Was it created *ex nihilo*? Does it appear out of nowhere? Is it simply the continuation of Israel? Paul taught that the Church is not a completely new creation, but it has been "grafted in" as branches of Israel were pruned off to make room for the Gentiles in God's redemptive plan (Rom. 11:11-24). As was mentioned earlier, Bosch made a strong argument for the Church being a solid continuation of Israel. Although this thesis will take the position that this is true, it will do so for different reasons than those of Bosch. Bosch gives much attention to perceived similarities, and much less attention to the differences. It is indeed through Israel and now through the Church that God has chosen to reveal Himself to the world. However, there are some sharp differences in how the Church goes about this—the break with the tradition of Law being primary. As mentioned previously, Moltmann pointed out that Jesus placed Himself in the slot that the Torah had previously held.

Whereas in the Old Testament the believers demonstrated their faith by obedience to the revealed Law, in the New Testament and thereafter, one gives evidence of faith through believing the gospel and becoming a follower of Christ in his Church. Now, it is the gospel that transforms. Luther described the Church as a holy little flock and a communion of saints that lives under the headship of Christ. One now lives out the message not in a faithful keeping of the Law, but in how one stands in relation to God's Son. Faith is involved in both instances, but the expression of that faith has changed. The message that is proclaimed is also quite different: "Repent, and believe the good news (Mk. 1:15b)." This is in every way a *New* Testament that is in effect.

Moreover, contrary to the claim of Bosch and Bowers, one can sustain the argument neither in the New Testament nor in church history that the Church plays a passive and centripetal role in participation in God's mission. The Church is, and always has been, a major participant in *missio Dei*. The New Testament calls the Church the "bride of Christ." Christ revealed himself in a body of flesh; He then took the Church into that metaphor and now reveals his "Body" through the Church. It is how He continues to "incarnate" Himself in the world today. (In fairness to Bosch, he is perfectly right in saying that God is the missionary *par excellence*. This is, after all, God's mission carried out through Israel and through the Church. It is not the mission *of* Israel or the mission *of* the Church. It is in fact God's mission *through* Israel and *through* the Church.)

Following Constantine, the Church partnered with the state and for centuries compromised its divine purpose in the process. Coupled with this movement was the increasing power of the Roman bishop. We looked briefly already at Cyprian's dictum *extra ecclesiam nulla salus*. The Roman Catholic Church claimed sole right to the term *ecclesiam*, and tied salvation to a specific culture—its own, rather than acknowledging the universal Church at large. Augustine had solidified the exclusive hold that the Church had on salvation, insisting that authority and holiness were both still inherent in the institutional Church. In 1302, Pope Boniface VIII declared, "Furthermore, we declare, we proclaim, we define that it is absolutely necessary for salvation that every human creature be subject to the Roman Pontiff."[73] Moreover, coercion—once a chosen tool for discouraging apostasy—later became a tool of oppression. By the time of Charlemagne, the masses were being "converted" at sword point. The policy of enforcing doctrinal purity by force devolved into evangelism by force.[74]

The earlier Church movement was correct in recognizing the important role that the Church is to play in God's carrying out of his mission. However, this role became far too hierarchical and institutionalized. In a chapter on Lutheran Ecclesiology, Veli-Matti Kärkkäinen says of Luther, "Luther stressed the noninstitutional character of the church; he disliked the word *Kirche* and preferred terms such as *Sammlung* (assembly) and *Gemeinde* (congregation). For him the church was in the first place a communion of saints, a gathering of believers."[75] As Luther wrote in the Smalcald Articles (3.12: 2-3), "...thank God, a seven-year-old child knows what the church is, namely, holy believers and sheep who hear the voice of their Shepherd... it consists of the Word of God and true faith."[76] The *Augsburg Confession*, article #7 presents the Church as "the assembly of all believers among whom the gospel is purely preached and the holy sacraments are administered according to the gospel."[77]

An emphasis on an *ecclesio*-centered model, in which church planting was the aim, aided the rapid expansion of the gospel to all parts of the globe throughout the nineteenth and early twentieth century.[78] Lutheranism also participated in this model, and reaped the benefits of creating a strong foundation of Word and sacrament wherever mission was done. The theological correctness of this would, however, be drawn into question in the twentieth century. First the collapse of Christendom, and then the decline of Enlightenment optimism purged the western church of a misplaced confidence. Missionaries had often equated Western culture with the message of the gospel and, consequently, the demise of that cultural hegemony shook the confidence of the Church in carrying out the mission entrusted to it.

A backlash from the non-Western world soon followed. As the newly planted church in these parts took form, the missionary moved from the role of church planter to manager.[79] A problem of indigenization developed, and the missionary too often looked little different from the colonial rulers in their societies. With the throwing off of colonial rule, there was also a desire on the part of the local church to throw off the yoke of an ecclesial colonialism and imperialism as well. In some parts of the world, there were calls for a moratorium on mission, such as that given by the All Africa Council of Churches in the 1970s.[80]

Mission work was sailing on a high tide of Enlightenment optimism between the late nineteenth century to the middle twentieth century. In Edinburgh, in 1910, the Protestant arm of the Church came together with an urgency for the cause of mission: to embrace the "unfinished task," and to design a strategy for a "final campaign." Edinburgh did not sense any need to engage in a theological justifying of mission. It was primarily a call to mission and a discussion of the "how to" of mission.[81] The watchword of that time was the "evangelization of the whole world in this generation," a phrase that had been adopted by the Student Volunteer Movement in 1889 and served as the title of a book written by John R. Mott in 1900. The theological issues for mission would surface later in the committee on Faith and Order. Mission activity was further encouraged in follow-up meetings through the International Missionary Council, founded at Lake Mohonk, New York in 1921. Soon, a worldwide movement was underway whereby distinctions between "sending" and "receiving" churches would be played down. The spirit evidenced much earlier in missionary statesmen like Zinzendorf and Carey was again influential, for here we also see evidence that the ecumenical movement of this past century definitely had its roots in mission.[82]

The International Missionary Council (IMC) held its first conference in Jerusalem in 1928 and its second in Tambaram-Madras, India in 1938. Both of these gatherings were extremely significant for the mission movement. Although the actual numbers were smaller in Jerusalem than Edinburgh, there was a much higher percentage of representatives from the world community, as more than one fourth of the delegation came from Asia, Africa and Latin America. With the spirit of the age leaning toward theological relativism, there was a fear that the agenda in Jerusalem would lead to what many thought would be a surrender to the "social gospel," and thus the conference issued strong statements to affirm the uniqueness of the Christian gospel. The first of the eight volumes of findings is heavy with references to sin and guilt and the need for conversion to the Christ who died and rose again to free us from our sin. In a reaction to the relativism of the day, the council stated that, "Its very nature (the Gospel) forbids us to say that it may be the right belief for some but not for others. Either it is true for all, or it is not true at all."[83]

The conference at Tambaram-Madras in 1938 drew an even larger delegation of the world community, with 60% of the delegates coming from Asia, Africa and Latin America. The issue of the relationship of Christianity to non-Christian religions dominated the discussion. Is there anything present in non-Christian cultures that evidence the prior work of God? Do these cultures offer something for the gospel to build upon, or is there nothing of value? The discussions centered on the theological relativism of William Ernest Hocking's *Rethinking Missions*, and Hendrik Kraemer's reply, *The Christian Message in a Non-Christian World*. While Kraemer was arguing the uniqueness of Christianity from a Barthian foundation, several Indian scholars of the day, in a very opposite approach, were attempting to relate Christianity to Hinduism in an organic manner.[84] One, Pandipeddi Chenchiah, in what he called "new-creation" theology, worked to fuse Christianity and Hinduism in an effort to create a third religion, based not on the doctrines, creeds or traditions of either, but on the experience of the "fact of Jesus" where regeneration is a biological process. Aspects of sin, forgiveness and reconciliation are missing; his is a cross-less theology. Chenchiah's hermeneutic is radically Marcionite, in the sense that he dismisses Peter, Paul and the other apostles, holding that Jesus and His demands alone are obligatory.[85] While disavowing the acceptance of either tradition, in practice he substituted the spirituality of Christianity with that of Hinduism. The debate over the place of non-Christian religions as a *preparatio evangelica* was heating up. In a brief statement at the closing session of the IMC Tambaram-Madras conference, the following words appear.

> National gods of any kind, gods of race or class, these are not large enough to save us. The recognition of God in Christ by no means robs a man of his nation or his family or his culture. When Christ is taken seriously by a nation or an ancient culture, He destroys no whit of good within it but lifts it rather to its own highest destiny. He does destroy exclusiveness, but in its place

He causes a new quality to grow—good will—a good will which is wider than national or cultural loyalties and corresponds to the largeness of God's love.[86]

With the birth of the World Council of Churches at Amsterdam in 1948, the International Missionary Council continued to play a decisive role for the organization in the discussion of and propagation of mission. In the immediate post-war era, the locus of mission was still in the Church and borne out in the multiplying of churches. With the advent of the 1960s, however, momentum was building to devalue the place of the Church, and some mission leaders were questioning whether evangelization was appropriate at all. Whereas the conferences in Jerusalem (1928) and Tambaram-Madras (1938) had affirmed the Christ-centeredness of the gospel, and explored God's heart for mission in all the world, later conferences became less "vertical" and much more "horizontal" in their approaches. In a later conference in Ghana (1957), evangelization was seriously downplayed, and by the time conferences in Bangkok and Uppsala were underway, there was no more talk of conversion or spiritual transformation in traditional terms. Instead, vague terms were being used, and "humanization" was being promoted as the goal of mission. Understandably, many evangelicals who had been invited to participate in these conferences were getting very frustrated, as well as many conciliar participants who also valued the role of evangelism in mission. The Church was becoming divided, and tensions were mounting. Debate was getting more heated, not only between evangelicals and conciliar members, but among conciliar churches themselves. This is the "crisis" church leaders, such as James A. Scherer, began to address.[87] This period saw the end of church-centered mission in the WCC.

Evangelicals responded with conferences in Wheaton and Berlin. At these conferences the motivation, means, and goal of mission were reassessed, and many in the conciliar churches appreciated the documents produced in those meetings.[88] Billy Graham was a major promoter of these conferences, culminating in the world conference on evangelism and missions in Lausanne in 1974. The Lausanne Covenant, a document that came out of that conference, was taken into consideration by mainline Protestants and Roman Catholics alike in their later conferences and gatherings, along with other major documents on mission and evangelization, such as the Roman Catholic *Evangelii Nuntiandi* and others on mission.[89]

Following these major debates, the Church started to turn once again to the model of a church-centered mission approach. Scherer calls this a return to the triad model of Luther: "Word—Church—Believer."

> Three main stages can be identified in the ecumenical development of mission thinking since 1948. The first stage, roughly from 1948 to 1961, is characterized by an emphasis on the church as the agent of God's mission. The concept of missio Dei begins to gain acceptance in ecumenical circles. The second stage, from 1961 to 1975, is marked by a shift toward the world as the locus for God's mission, with a marked displacement of the church from its earlier place of centrality. The mission of God is now given a distinctly new and different connotation. These years represent a particularly troubled period for ecumenical missionary thinking, a period that produces a disquieting response from the side of Lutheranism. The final period, from 1975 to the present, is notable for its reaction against the one-sided worldly orientation of the previous period. The church is once again affirmed as a valid instrument in the mission of God, Christology is given a more central role, and ecumenical mission is seen as moving toward a synthesis between the previously opposed viewpoints.[90]

Scherer sees the "church as agent of God's mission" and the "world as the locus of God's mission" as opposing viewpoints. However, one does not have to see these positions as totally antithetical, although the often extreme ways in which these emphases exhibited themselves in the thinking and activity of the Church did in fact lead to differing outcomes and considerable debate about the nature of *missio Dei* and its goals. The final period referred to by Scherer has been a welcome change from the previous two extremes; however, we are still not close to total consensus in the world Church as to mission's purpose. On one side of the spectrum, the Church is about presence and social movements, and on the other side, the Church sees mission functionally expressed in methods of church planting and more effective proclamation of personal salvation. In between these extremes are varying perspectives that lean to one side or the other. The difference now is that the Church is less inclined to see the *ground and goal of mission in the Church or in the world* and is more inclined to see the ground of mission *in God himself* (*missio Dei*), with the goal being *the Kingdom of God* (*regnum Dei*).[91]

Regnum Dei

Regnum Dei is concerned, naturally, with the reign of God, or the *basileia tou theou*. This concept of the *basileia tou theou* is central to the life and teaching of Jesus in the New Testament. In Jesus, the Kingdom—or reign—of God is the expression of God's love and mercy, the focus of each of his parables, and is evident in every act he carries out in opposition to evil. Although *regnum Dei* is certainly present in the Old Testament as God leads Israel and teaches them of justice and righteousness, and reveals his covenant in suzerain/vassal form, etc, it comes to fruition in the ministry of Jesus. The New Testament expresses the Kingdom in a number of ways, sometimes paradoxically.

> Visions of God's kingdom vary widely, and often they are linked to visions of the end times... It is in the world but not of it (John 18:36). It belongs to the little ones, but those in it are greater than the greatest ones (Matt. 11:11; 18:1-4). It comes as a free gift but demands all that we have (Luke 12:30-33), and only the truly righteous will enter it (Matt. 5:20). It is God's very reign but works in hidden ways (Matt. 13:33). It is already present (Luke 17:21) yet still coming in the future (Matt. 6:10). It does not consist of talk (I Cor. 4:20), but it must be proclaimed (Luke 4:43...).[92]

In the life of Jesus, we see the Kingdom of God arriving. Here we can find a great help in the "already" and the "not yet" categories. One often sees the phrase that the Kingdom of God is "breaking into our world." Taken literally, that wording could imply that the Kingdom is an outside force that has no place here in our world until it "breaks in" and enters like a thief. Though not entirely correct (God is certainly already here!), there is a sense in which God does indeed enter into the realm of the "prince of this world" and exert his authority over *evil and all of its manifestations*. This inbreaking of God has been termed *missio adventus*, and includes the incarnation, the coming of the Spirit at Pentecost and His work through the church. "*Missio adventus* is, then, God's mission as it brings unexpected surprises, radical changes, new directions, almost unbelievable transformation in the midst of human life: personal, social, and structural."[93]

What we need to keep in mind is how the Kingdom is the *goal* of mission. Jesus taught us to pray, "Thy kingdom come, thy will be done, on earth as it is in heaven." Jesus kept the Kingdom in the forefront of His teaching and action. In this prayer, it is assumed that just as Jesus inaugurated but did not bring the fullness of the Kingdom, so it is with our involvement in *missio Dei*. We do mission in dependence upon God's work and timing. Bosch comments in *Transforming Mission*,

> As we pray "your kingdom come!": we also commit ourselves to initiate, here and now, approximations and anticipations of God's reign. Once again; God's reign *will* come since it has *already* come. It is both bestowal and challenge, gift and promise, present and future, celebration and anticipation...We have the firm assurance that its coming cannot be thwarted.[94]

God has already acted in kingdom ways through his Son, and after Jesus' ascension, God continues to reveal His kingdom activity through His church as He fills and empowers the Church in His Holy Spirit. In this way, Christ could say to his followers, "I tell you the truth, anyone who has faith in me will do what I have been doing. He will do even greater things than these, because I am going to the Father (Jn. 14:12)," precisely because this same Spirit that empowered the ministry of Christ is now given to the Church, and the works of Jesus are multiplied through his followers. Does it not then follow that as Christ's first coming into the world was an eschatological event, so that event continues even now as Jesus reveals himself through his Body, the Church, as it expresses itself in *missio Dei*? This certainly can be said, because *missio Dei* is the work of God, not the work of his created beings. The eschatological aspect of *ecclesia Dei* in *missio Dei*, though not synonymous with it, is both the present foretaste and the anticipation of the future fullness of *regnum Dei*.

One of the ways that God reveals his Kingdom today is through the Church being the Church. When the Church is about exemplifying the Body of Christ and personifying the character of Jesus in the world, there is an opportunity for us to be God's "yes" and "no" (to use Bosch's terms). "...[O]n the one hand we assert God's 'yes' to the world as expression of the Christian's solidarity with society, we also have to affirm mission and evangelism as God's 'no', as an expression of our opposition to and engagement with the world." In identifying with the world, we must also beware lest we become what Moltmann referred to as a "religion of society."[95] The doing of good in this world is affirmed in the work of the Kingdom; and the evil that is in the world is opposed. The Spirit of Jesus challenges the Church to live out its role as ambassador of the Kingdom, not only in calling our attention to the suffering of the oppressed and marginalized, but also in calling us to work for the redemption of those who are in bondage to their perceived need to oppress. In looking at the scenarios of slave/master, male/female, racial issues, poor/rich, etc., one can criticize Liberation Theology movements for focusing exclusively on the suffering of the victims of oppression. If the Church only concerns herself with the suffering of the oppressed, then one never addresses the real cause of suffering. Indeed, we who call ourselves the Church must do more than simply dress the wounds of the suffering. Though the importance of such Christlike witness is paramount, we must also be careful to address the *causes* of suffering. If the suffering ones are ever to truly be free, we must confront the need also to liberate the oppressor—from his sinful and depraved need to oppress.[96] Here is where the power of the gospel can genuinely be felt—as the need for the transformation of those bound in an evil need to wield power over the powerless is confronted (God's "no" to the world) and the gospel does its work of transformation upon them. Here is where both the "charity" and "liberation" models fall short. Simply throwing money at problems or "removing" oppressors by whatever means deemed necessary, neither is an adequate representation of the Kingdom of God as we see it in the New Testament; at the same time, simply preaching to "souls" leaves us with an equally inadequate picture. Jesus did not separate the spiritual and the material as we have done, but held them together in synthesis. Like the inside and outside of a jar, one without the other was unthinkable to Him.

This is something that Paul apparently understood, as he wrote to his friend Philemon concerning the runaway slave, Onesimus. Paul wrote to Philemon to announce that Onesimus had become a brother in Christ; consequently, Philemon was no longer to treat him as only a slave. Paul did not ask Philemon to free Onesimus, *per se*, but to treat him as a brother in Christ. What would that entail? It would entail Philemon's exchanging his sole role as a master for the role of a brother—it is a "coming down" for Philemon, a very Christ-like and *kenotic* act—a giving up of power over another in exchange for equality with the other before God. To confess Jesus as Lord at times means to be counter-cultural and rather revolutionary.

Moltmann pointed out where this understanding of the social element of mission has gone wrong when he said that to equate mission and the Kingdom *only* with social justice is to create a "religion of society," as opposed to a living faith of the Crucified One.[97] Though working for human rights and justice are undoubtedly the will of God, this alone does not make the Kingdom. Certain forms of Liberation Theology have made the mistake of confining the expression of *regnum Dei* to only a lower story existence. One example of this could be some of the expressions of Minjung theology in South Korea. David Kwang-sun Suh has written of his experience of growing up under the Japanese occupation in a conservative church which his father pastored—a church that preached repentance and personal faith but took little or no interest in political involvement. Suh felt that a church concerned only with personal salvation, a church that was not concerned with living in this world, was not helping the people. This was a kind of Christianity that was out of touch with the needs of the people, and, consequently, was a poor representation of why Christ came. Suh wanted an expression of Christianity for the *minjung*, for the people, something that would address their *han*, their unresolved deep suffering and agony of heart. In Christ, he saw the perfect model of one who could identify with the *han* of the *minjung*, and one with whom they in turn could identify.[98] There is no doubt that this expression of Christianity had a great deal to do with how Christianity has prospered in South Korea. There was a deep identification made between Christ and the felt needs of the people in addressing their *han*. This parallels in many ways with some forms of Black Theology. The question that one needs to ask here, however, is one that Dr. Paul Martinson asked in a class discussion at Luther Seminary, "But where is the redemption in this?"[99] There is an important difference between seeing a "personal salvation" expression of Christianity alone as *insufficient*, and seeing personal salvation as *insignificant*. Without the aspect of salvation through a reconciliation of creation with the God who is offended by our sin, the cross experiences a radical reductionism, and Christ's identification with the suffering victim becomes nothing more than a different kind of sentimentality. Further, in this reductionism, Christ's work relates solely to our "lower story" existence: human to human, and even then it is powerless to be anything more than an inspirational symbol. It can do nothing to *resolve* the pain and the suffering that our sin has created in the heart of God, nor does it free us from the power of our sin and/or its eternal consequences. To be truly effective, the cross must call for and enable a genuine repentance, a U-turn, with an accompanying conversion and transformation of the *whole* person. As Paul wrote to the Corinthians,

> Therefore, if anyone is in Christ, he is a new creation;

the old has gone, the new has come! All this is from God, who reconciled us to himself through Christ and gave us the ministry of reconciliation: that God was reconciling the world to himself in Christ, not counting men's sins against them. And he has committed to us the message of reconciliation. We are therefore Christ's ambassadors, as though God were making his appeal through us. We implore you on Christ's behalf: be reconciled to God. God made him who had no sin to be sin for us, so that in him we might become the righteousness of God. (2 Cor 5:17-21)

The work of Christ on the cross is intended to effect in us a total transformation—a transformation that is centered first on the sin question. The words, "who reconciled us to himself through Christ," give us the starting point. There can be no true and lasting reconciliation on the horizontal level without the vertical relationship with God being resolved. Our reconciliation with others is rooted in our reconciliation with God. The words, "All this is from God..." point to the divine initiative of God's grace reaching out through Christ to His lost creation, which in turn becomes the model for the participation of the Church in the *missio Dei*. Without a resolution to the sin question, there is no real remedy or healing for the divisions within humanity either (the horizontal aspect). Jesus became sin on our behalf in order that we might become the "righteousness" of God. The word Paul uses here is dikaiosune. There is some debate regarding whether this "righteousness" refers back to the righteous *standing* of the sinless Christ before God, or instead to the *doing* of righteousness (justice). Although either meaning is possible in dikaiosune, in this passage where Paul parallels the sinless Christ to our becoming the "righteousness of God," it is likely that his primary intent is to present Christ's sinless state to us as a picture of what we become before God through Jesus Christ. Moltmann refers to this same 2 Corinthians passage in *The Church in the Power of the Spirit*,

> In this theological dimension of Jesus' passion, it is completely clear for the first time why the church of Christ lives, believes and hopes from the sacrifice on the cross. It is the fellowship of the godless who have found fellowship with God through Jesus' abandonment by God. It is the fellowship of the sinners who through the one who for them was made sin have

arrived at righteousness. It is the fellowship of the accursed, who were blessed through the accursed death of Jesus as their representative and who become a blessing. And because the Father is reconciled to 'the world' through the death of the Son, its new life must also serve the reconciliation of the world. In so far as, with the epistle to the Hebrews, we can term Christ's sacrifice on the cross a priestly ministry, its consequence is the priesthood of all believers. They are all "ambassadors of reconciliation" in Christ's stead. They live in fellowship with God by virtue of Christ's giving of himself for them. Because of this their life is also destined for self-giving—they are destined to love, to be representatives and to intercede. That does not divide them from mankind or raise them above others. What is true of Christ in this respect—that he 'had to be a merciful and faithful high priest in the service of God', and that it is only through his experience of suffering and temptation that he can help those who suffer and are tempted (Heb 2.17f.)—applies in its corresponding degree to them too. The priestly ministry of the representative can only spring from *sym-pathy*, from 'suffering with' (cf. also Heb 4.15)...

The church is called to life through the gospel of Christ's self-giving. Hence it is fundamentally born out of the cross of Christ. At its centre is "the word of the cross" and the eucharist with which the death of Christ is proclaimed. It is from the cross of Christ that there develops the fellowship of the godless with God. What makes the church the church is reconciliation 'in the blood of Christ' and its own self-giving for the reconciliation of the world.[100]

Put into other words, Moltmann links the "righteousness before God" with the "righteousness of God" that is to be *lived out* in this world in solidarity with those who suffer. Our identification with the holiness of Jesus—which has become possible for us only because of the cross—certainly does not preclude our also becoming like Him in the *doing* of righteousness. On the contrary, it demands it. At the same time, somehow the pain and suffering of Christ has to heal our pain in *more* than a "this worldly" sense. If this is *not* to be the case, then Paul's words apply: "If only for this life we have hope in Christ, we are to be pitied more than all men (I Cor. 15:19)."

The goal of *missio Dei*—experiencing the fullness of *regnum Dei*—cannot be divorced from reconciliation with God. We must not separate the vertical and horizontal aspects of salvation from each other. This is *not* to say that those still alienated from God do not receive some of the positive affects of the *regnum Dei*. It *is* to say that the suffering of this world is rooted first in our alienation from God, which results from our sinful and rebellious nature. There can be no end to suffering between human beings apart from the reconciliation of humanity with our Creator through the suffering of His Son on the cross. This message of reconciliation is proclaimed in word and deed. To look again at Moltmann's statement quoted above, "The church is called to life through the gospel of Christ's self-giving. Hence it is fundamentally born out of the cross of Christ. At its centre is 'the word of the cross' and the eucharist with which the death of Christ is *proclaimed*. It is from the cross of Christ that there develops the fellowship of the godless with God. What makes the Church the Church is reconciliation 'in the blood of Christ' and its own self-giving for the reconciliation of the world."[101]

The New Testament places the suffering of God and His Son squarely in the midst of human suffering. God did not save us "at arms length." Instead, He took flesh and dwelt among us. The Trinity entered the human world, stood in solidarity with us against sin and evil through the incarnation of Jesus Christ, and bore the suffering of all human sin on our behalf. This suffering in Jesus Christ became a watershed in Martin Luther's understanding of the righteousness of God. His view of God's righteousness changed from a righteousness in God's wrath *toward* us, to a righteousness in God's grace *for* us. Thus, the theology of the cross became a central aspect in Luther's understanding of God and the Church.

The Japanese theologian Kazoh Kitamori did a wonderful service to the Church in bringing new depth to this concept, and greater prominence to the fact that the Divine suffering was a suffering not only of Jesus Christ, but of God the Father as well. In his *Theology of the Pain of God*, he maintained that suffering is part of the eternal nature and character of God. His "embracing completely those who should not be embraced" causes the suffering and pain of God.[102] God can embrace us because His love totally overcomes His wrath. Kitamori depicts this as a struggle of the *God of wrath* against the *God of love*. God works the whole process *within himself*, and His suffering never goes away because He always loves us. This theology is correct in linking the suffering of God with that of humanity, and yet it sparks debate when Kitamori locates this suffering in the *eternal nature* of God.

> The pain of God is part of his essence! This is really the wonder. God's essence corresponds to his eternity. The Bible reveals that the pain of God belongs to his eternal being. "I am the first and the last, and the living one" I died, and behold I am alive for evermore (Rev. 1:17-18)...The cross is in no sense an external act of God, but an act within himself...The question in regard to the salvation of the world, according to him [Luther] is not the relation between God and the world, or God and Satan, but the relation between God and God to the world.[103]

C. S. Song challenges Kitamori on this point, saying that the above paragraph leaves the work of the cross and the suffering of God totally divorced from the human world. God is wrestling with His eternal suffering through an *interior* process of His love overcoming his wrath, cut off from the realm of sinful humanity. The cross and the sacrifice of the cross, in the end, is left short of its full meaning, because the whole issue of God's wrath was settled *within Himself*. It then becomes possible for God to resolve the whole issue of the fall of humanity from a distance. This is why, says Song, that Kitamori can also say that the story of the New Testament would be more appealing if it stopped at the cross. Kitamori confuses the eternal and absolute God with God's wrath, to which he also attributes absoluteness and inflexibility.[104] Song does raise a weighty point when he says that Kitamori confuses God's eternal nature and God's suffering. If God's suffering is indeed part of His eternal nature, there can be no resolution to it. Moreover, suffering would have to be a good thing if it is part of God's very essence. "His God is not only the God who has pain, but the God who is pain."[105] However, Kitamori is saying this to stress how God's suffering is directly tied to His love for us. This suffering of God is directly tied to His human creation, not divorced from it. Song also levels the same critique at Moltmann's *Crucified God*. "What we have in Kitamori and Moltmann, it seems to me, is a theology that loses sight of human beings by trying to say too much about God."[106] Actually, Kitamori is doing anything *but* removing God from the pain of human existence.[107] He is in fact crusading against the overly transcendent God of "liberal theology since Schleirmacher."[108]

While acknowledging what Kitamori calls their delightful soprano of "God is love," he points out their inability to hear the tone of bass, "which is the pain of God sounding out the depths." His first target is Karl Barth. He quotes from several of Barth's works to demonstrate what he considers examples of a law vs. gospel theology, and a theology of a God without pain. For example, Kitamori quotes Barth's *Church Dogmatics*, (Vol. II. part. 1, page 612), "God is a total person without tearing and pain" (*ein Ganzes ohne Risse und Schmerzen*), and then he comments, "It is obvious that a God who does not embrace is a God without pain."[109] Kitamori clearly maintains that God's suffering comes precisely because of His "embracing that which should not be embraced." He would agree with Song that what we see in the Bible is a God who *does* suffer—not a God whose crucifixion has no relevance outside of Himself, but whose cross is precisely on our behalf. The fact that the atonement was substitutionary draws God into our suffering, and draws us into His. And yet, redemption had to happen within the Godhead; humans can contribute nothing to it. Song continues, "... there must be a difference between the cross that God in Christ is bearing for the pain and suffering of this world and the cross that embodies the conflict between God's love and God's wrath, between God the "Father" and God the "Son," to use the traditional Trinitarian language. The cross in the former sense is redemptive or salvific, but the cross in the latter sense is an external symbol of the struggle within God's own self, that is, God against God's own self."[110] And yet, *why* must there be a difference? Why must we view these two truths as an irreconcilable dialectic, rather than as a synthesis in Christ? Cannot the cross be simultaneously redemptive for humans *and* an external symbol of the "abandonment" (to use Moltmann's term) of the Son by the Father? Is there really a conflict here? Kitamori is expressing dissatisfaction with merely abstract discussions of "essence" and "begetting." He is forcing these concepts to be incarnational. Commenting on this point in Kitamori's third chapter, Paul Martinson put it well, "There can be an incarnation without a cross, but not a cross without an incarnation."[111]

Thus, the Church also reflects the suffering of the God who *completely embraces that which should not be embraced*.[112] By definition, this God embraces not only the righteous, but the unrighteous. His Church must do the same. *Missio Dei* expresses itself through *ecclesia Dei*, toward the goal of *regnum Dei*. As a channel of *missio Dei*, *ecclesia Dei* needs to be an expression of *regnum Dei* on all fronts—engaging, even embracing the world on each of those fronts. An abstract, all "upper story" or "from above" Kingdom does not touch us down here. On the other hand, a strictly "lower story" or "from below" Kingdom does not communicate the desire of the heart of God to embrace his suffering world in love, and will never truly evidence God's presence in His creation. The tension between these two positions—the biblical call for justice in the everyday realm (lower story) and the need for personal justification before God (upper story)—has been a tenuous topic for the Church at large to manage. We are prone to land on one side of the dialectic or the other. Our world needs a theologically rooted, Christ-centered synthesis, in which the Church boldly yet humbly participates in the fullness of God's mission, the goal of which is an ever-increasing experience of His Kingdom. Since the latter part of the twentieth century, the Church has expressed almost unanimous agreement that such a holistic approach is called for in the gospel, yet there is still disagreement on what this synthesis would look like. Listen to James A. Scherer as he asks the question, "Does the goal of mission remain making converts and planting churches wherever they do not exist, or does the expectation of the kingdom shift the church's priorities to activities which somehow anticipate a 'new heaven and a new earth'? If church reproduction is no longer the final goal, can it be properly described as a still valid intermediate goal?"[113] But do these kinds of "either or" questions not cloud the issues at hand? One must be careful to emphasize *regnum Dei* neither at the expense of *ecclesia Dei*, nor of *ecclesia plantatio*. The mere fact that church planting will not be carried out in the *eschaton* does not lessen its importance now any more than the *eschaton* negates the validity of the struggle of justice in the present time. Both are part and parcel of *missio Dei* today, in spite of the fact that neither will continue to be necessary once the fullness of the Kingdom of God arrives.

So how do these doctrinal categories integrate? What priority, if any, should be given to each? We have argued that they do not stand apart from each other. They are interdependent; and yet both *ecclesia Dei* and *regnum Dei* find their essence and *raison d'etre* in, and flowing out of, *missio Dei*. Still, there is a role that each must play. When the Church of the nineteenth and early twentieth centuries considered *ecclesia Dei* to be the starting point, as the ground and the source of mission, the focus was on the sending Church and the emerging Church, newer and older, etc. In such a scenario, it is easy to see no value in the host culture, and there can be a tendency to discard everything in the host culture as irredeemably evil (the perceived need for a *tabula rasa*). For this reason, it was easy for the mission ventures of the past to equate themselves with expressions of Western cultural superiority. (This is, thankfully, an increasingly difficult posture to take as the non-western Church experiences resurgence and takes ownership of its place in *missio Dei*.)

Moreover, when the Church is the ground and source of mission we can also come to see mission as only an added function, and not always an important function, of the Church. The gospel becomes interiorized in the Church. The words hurled at William Carey by the hyper-Calvinists of the Northampton Baptist Association come to mind, "When God pleases to convert the heathen, He will do it without consulting you or me." Carey insisted that the Church had a role in the mission of God, as the title of his published work illustrates: *An Enquiry into the Obligation of the Church to Use Means for the Conversion of the Heathens* (1792).[114] The Church is not incidental, let alone dispensable, to *missio Dei*. God could do it without us, but He has chosen to call us to collaborate with him in mission—His greatest work.

Martin Luther asked in his Large Catechism, why do we pray that the Kingdom will come, if it indeed comes of its own power? The answer is that we pray that his Kingdom reign will first come to our hearts and lives and that his Kingdom will be revealed in and through us. When the question is posed, "What is the Kingdom of God?" Luther answers that, as expressed in the Creed, it is first God's sending of his Son and Holy Spirit, to bring the Church to himself and under his rule, and to save humanity from the consequences of our sin.[115] This is evidenced in Paul as he called the Church to imitate him, not necessarily in detail and method, but in passion for the lost, "that they may be saved" (I Cor. 10:33). This necessitates, of course, that we see the gospel and the Christian faith as something "so vital that without it men will perish."[116] It requires that we see humanity as lost. As Luther argued in his response to Erasmus in their debate on free will,

> It is, moreover, a mere dialectical fiction that there is in man a neutral and unqualified willing, nor can those who assert it prove it. It is the result of ignoring facts and paying too much attention to words, as if a thing were always in reality just as it is represented in words. There are innumerable examples of this in the Sophists. The truth of the matter is rather as Christ says, "He who is not with me is against me" (Luke 11:23). He does not say: "He who is not with me is not against me either, but neutral." For

if God is in us, Satan is absent, and only a good will is present; if God is absent, Satan is present, and only an evil will is in us. Neither God nor Satan permits sheer unqualified willing in us, but as you have rightly said, having lost our liberty, we are forced to serve sin, that is, we will live sin and evil, speak sin and evil, do sin and evil.[117]

If we hold to the bondage of the will, as both Luther and Calvin did, then we must see humanity as eternally lost apart from Christ. God calls the church to participate in mission "that they may be saved."

Finally, if indeed *regnum Dei* is the goal of *missio Dei*, and *ecclesia Dei* is to be engaged in Kingdom living before a watching world, this will require opposing all that is evil in the world, and promoting all that is good. This may entail finding a cure for a dread disease; it may be feeding the hungry and empowering the poor who have no voice. It may be evangelizing the oppressor and liberating the oppressed. The word for justice in the Old Testament Hebrew combines the concept of righteousness with justice. The writers use the same word (tsedeq) for doing justice and being righteous.[118] This is similar to *dikaios* or *dikaiosune* in Greek, which carries with it at times the nuance of justice on behalf of those who do not have power (John 5:30). We translate this word as "righteousness," but it has within it also the "doing" of the "right." Jesus is of course the greatest model of justice of all kinds, and God calls us to image Christ's justice before the world, becoming like Him. "God made him who had no sin to be sin for us, so that in him we might become the *dikaiosune* of God (II Cor 5:21). Jesus calls us to be in the world, but not of it. Jesus identified with those who suffer, while avoiding the evil that contributes to or causes the suffering. We must do the same. As Moltmann said, a church can so identify with the world that it becomes nothing more than a human religion. Mission without righteousness, without justice, is powerless to save or deliver. On the other hand, a church that isolates itself from the suffering of the world runs the danger of being so out of touch that it is living in disobedience to the calling of God to be a reflection of his love and mercy to the world—so "heavenly minded" that it is "no earthly good." The servant is not above its master, Jesus said, "As the Father has sent me, I am sending you" (Jon. 21). How did the Father send the Son? Into the world. We are God's "yes" and God's "no" to this world. This is not out of a sense of superiority or arrogance, but only in the deepest humility. We are unworthy of such a task. Our authority is not our own. We are only the messengers.

Is there one part of this triad one should prioritize above the others for an appropriate missiology? I have argued here that *missio Dei* must be the ground and source of mission. Rooting mission praxis anywhere else will have the effect of limiting the scope and involvement of *ecclesia Dei* in the world and will serve to limit what constitutes the manifestations of *regnum Dei*. The key to keeping these latter two parts of the triad in proper perspective is to have the constant realization that mission is rooted in the heart of God, and is not an addendum or an option for the church. Further, mission from the standpoint of the church must take its cue in how both the Old and New Testaments express God's purposes and the revelation of himself to his creation. The theme of the *basilèia tou theou* was very central to the life and ministry of Jesus, and this must be true with us as well. In fact, more than Paul (a standard model for mission) Jesus himself gives us the most complete picture of what *missio Dei* looks like.

If one becomes preoccupied with "Church" or even with expressions of "Kingdom justice" without rooting such categories back into *missio Dei*, there is the danger that these can become what we have referred to as either upper or lower story categories only. Though the goal of *missio Dei* is *regnum Dei*, we must always bring our actions on behalf of the Kingdom back to the God of the Scriptures and critique those actions in the light of God's already revealed activities. Both *ecclesia Dei* and *regnum Dei* must find their *raison d'être* and their essence in the *missio Dei* depicted in the Bible. As Kähler said, "Mission is the mother of the church."[119] Our self-understanding is rooted there, in our "mother." There is nothing that we have that we did not receive in grace. Consequently, there is no room for arrogance or superiority. Nevertheless, neither must mission be done in timidity. Neither the message nor the mandate originates with us. Thus, as Paul quoted from Jeremiah, "Let him who boasts boast in the Lord (I Cor. 1:31)."

CHAPTER TWO

Rooting the Message in Culture: Models of Contextualization

If, in fact, mission is rooted and grounded in the Trinity (*missio Dei*), and if the Church is indeed God's chosen and primary means of revealing and bringing about His Kingdom (*regnum Dei*), we must then ask how does *ecclesia Dei* respond to and collaborate with *missio Dei*? How, as God's agent, is the Church to engage the world appropriately and effectively with the gospel of Jesus Christ? This engagement must take place in actions, signs, symbols, ceremonies and grammatical constructions understandable to the various peoples of this world. As the Church has sometimes boldly, at other times reluctantly, taken on this challenge, a number of theories and practices of contextualization have surfaced. This has resulted at times in serious debate between the practitioners. A prominent example that we will consider briefly from the seminal years of modern mission is the work of some of the Jesuit pioneers, Robert de Nobili and Matteo Ricci. Jesuit missionaries earned a reputation for their experimental and novel approaches to mission, drawing them into heated and protracted controversy.

The contextualization debate has not been limited to the Roman Catholic Church, however. On the Protestant side, the International Missionary Council and the World Council of Churches also wrestled with this challenge, and in turn, the Evangelical community has carried out its own inquiry, particularly within the context of the Lausanne movement. Thankfully, these scholars of differing theological persuasions have not conducted their investigations in total isolation from each other. Thankfully, these successive deliberations have played off of and informed one other.

Stepping into this debate, we will look briefly at a number of modern and critical expressions that have become foundational for mission practice and theology, such as: contextualization, indigenization, enculturation, inculturation and incarnation. To what extent do the issues surrounding these terms inform how one does mission work? In contemporary mission studies and articulations, these terms have become very critical in guiding missiological theory and praxis. At times, missiologists employ them rather distinctly; while at other times, they use them interchangeably and rather loosely. This chapter will give a brief but critical definition of each of these terms, as well as their theological underpinnings and *raison d'être*. We will see that each of these respective methodologies identifies itself with a particular tradition within the western church, each in turn claiming to be its originator, or at least emphasizing one above the others. Accordingly, we will also give the ecclesial and theological location of these diverse approaches, and the reason for the emphasis attributed to one or a combination of these within a given tradition. Finally, this chapter will offer a theological and missiological argument for an approach considered most appropriate for the mission of the Church today.

There is widespread agreement in the Church that the contextualization of the gospel is not optional; but is imperative, having its basis in the *missio*—in the incarnation of God (the *sending* of Himself) in His Son, Jesus Christ. Jesus immersed Himself fully in human ethnicity and culture, becoming God's visible presence among us. As Jesus Christ "took flesh and dwelt among us" (Jn. 1:14), He entered our history, died, rose again and ascended back to the Father. Yet, there is still a continued visible manifestation of the presence of God through His auxiliary chosen means—the Church. Here He engages the world through His Word and the sacraments. This is the post-resurrection and earthly expression of "his [Christ's] body, which is the church" (Col 1:24). How well we carry out this role will determine, largely, the degree to which the world will be able to *recognize* that "the Father has sent the Son" (John 17:23). For this reason alone, proper contextualization of the gospel is an issue of monumental importance.

There has never been a time when contextualization of God's message for the world, in some form or another, has not taken place (although we probably came close to this in the nineteenth and first half of the twentieth century).[120] But it is only recently in the history of the Church that this process has been recognized as a Church-wide missiological discipline *per se*, where it has been deliberately tried, tested, researched and discussed to the extent that we see today.

The very first time that the Church as a whole had to deal with contextualization was at the Jerusalem Council (Acts 15), where the debate focused upon the incorporation of the Gentiles into the Church. Was the revelation of God's self to Israel some kind of static entity to be passed on without alteration, or would its form have to undergo change as it found a new home and expression among the Gentiles? If it did undergo change, to what extent would it change, and on what basis? Could one differentiate this revelation into a "kernel and husk," or would a complete rethinking of not only the form but also the content of the revelation be in order? Still yet, would it emerge somewhere in between? These are some of the issues that the Church has wrestled with over time, *inter alia*, "what is mission?" and "where is the source of mission?" The twentieth century brought us little agreement on these issues and the attempted resolutions to the problems have ranged across the spectrum from fossilized conservatism to outright revolt.

Apart from the Scriptures themselves, and apart from the writings of some of the early Church Fathers (e.g. Justin Martyr), it was perhaps in the sixteenth century work of the Jesuits—Robert de Nobili in India, Allesandro Valignano and Matteo Ricci in China—that this issue of contextualization became a topic of hot debate.[121] These attempts sparked the Chinese Rites Controversy in the Catholic Church that exploded after the death of Ricci. The first challenges to the Jesuit attempts were by individuals from other Orders—Dominicans and Franciscans—many of whom had only been working in China for several years. Interestingly, the first Dominican to come and work in China, an Italian by the name of Angelo Cocchi, was in favor of Jesuit practices and recommended to the Dominican authorities in Manila that these practices be followed. Those who arrived after Cocchi, however, felt compelled to challenge the Jesuits at every turn.[122] Their challenges came under three headings. Andrew C. Ross lists them as follows:

> The first was that the Jesuits did not insist on the positive precepts of the Church, such as were imposed on the Indians in "New Spain" and in the Philippines. The second was the issue of the Chinese terms used for God, soul, angels and other Christian theological terms. The third was the participation by Christians in the rites for honoring the dead and, in the case of the literati, the rites honoring Confucius.[123]

In addition to these points, there were other complaints to Rome: for example, that certain fast days were not observed in the Church in China (as they were in the Philippines and other Spanish dominions), that the Jesuits did not use prescribed rites for baptism of women, and that the Jesuits did not proclaim that Confucius was in hell. Such controversy makes it clear why Valignano did not want Spaniards of *any* kind, even Jesuits, in China. Spanish dominions were under Spanish rule and the conquistadores made sure that their dominions came into line with the customs of old Spain. The mendicant Orders did not have patience for the lack of such discipline in China. From this, Ross explains that even more than the differences in Orders, the Spanish milieu created the problems. Laying out the background of this conflict in his Introduction, Ross points out that,

> From its inception, the Society of Jesus had problems with Spain which were to last for centuries. The Spanish church was inextricably involved with the Spanish crown. The Spanish Inquisition had become a royal institution, despite its technical ecclesiastical status and a most important tool of royal policy and control over the newly united and reconquered Spain. Its authority was extraordinary and it did not recognize any spiritual authority beyond itself—not even that of the Pope, although nominally recognizing the authority of Rome. During this time as a student, the ex-soldier, Ignatius Loyola, had fallen foul of it on occasion. After his Society was recognized as an Order, it was still suspect in Spain...Most important of all, however, was its [Spain's] profound objection to the Jesuit claim...of a direct and special relation to the Pope. This special relationship, the Jesuits insisted, meant that they were not subject to the Spanish Inquisition...Dominican and Spanish suspicion of the Society of Jesus is thus built into the story of the Society from the beginning.[124]

Responding to the charges, the Jesuits offered a careful and rational defense for their actions. (1) They had pared down baptismal rites for women to the bare minimum because there were cultural taboos about touching women. (2) Fast days where people abstained from work would require a clash with Chinese authorities, and fasting was harsh for people who lived on a subsistence diet of rice and herbs. (3) To say that Confucius was in hell might actually violate the Catholic position on the fate of those who had not heard the gospel, but had followed the light they had been given. To clash with the Chinese over such issues meant to the Jesuits that they would be clashing unnecessarily over issues that were *not central to the gospel*.[125] Also, the Jesuits had in fact instructed Chinese believers to eliminate some Chinese practices, and they called for modification of others. These seventeenth century accusations and consequent defenses have continued to shape the contextualization debate in the Church ever since.

Without going into a lot of detail here, suffice it for now to say that basic to this discussion were questions such as: are Confucianism and Christianity in opposition to each other, or are they compatible? Are ancestral rites religious and pagan at their core, or are they merely continuations of filial respect paid to one's elders in this life? The controversy over the practices of Ricci and Valignano eventually resulted in Rome condemning them as religious and banning their continuance. This was not the end of the story, however; this prolonged and bitter debate would continue until 1939, when Rome would eventually reverse its stance. Even so, the controversy will likely never fully resolve itself.

So then, what exactly was the philosophy that shaped the Jesuit approach to proclaiming the gospel message? These sixteenth century pioneers recognized that although the *core message* that they brought was in itself "static," in order for it to be *accepted* by cultures that were different from the West, missionaries would have to make accommodations to those cultures. The Jesuit missionaries had shaped their missiology around the "kernel and husk" idea. One must not tamper with the kernel itself, but the husk was of lesser value and could accommodate itself to the new culture.[126] They were able, unlike the Spanish mendicants, to separate European culture from the gospel they offered. With this model, the primary focus of mission was on the "sending" church, with a secondary focus on the "receiving" culture. In India, in the case of de Nobili, the gospel had to make accommodation to the caste system (specifically to the Brahmin portion of it), as he utilized an early version of the "homogeneous unit principle" that would find popularity (and stir controversy) in the twentieth century through the work of Donald McGavran.

The accommodations of these early Jesuits produced a reaction of fear and strong opposition from other orders of the Catholic Church. The Franciscans and Dominicans, for example, were highly skeptical of this process. Theirs was a method much more characteristic of the "Christ against culture" stance described by H. Richard Niebuhr.¹²⁷ Accounts of one Dominican who worked in the region say that he "set about overthrowing every idol wherever he could lay his hands on them. The mandarins soon laid their hands on him, and he was speedily ejected."¹²⁸ The Jesuit appreciation for cultures was in part responsible for the society's eventual political fall in 1774, until the order again achieved renewed strength in the twentieth century.¹²⁹ Where others saw syncretism, the Jesuits saw accommodation. Were the Jesuits compromising the gospel in their zeal to accommodate? Had Rome granted them total freedom, would the uniqueness of the claims of Christ have been totally lost? The Jesuits, in spite of their practices of accommodating to culture, still employed confrontation of Christian doctrines against Buddhist ones. Ralph R. Covell points out that the nature of charges brought against them by opponents in the Chinese court clearly portray the serious commitment the Jesuits made to the faith. The following are accusations directed against Adam von Ball Schall, a leading Jesuit and director of the Bureau of Astronomy, in 1655. Covell quotes here from Arnold Rowbotham's *Missionary and Mandarin*.

> 1) Preaching Christ crucified, 2) baptizing annually two or three hundred converts, 3) claiming that the emperor had accepted Christianity, 4) preaching that Adam was created of God and was the father of the human race, 5) seducing people by the preaching of repentance and by the administration of baptism and anointing, 6) preaching that Heaven *(T'ien)* is the seat of God and not God himself, 7) forbidding the worship of ancestors, 8) holding, four times a year, suspicious meetings with Christians and collecting money from them, and lastly 9) having suspicious relations with the Portuguese at Macao.¹³⁰

Though the Society of Jesus was undoubtedly on a learning curve, it would appear they strove to preserve the core elements of the gospel message. Nevertheless, one of the important points that surfaces here is the issue of connection to a foreign power, a serious problem that would have grave consequences for the work of the Church over the long haul, not only among Roman Catholics, but with Protestant work as well. For the purposes of this particular chapter, however, let it suffice to say that these early pioneers of accommodation laid a valuable groundwork that served many generations of missionaries to come.

In the wake of the Enlightenment, accommodation (and the Protestant equivalent: indigenization) was widely practiced. Cultures and people groups became the "objects" of "discovery," setting the stage for colonization and research by Western powers. Throughout this era too, the "sending" culture remained the standard for the communication of the gospel, and missionaries still viewed the indigenization process as a gracious act extended to the needy "host" cultures. The patronizing nuance remained unchanged.

Next, we enter the period of colonization (1800-1950)—a period which has been labeled by Paul Hiebert as the "Era of Non-Contextualization."[131] Why, after a degree of openness to indigenization in earlier periods, did the process come to a halt? Hiebert cites three primary reasons for this, the first being colonization. With colonization came the flawed perception that "the West was best"—a view of cultural superiority. A corollary to this was the thinking that the gospel in the West had already undergone an indigenization process, and had already achieved its perfected form that could now be merely "put into" another culture. This leads us to the second contributing factor: a Darwinian view of culture. If social Darwinism were in fact true, there would be no need to pay any attention to a "more primitive" culture, since it would be in the process of development. It would be only natural for it to shed its own skin and become like the West. The third reason given by Hiebert is the triumph of science. Because the West had clearly "won" in this category, it was very easy to associate the gospel with a "superior" form of Western thinking that would ultimately serve as the salvation of the world.[132] It was the notion of many in the Church that the world was truly on its way to the "Christian Century." That sense of inevitability that Marx applied to his economic theory found expression in the thinking of many toward mission. In light of such progress-oriented theology, it is easy to see why the Church might view any form of contextualization as largely unnecessary, and perhaps even unwise. This unfortunate reality led, in turn, to the belief that the best approach to mission work was to view all other cultures as evil, to strip away as much of the culture as possible, and to seek to build the Church upon a *tabula rasa*, or clean slate. Surely, it was thought, nothing could be worth keeping in a "primitive" or "pagan" culture. The *intended* effects were to elevate culture to Western standards, and to prevent syncretism (the thing feared most by those who opposed any sort of accommodation). The *unexpected* effect was that quite frequently this approach actually *fostered* syncretism. The suppression of the basic elements of the "native" culture served only to drive them underground and out of the view of the Western missionary. Knowing that they could not discuss cultural issues with the missionary, the people adopted the Western forms when in public, and then went home and did things their own way—in their own cultural forms. A secondary, but equally tragic, down side to this approach was the perception of the local people that the gospel was a Western, and consequently foreign, religion. Thus, the need appeared once again to bring the local people and their culture back into the process, as partners, in mission. The next major phase of this process is contextualization.

"Contextualization" has become a sort of umbrella word for many different sub-models that incorporate a meeting of theology and context. The term as we know it today surfaced in the deliberations of the Theological Education Fund (TEF) under the World Council of Churches in 1971-1972, and was a driving force in the resulting TEF document, *Ministry in Context*.[133] This movement was a response to a growing recognition that the accommodation/indigenization model held to a static view of doctrine and did not take adequate account of the "receptor culture." The forms, theological expressions, and educational method were all Western expressions and were often alien to the culture in which they were to take root. The document's formulation of a two-premise (theology and context) approach to transplanting the gospel addresses this deficiency in some detail.

The *Ministry in Context* document called for a "contextualization" of theology as a response to the mission imperative. Evangelicals especially have often missed the radical nature of its content. The goal was to make Christianity relevant to all ethnic groups, or to make a new Christianity that is relevant. As Europe was moving into a post-Christian era, liberal theologians were ready to give the Christian faith a major overhaul. The document targeted four areas for attention: missiology, educational structures, theology and pedagogy.

There were three separate mandates that came out of the Theological Education Fund: "advance" and "rethink" were the first two.[134] The *Ministry in Context* document incorporated the third mandate: to "contextualize." Missionaries were to apply the contextualization concept to pedagogy and theology, the result being such that "doctrinal theology" and "contextual theology" came forth as two dialectical partners and both became a source for a "comprehensive theology."[135] At the same time, both are relativized for the sake of this process. Either must be open to change. This is in stark competition with the earlier form of doctrinal theology being "static" and a lone source for theology. In contextualization, culture is to speak back to doctrine, and doctrine is to be open to change.[136] In the process, what often happened was that the "text" (of Scripture) itself became a *relative* text, and there was little accountability left for culture. In contrast, the earlier indigenization process, as far as it went, held to the absolute nature of Scripture. With "indigenization," the focus was simply on communicating the gospel in terms already present in the culture and working for local leadership. It was "clothing" the gospel in the dress of the local people. Contextualization went beyond this. The more radical "rethinking" of theology under the TEF document denigrates any and all forms of an absolute. In effect, what may have been an attempt at constructing a new method ends up being the construction of a new theology altogether. Whereas before, the culture was losing out to the biblical text, now we see the biblical text losing out to culture, at least in the more radical forms of contextualization. We are witnessing a new way of looking at mission; we are observing an epistemological paradigm shift.

In discussing the genesis of this new contextual theology, Bosch refers to the categories of Justin Upkong.

> Upkong...identifies two major types of contextual theology, namely, the indigenization model and the socio-economic model. Each of these can again be divided into two subtypes: the indigenization motif presents itself either as a translation or as an inculturation model; the socio-economic pattern of contextualization can be evolutionary (political theology and the theology of development) or revolutionary (liberation theology, black theology, feminist theology, etc.).... In my view, only the inculturation model in the first type and only the revolutionary model in the second qualify as contextual theologies proper.[137]

Political and developmental theologies have been viewed as serving the interests of the West, and so Bosch agrees with Latin American liberationist theologians in eliminating these options from the contextual family, and the translation model would not go far enough to be seen as true contextualization. In *An Open Letter to José Míguez Bonino*, Moltmann wrote, "the most decisive difference between the Latin American theology of liberation and political theology in Western Europe lies in the assessment of the various historical situations."[138] Emilio A. Nuñez C. explains, "According to liberation theologians, European political theology—precisely because it is not Latin American and because it has been formulated in a context of affluence—cannot understand the economic and social problems of our people."[139] Liberation Theology, as a revolutionary breed of contextual theology, speaks back to those with power, and seeks to bring about a change in the status quo. Moreover, it redefines salvation as liberation for the oppressed and the poor, often in terms of outright political revolution. Although originally hailed as the most prominent expression of contextualization, ironically, Latin American expressions of Liberation Theology utilized European political and theological models to produce this construct. Marxism, for example, figured prominently in many of its expressions. Bosch said of this new contextualization epistemology, "Like Marx, it says, 'The philosophers have only tried to interpret the world, the point, however, is to change it.'"[140] This too has an echo of Moltmann in it, as he wrote, "The theologian is not concerned merely to supply a different *interpretation* of the world, of history and of human nature, but to *transform* them in expectation of a divine transformation."[141]

Gustavo Gutiérrez, a Peruvian Roman Catholic (sometimes referred to as the "systematic theologian of Liberation Theology"), brought the most attention to this Latin American movement, and initially gave the best articulation of it.[142] (Others would include but not be limited to Juan Luis Segundo of Uruguay, Presbyterian Rubem Alves from Brazil; the Spanish Jesuit living in El Salvador, John Sobrino; and Brazilians Hugo Assmann and Leonardo Boff.) Gutiérrez argues that Christians must cease doing theology on the basis of interpreting Scripture, and must instead base theology on "critical reflection on liberating praxis."[143] The Liberation Theology movement influenced Jürgen Moltmann's theology,[144] and he in turn inspired it;[145] however, Moltmann remained a more God-centered force for liberation, whereas the bulk of the movement became much more anthropocentric in its approach. Salvation became a process of human effort in human history, and the vertical dimension of salvation, the God-centered focus of liberation, was de-emphasized (again, the lower story severed from the upper story, for the most part). In the process, "Thy Kingdom come" becomes a human effort, something we bring about ourselves. The reason for this, says Bosch, is found in the move of contextualized theologies away from rooting life in truth and eternal principles, substituting this approach with action stemming from observation of specific, non-static environments and contexts.[146] In the attempt to liberate cultures from dogmatism and the magisterium of Western forms, the "kernel" or revealed truth of the gospel was sacrificed and the "husk" was enthroned. That which *should be unchanging* (the biblical truths that unite the world Body of Christ) was changed, and ever-changing cultures became the new absolute for an ever-changing hermeneutic.

Another serious problem that surfaces in this context is that once a "contextual" theology roots itself in its localized culture, rather than in the universal Scripture, it leads to what Moltmann termed a "provincialization of the theology."[147] Such a potential surfaces also in C. S. Song's transpositional theology of the "flat-nosed Christ." The problem does not lie in the need for Jesus to be accessible to all cultures. Rather, the problem surfaces when God is so defined by a local people that He loses all historical significance and Jesus ceases to be an historical person in flesh and blood with Jewish features. Jesus, and His teachings can lose their concrete historical reality, and local context then becomes the overriding hermeneutical principle. The end product is a phantasmal Docetic Christ whose only reality is ideological.

A Roman Catholic parallel to contextualization was "inculturation." In 1977, Pedro Arrupe, then Jesuit superior-general, introduced the term to the Synod of Bishops. It has since become the most common definition, at least in Roman Catholic circles.

> Inculturation is the incarnation of Christian life and of the Christian message in a particular cultural context, in such a way that this experience not only finds expression through elements proper to the culture in question, but becomes a principle that animates, directs and unifies the culture, transforming and remaking it so as to bring about a "new creation."[148]

The Apostolic Exhortation of Pope John Paul II in 1979 (*Catechesi Tradendae*, "Catechesis in Our Time") took up the term "inculturation," giving it widespread exposure. Inculturation is the theological adaptation of the earlier sociological concept of "enculturation," which had found a home in anthropology. Enculturation is the process of forming a worldview as one grows up, shaped by one's own cultural environment.[149]

Like contextualization, inculturation recognized the great role that culture plays in people's understanding of the gospel, and the inadequacy of accommodation. Aside from the greater role that it gives to the "three legged stool" of Catholicism (Bible, Pope, Church Tradition), it is so much like the contextualization model, Protestants gave little reaction to it.

The other category mentioned above is incarnation. The incarnational view developed as Protestants considered the inadequacies of indigenization. Its premise is that as God has already incarnated Himself into our world and clothed Himself in humanity, the world really must *remain* the focus of mission. Theology is *for the world*. We no longer need to look to systematic doctrinal categories to interpret the biblical text for us; interpretation of the text must find its source now *in the world*, and the *issues* of the world. The missionary first must examine the issues, and then go to the biblical text. The text sits under the authority of culture. *The world, then, informs the biblical text, rather than the other way around.* This conforms to the view of earlier liberal scholarship that all of theology is not only influenced, but in fact is determined by the context from which it evolves. The message is never a "pure" message that sits above culture and history. The recognition of the way in which environment conditions theology became the received view in critical theological circles in the nineteenth, and more particularly in the twentieth century.[150] This approach is different from taking the questions of the world to the Bible and seeking normative answers: it is instead using the needs and ideas of the cultures of the world as a *magisterium* for biblical hermeneutics. In the former, the Bible remains the source and norm for social action, in the latter, the dictates of a culture become the primary, and ever-changing norm for interpreting what the Bible means and says. (As we will see shortly, this dialectic of Bible and culture can express itself in destructive ways at *either* end of the spectrum.)

Incarnation serves as a sort of subsystem of contextualization, and since world issues are driving it, it expresses itself in more radical and revolutionary forms. Says Aram I, the Armenian Catholicos of Celicia, "... the question is how to liberate, transform and reorient the cultures."[151] In describing this model, he continues:

> The gospel is affirmed *through* cultures, not *in* cultures. Culture is only an instrument, framework and context to embody and articulate the gospel. During the colonial era, mission emphasized the text and ignored the context, while during the post-colonial era, mission focused on context to the extent of losing sight of the text.[152]

With this new emphasis on *the world being a source* of theology, there was also an emphasis upon the necessity of reading the "signs of the times." The question became one of reading the needs of peoples in each time and in each context. Meeting these needs became mission. (This reading of signs has many pitfalls. For example, people in the West, and some even in its colonies, saw colonization as the will of God. The Nazis also saw their "signs." etc. By what standard are the signs tested?)

It will become obvious at this point that a major blurring is taking place in regards to the historical distinction of general and specific revelation (even a hostility, in some cases, toward holding these as separate categories), as well as a blurring of form and content. In the rush to value the human in the communication and consequent appropriation of the gospel, there is a "rethinking" of revelation as well, by Catholic and Protestant alike. Whereas at one time the "human" in the world was disparaged and destroyed in many of the expressions of mission, the "human" has since then been put on the same level of authority as God's own revealed written Word. One can do this only if one sees the world as "God's world." But what does one mean by "God's world"? In the minds of some, the fact that "This is my Father's world" has legitimized the shift from a view that the world is fallen, corrupted, and must be redeemed by a momentous act of God, to a view that the world is basically good and simply needs help in becoming "humanized." This is a major paradigmatic shift. It is an elevation of fallen creation through action that is chiefly anthropocentric. "Doing of theology" now takes on a new expression in "making this world a better place for humanity." Religion as expression of human culture is then no longer seen as idolatry, but is instead a *proto-evangelium* that needs only to be fulfilled and completed by the work of Christ (and in some cases, it is not even necessary that He be known.)[153] To the degree that human creatures possess the image of God and have the Law of God written upon their hearts, there is without question a degree of truth in this. Certainly, such action is consistent with the Kingdom of God coming to earth through his Church, and even at times *apart from His Church*, and yet should one interpret such revelation alone as salvific? Many would argue so. What then becomes important is not the object of one's faith, but the mere fact that faith exists. The question becomes one of "What is driving your theology of hope?" These are precisely the kinds of issues that are fueling today's missiological debate.

We can also, and indeed must, approach this question from another standpoint: if in fact the Son of God has come to earth as Savior, what visible difference has this salvation made in the world, if any? How is the world different today because of His coming? We cannot simply critique the process of "humanization" without also asking this question. Furthermore, if, in fact, His coming *should* make a difference in our world, then how is that difference to come about, if not through those who call themselves His redeemed followers? Should the Body of Christ not manifest the evidence of the Kingdom of God toward a suffering humanity? How does a doctrine of total human depravity integrate with a tangible manifestation of God's Kingdom and will toward "the least of these"? Should not the aforementioned "momentous act" of God crucified and resurrected express itself in forms that result in liberation from injustice and poverty *precisely* because one's soul has been transformed through the power of that "momentous act"?

Let us then turn our attention to a couple of Evangelical interpretations of contextualization. In Bruce Fleming's discussion of the models some years ago, he constructed a helpful graph, which included four expressions of contextual theology, ranging as follows:

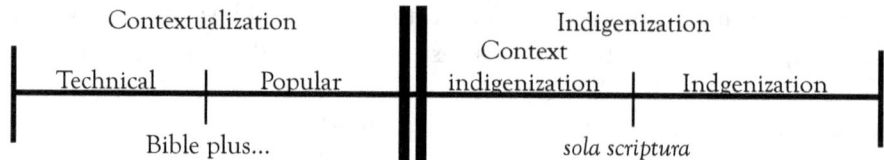

Commenting on his graph, Fleming explains, "The further one goes from right to left, specifically from the break in the middle of the graph the more one supplements the Bible with other thoughts."[154] On either end of the spectrum, one finds a predominant emphasis played out either by culture (Technical Contextualization), or text (Indigenization). Under "Popular Contextualization," for example, he would place someone like Kosuke Koyama. Koyama opened his book, *Waterbuffalo Theology*, with the stated intent of developing a Third World theology.[155] As a missionary in Thailand, Koyama concluded that rather than expounding upon the works of Western theologians—such as Augustine, Barth, and Rahner—his first task would be to "raise issues."[156] Although these Western theologians would be helpful in knowing what issues to raise, their theology was not the answer to the needs of the farmer working his waterbuffalo in the rice paddies.

Fleming quotes Koyama's interpretation of the Theological Education Fund document as follows:

> ...contextualization of theology is something more than taking the historical and cultural context seriously; it is letting theology speak in and through that context. This much is already a tall order indeed. The TEF concept of contextualization "seeks to press beyond" this. Theology must consist of critical accommodation. This is *authentic contextualization.* TEF theological reflection locates the ultimate moment of such contextualization in the incarnation of Jesus Christ.[157]

Fleming then goes on to comment that Koyama agreed with the "technical contextualizers" to the degree that theologians had to take an active posture as they "incarnated the crucified Christ."[158] Yet, Koyama differed from the TEF in feeling free to interchange the terms "contextualization" and "indigenization." Koyama also appeared to place more of a stress on grassroots theologizing. Fleming draws another quote from Koyama as an example of Koyama's distaste for the modification of existing theologies.

> Chinese theology cannot come out instantly when theology is cast in the Confucian category from a neo-Platonic category. If that were all it took to contextualize theology, it would not be such a difficult arrangement. It is, in reality, to do with the emergence of theological work engaged in by a Chinese crucified mind.[159]

In his footnote on this quote, Fleming points to the work of Lynn A. DeSilva as an example of Koyama's approach. He quotes DeSilva's comments on work in Sri Lanka, "As a result of these efforts there is now emerging an indigenous expression of the Christian faith based on a theological structure oriented to the conceptual framework of Buddhism."[160] In such examples, culture does have a major role as a source of theology, but it is less of a factor than you would find in the case of the Technical Contextualization model.

To the right of the double lines in the above chart, the "Context-Indigenization" model values culture highly in the interpretive process, but not to the extent of actually becoming a *source* for theology. (In a moment, we will discuss a model similar to this, proposed by Paul Hiebert.)

A number of things come to the fore while reflecting upon this entire spectrum of approaches to contextualization. First, in the deliberation of the TEF, one sees a *much needed* rebellion against a static systematic/biblical theology running roughshod over culture; and yet, rather than attack the *way* in which systematic or biblical theology is carried out, the TEF approach reduces special revelation in the written Word of God to the level of human culture. Consequently, one comes to view the Scriptural text as relative. This led to a further fragmentation of the Church as each culture became its own individual standard and its own defining force for doing theology. In this process, the Bible was moved from a position of *norma normans* to *norma normata*. Historically, the Bible has been the "normative norm" to which the Church was bound. The confessions of the Church were the "normed norm" or the Church's interpretation of the Bible; the first is a Divine work through a human element, the second is a human work in response to the Divine. Consequently, the Bible has a Divine and absolute authority, whereas the Confessions, or interpretation, haVE only an ecclesiastical and relative authority.

Over the course of history, the Bible has held this position of the absolute and unchanging standard. At times, the councils which produced the confessions have been elevated to a status equal with the Word of God, but in the modern period we actually saw the opposite: the Word of God was reduced to a position equal with culture and subservient to the ever-changing fads of hermeneutic.

When the possibility of an unchanging absolute disappears, it becomes more difficult for the universal Church to have a unifying standard to which all subscribe. As each church body becomes at the same time autonomous and relative, we drastically reduce, or even lose, the possibility for mutual critique and edification. Moreover, the Church also becomes more vulnerable to unhealthy kinds of syncretism,[161] which is already at the point of being out of control in many parts of the world today. (One need only look to the materialist/consumerist culture that has found a home in the church of the West. What theology will such a culture promote in the world?) Whereas once we fostered syncretism by a *denigration* of culture, today missionaries foster unhealthy syncretism by giving culture a supremely defining role as an actual *source* for theology. In so doing, culture usurps the place which rightly belongs only to the Bible.

Certainly, the old model of indigenization did not go far enough. The setting of Christendom allowed missionaries to minister from a position of power, as they carried with them the authority of the king's sword. Thankfully, the situation is far different today. The effective missionary today must come in personal weakness as a learner. The power no longer comes with her or his passport, but in the gospel alone. Missionary and national come together before the gospel of Jesus Christ, as He is revealed in the unchanging Word of God—the *norma normans*. This unchanging Word needs to be the sole and unchanging source both for changing culture and for changing how one does theology. Neither of the latter two should have the status of an absolute, just as the status of the unchanging Word should not be reduced to that of a relative entity, on a par with human culture. Thus, an absolute and normative standard is imperative for genuine unity in the universal Body of Christ. But that standard is not to be a Western, African, Asian theololgy or any other type of theology to which all others must conform. Theology is not the Word of God itself (*norma normans*), but is our interpretation of that Word (*norma normata*). Thus, we sacrifice *Sola Scriptura* at our peril. What is now needed, however, is a better method of rooting the Scripture in a culture—a method that values cultures enough to allow it to express God's truth in ways understandable to its people. At the same time, this method must not compromise truth; it ought to allow the Scripture to become the sole norm for a critique of and transformation of that culture, independent of the proclaimer or the hearer.[162] As will be seen in a moment, this process also needs to be *locally* driven.

Secondly, the emphasis in mission should not change from Luther's question "How is one made right with a Holy God?" to "How does one get along with one's neighbor?" The vertical aspect of salvation, reconciliation with God, needs to inform the horizontal, reconciliation with my neighbor. Just as the "vertical" question does not stand alone and apart, but is borne out in the "horizontal" aspect, so the "horizontal" does not find resolution apart from the "vertical." Barth expresses this in his exploration of justice flowing from justification.[163] He is correct in so far as he asserts that justification needs to remain primary. As discussed earlier, a theme of "humanization" cannot replace the preaching of the gospel unto repentance and conversion, any more than one can consider redemption to be only a spiritual matter.[164] True humanization (that which is in accord with the Kingdom of God) can fully emerge only out of a response to the death and resurrection of Jesus Christ in repentance and conversion through faith.

The conference at Melbourne declared that victory in countries struggling for liberation was "the glory of the resurrection of Jesus Christ." This is theological reductionism. Liberation from oppression is without a doubt an important and essential part of the work of the Kingdom. The oppressed and those "on the periphery" are always on the heart of God, and although such a movement may be cause for rejoicing, it is not to be equated with "the glory of the resurrection of Jesus Christ." To do so is to fall into the dangers of what Moltmann called a "religion of society." Moltmann asks, "... can the church of the crucified man from Nazareth ever become a political religion, without forgetting him and losing its identity?"[165] The complete and true gospel is more than human endeavor for justice on earth; the vertical (with God), as well as the horizontal (human with human) aspects of salvation must be included.

Now let us turn our attention to our second example of Evangelical contextualization. In response to this, and other problems that have surfaced in the contextualization debate, Paul Hiebert has proposed a model called, "Critical Contextualization."[166] This method states that one begins with a thorough (and *non-judgmental*) examination of the cultural forms of the people. At this point, there is to be *no evaluation* of the forms, only an examination and explanation of the "hows" and the "whys." The second step is for the missionary to conduct a biblical study of the issues that the original cultural forms address. For example, if one were to investigate the cultural form for the funeral, then the missionary would conduct a biblical study of death and the afterlife. Again, there is to be *no judgment* of the cultural forms at this stage, only a presentation of what the Bible teaches about the issues themselves. *The people* are to then draw a comparison and see to what extent the cultural forms agree or disagree with the biblical teachings on the issue. The missionary can be involved, but *it must be a locally driven process*. Finally, the decision is made *by the people* as to what can be kept in the local forms, what must be discarded, what can be substituted etc. In this manner, both the local culture and the biblical text receive respect and value. Neither sacrifices itself to the other, which is only as it should be. At the same time, God's written revelation to humankind—the biblical text—is still the source of faith and the standard by which one evaluates community life. It is the primary source for our understanding of who Jesus is and what He taught. The text does not go through any kind of reductionism, but is valued to be what it is—the inspired Word of God. Hiebert's proposal is a response to what has often been termed "uncritical-contextualization," where culture is valued over text, and the gospel becomes captive to culture.[167] Rather, it must be the other way around—the culture must be captive to the gospel so that the culture is accountable to, and transformed by it. This transformation is to be, however, a process of the Holy Spirit *via* those who can discern the culture best—the people themselves. The missionary determines neither what is to be transformed, nor how.

As can be seen in Hiebert's model, true contextualization goes beyond accommodation/indigenization. The local people and their culture fully engage themselves in the process of rooting the gospel of Jesus Christ into their local soil. There is now a gentler kind of dialectical process going on that ultimately does injustice to neither side. Both culture and biblical text gain a hearing, and both the missionary and the culture subject themselves to the potential for change as the Holy Spirit speaks to them through the biblical text. Thus, there is no "sender and receiver" or "subject and object" relationship between the culture and the missionary, but, instead, full partnership in the gospel.

In light of these various issues I would propose an approach similar to the above-mentioned Context-Indigenization model as a form of mission that does biblical justice to both human culture and doctrine. While preserving the absolute nature of Scripture, it prevents our theological indigenization process from taking on a static and totalitarian role in culture. It still allows appeal to an absolute standard without any culture having to bow before the foreign cultural trappings in which the gospel comes to them. In the past, mission had a decidedly Docetic emphasis, and this certainly needs to be discarded. We need to value the human role in the transmission and assimilation of the gospel into our being. As Koyama rightly saw, the Thai people did not need to hear Barth and Brunner, they needed a gospel that spoke to them in the rice paddy, and which valued who they were. Finally, doctrinal theology and context must sit under the authority of the biblical text. Mission is not all about propositional truth, but neither is mission truly *missio Dei* if there is no propositional truth. Revelation is not *only* cognitive knowledge of God, but, at least in part, it <u>is</u> that. The God who has revealed Himself to us is *unchanging* in essence, and yet He is also *changed*, *via* His incarnation and becoming "sin for us" that we might "become the righteousness of God." He is the "Changed Unchanging." This concept can serve as a guide in the earthly and ongoing work of *missio Dei*. The core essence does not change, and yet neither is the "Unchanging" unaffected or apathetic regarding the object of His affection.

The text which we have discussed is not to be equated with the Text-Writer (God), but it is the Testament of His will (just as a certified Last Will and Testament is the legally binding revelation of the will of the one who made it), and thus the Bible serves as the unchangeable revealed standard for *missio Dei*. In this sense, Luther and others were right to promote *Sola Scriptura*. Where change comes in is in how the text is used, and this is also where the debate happens. Is the biblical text relative and subject to culture? Or is it a static text, which once indigenized in the West, is now a tool for the missionary to promote at the *expense* of culture? Still, is the biblical text the standard by which missionary and culture come together in partnership, with each open to change before the text? Is each allowed to experience the wonder of Acts chapter 2? Upon hearing the followers of Jesus, "God-fearing Jews from every nation" responded thus:

> Utterly amazed, they asked: "Are not all of these men who are speaking Galileans? Then how is it that each of us hears them in his own native language? Parthians, Medes and Elamites; residents of Mesopotamia, Judea and Cappadocia, Pontus and Asia, Phrygia and Pamphylia, Egypt and parts of Libya near Cyrene; visitors from Rome (both Jews and converts to Judaism); Cretans and Arabs—we hear them declaring the wonders of God in our own tongues!" Amazed and perplexed they asked one another, "What does this mean? Acts 2:7-12"

The text was not relative in this instance, but the language in which the text was heard was. The resultant interpretations of the phenomena were also varied; some thought, "They have had too much wine (2:13b)." Others asked that the true meaning of the message be explained. This idicates that we need to take into account not only how one communicates a message, but also the reception of that message. People often assume that if a message is clearly presented, the listener will clearly perceive. However, as Robert Schreiter has pointed out, one must take account of the universe in which the message is taking root as well as the universe from which the message has come. How will the message relate to other meanings in the culture?[168] Schreiter offers the following example:

> A noted Bible translator told of his experience of presenting a fresh translation of the Psalms and the New Testament to a Thai university student. The student was not a Christian, and the

intent of the gift was to see if the translation was intelligible to a non-Christian, not just syntactically (at the level of the correct grammatical usage), but also semantically. A few weeks later the translator encountered the student again and asked what he thought. The student admitted to having read the four Gospels and was at that point reading the Acts of the Apostles. "What a wonderful person, your Jesus!" the student exclaimed. The translator, clearly excited by the response (for he is also a devout evangelical Christian and saw a potential convert here), asked the student to elaborate. "What a marvelous story," he continued, "of how your Jesus was born, lived, died...was reborn, lived, died...was reborn, lived, died... was reborn lived, and then—in the Acts of the Apostles—ascended into Nirvana! Just four incarnations to reach Buddhahood, and it took our Gautama a thousand lives to achieve that!" No doubt the more exalted language of the Gospel of John contributed to this reading of the spiritual maturation of Jesus....[169]

Much more work needs to be done in regards to the reception of the gospel message. This is true not only in the case of written communication, but in symbols and ceremonies as well. Form does not express the same content in all cultures. To refer to another illustration by Schreiter:

An interesting and somewhat embarrassing case arose some thirty years ago when the Roman Catholic cathedral was built in Kyoto. One of the stained glass windows had a portrait of St. George slaying the dragon. This image of St. George goes back to an amalgam of pre-Christian, Eastern Mediterranean lore. The problem in its context in Kyoto was that the dragon is not a symbol of Satan or of evil. Throughout East Asia, the dragon is a symbol of royalty and of heaven! Needless to say, the window was removed.[170]

This is a good example in two ways: one, it demonstrates how easily we assume that our traditions, our symbols and even our concepts are supracultural. How far from the truth that is. Although the gospel in itself is supracultural, the expressions that we give to it are not. Secondly, the example demonstrates how important it is for us to be responsive to the culture in which we work. In this instance, the gospel remained—the window went.

The primary purpose of the Church being left in this world is that the glory of God might continue to be manifested in human flesh. The Roman Catholic Church once saw itself as the *societas perfecta*. With Vatican II, it redefined itself as the "pilgrim people (in *Lumen Gentium*)."[171] What this new definition means is still being worked out. How is a "pilgrim people" different from any other "people" on this earth? The difference is not discerned in looking to the people themselves; Christian people are not inherently better than any other. The difference is in the intent of God for His Church—in the role that He has given to His *ecclesia*. That role is to image Him in our world. The Church is not yet the *societas pefecta*—that is still an eschatological reality. (As Schreiter commented on this Roman Catholic deliberation of what the Church is, "Instead of being an already perfected society, the church as the pilgrim people of God saw itself perhaps as the vanguard of that perfect society, but in highly modest and provisional terms.[172]) Neither are we the *regnum Dei*—rather, we point to it. We must value the place of *ecclesia Dei*, the role of God's Church, as He calls the world to this place of fellowship—a fellowship not in *retreat from* the world, but instead, an oasis of God's love within it. Some contextualization models have no place for the Church in their theology; when this is so, this is a major lacuna in our theology. The role of the Church is to affirm humanity without forgetting that the world and the Church is not the same thing. The Church points the world to its Creator God. In this sense, there is a sacramental element to our calling. The Church is a servant to the world (thus the call for the crucified mind) that the world might come to participate fully in the grace of God. In affirming the image of God in His creation, we must also see His creation as "lost and without a Shepherd." Jesus told us that He came to seek not those who are well, but to "seek and to save that which was lost." Our role is to "compel them to come in," not with the sword of Charlemagne, but with the good news that Christ died to save us all from sin and its evil consequences (in all forms). Our role is to speak and act out His love to the world. This is to be done in humility and service, not in timidity and fear. It is to be done in boldness that is rooted not in the self, but in the One whom we serve. The importance of this role necessitates great communicative care so that those who hear can hear him "in their own tongues." The result will hopefully be, "Amazed and perplexed they asked one another, 'What does this mean?' (Acts 2:12)"

CHAPTER THREE

Buddhism as a Missions Movement in Northeast Asia

> The history of Buddhism, at least from the time of its founder to the tenth century A.D., makes it plain that it was one of the great missionary religions in the world. Buddha himself, among other things, was an untiring evangelist, and to him the raison d'être of the Buddhist Community, more particularly its monastic orders, was the conversion of the whole world.
> Joseph M. Kitagawa, Religions of the East[173]

Buddhism was breaking ground in China at roughly the same time the Christian era was getting underway. Some have referred to what followed as the "Indianization of China." The late Dr. Hu Shih for example, presented an address on this theme at the Tercentenary Celebration of Harvard University in 1936. In that address, Hu Shih contended that pre-Buddhist Chinese religion consisted primarily of the following three things: "the worship of ancestors, of natural forces and T'ien or heaven; of belief in the efficacy of divination; and of some vague concepts of rewards and retribution."[174] As Buddhism entered Chinese society, it brought to the people a worldview much more elaborate than what they had heretofore known, introducing them to multiple heavens and hells containing myriad deities with varying degrees of sensibilities and passions. Buddhism replaced their comparatively vague notions of rewards and retributions with an "all-pervasive force called karma, which operated inexorably to reward good deeds with meritorious rebirths, and evil deeds with rebirth in one of the evil modes of existence." [175] Along with this came the otherworldly concept that life in this world is only a mirage or shadow; consequently, sensual desire is something to suppress, or better yet, eradicate. In fact, withdrawal from society and family to a life of celibacy and mendicancy was preferable. Moreover, since rebirth is the fate of every human, and since some of our relatives may come back as animals, a vegetarian diet may be advisable.[176] By the time of the T'ang dynasty (618-907 AD), Buddhist ideals had permeated all of Chinese society.[177] According to Kenneth K. S. Ch'en, Hu believed Buddhism to be "one of the greatest evils to have befallen China."[178] This, says Ch'en, is because Hu failed to balance out his address with a treatment of the other side of the story: how Buddhism underwent change as it rooted itself in China. Thus, while there was indeed an "Indianization" of China, there was a "Sinicization" of Buddhism as well.[179] While not ignoring the former, the Sinicization of Buddhism will be of more interest to us in this chapter.

The questions that we will raise in this section stem from a curiosity regarding how religions are "re-rooted" (to borrow Koyama's expression[180]). We undertake this investigation in the hope that a look at the transplanting of Buddhism into Northeast Asia, followed by a comparison (in the following chapters) of that process with the later "re-rooting" of Christianity in the region, may reveal insights that will be informative about the transplanting of religion in general and about Christian mission in particular.

Considering Buddhism in its earliest context, it originated as a reform movement within Hinduism, similar to Protestantism in Christianity. Some forms of Hinduism taught that salvation could come through rituals, as prescribed in the sacred literature, the Vedas. According to this line of teaching, the rituals themselves contained magic powerful enough to influence even the gods to do our bidding. Other forms of Hinduism pursued a more philosophical course, seeking the union of one's self or "soul" (*atman*) with Brahman, the ultimate reality. According to the Upanishads, once one achieved such union, that person was free of the cycle of birth-death-rebirth, or *samsara*.[181]

Although much of Buddhism is a carry-over from Hinduism, the teachings of Siddhartha Gautama (the "Buddha" or enlightened one) differed significantly from Hinduism on some key points. For example, he challenged the authority of the sacred canon of literature, the Vedas, and disagreed with both of the above-mentioned Hindu means to salvation. In their place, he introduced a rigorous spiritual lifestyle, substituting conduct as the primary avenue to spiritual achievement.[182] Further, he rejected caste, instead accepting all types of people into his community of followers.

Joseph Kitagawa points out that historians maintain that this community, called the *sangha*, was likely based in name and form upon the political *sangha*, evident in northern India during that time. The *sangha* became a primary missions strategy through which the Buddha hoped to transform society gradually, "not by legislation and coercion but by the permeating influence of the Buddhist Community, as well as by individual conversion and moral persuasion."[183]

In its early expression, Buddhism was a religion of individual effort and advancement—"concerned each with his own salvation in following the path the Buddha had trodden."[184] Buddhism was, and is, a religion that incorporates strong denials (for example: *anatman* or "no *atman*"; no material reality; no use for the gods, etc.) and yet it just as vigorously avoids practices of the extreme ascetics. It is what the Buddha liked to think of as the "middle way"—a middle way between luxurious self-indulgence, and extreme self-denial. However, in one sense the Buddha *added* to Hinduism. Ch'en explains,

> "Karma" to the Indians means the deed performed and the results that arise from it. To this conception of karma, the Buddha made a significant addition. He taught that karma involved not just the deed and the reward but also the intention behind the deed. For karma to be generated there must be intention, and he considered this intention much more important than the deed. If the deed is unintentional, he said, no karma is generated, but if intention is present, then karma is produced even though the deed itself is not actually performed. The Buddhist definition of "karma" is therefore "intention" plus the bodily action that follows the intention.[185]

As a reform movement, Buddhism eliminated parts of Hinduism with which it disagreed, kept other elements and expanded on still others. Also like other reform movements, Buddhism has its canon. The early texts of Buddhism are a compilation of monastic perceptions of the teachings of the Buddha. These are Pali texts, referred to as the *tripitaka* (three baskets).[186] "This with its three main divisions, the sutras, containing what claim to be Sakyamuni's [the Buddha's] own words, the *vinayas*, giving the monastic rules, and the *sastras*, dialectical essays and dialogues by famous early teachers, achieves a bulk which is simply stupendous, so that the whole Christian Bible plus the writings of the Fathers cannot compare in size."[187]

The *tripitaka* has long served as the core of the Buddhist canon, at least for its more conservative expressions.[188]

Although a number of different traditional Buddhist sects developed from the start,[189] the predominant manifestation of this earlier and more conservative tradition had as its goal the salvation of the individual through practice of the Four Noble Truths. Briefly, they are: (1) life is suffering, (2) the cause of suffering is desire, (3) cessation of suffering is brought about through the elimination of desire, which is achieved by, (4) the practice of the 8-fold path—a series of exhortations on right thinking, morality, and actions. According to the Theravada tradition (described below), the only way one can reasonably attain these goals is through a life of this-world denunciation. Thus, the life of the monk is the ideal.[190] The average layperson, however, could never hope to achieve such a standard while encumbered by the demands of daily living. Such a dilemma led, in the 2nd and 1st centuries BC, to subtle changes within Buddhism.[191] Many in that day, perceiving that the rigors of Buddhism were too strict and out of touch with the realities of the average layperson, called for a "Greater" or "Wider Vehicle" (Mahayana), seeking to apply Buddhism to a broader spectrum of life. Those who still favored a conservative and traditional approach to the religion declared the majority to be heretics and broke off to form its own wing. The Mahayana Buddhists labeled this conservative wing Hinayana, "The Little Vehicle," which at one time enveloped as many as eighteen schools, the most dominant being Theravada (Tradition of the Elders).[192]

Mahayana has impacted Buddhism in a significant way. One of its more revolutionary features was its insistence upon an open canon, declaring that Buddhist knowledge was much larger than what Siddhartha Gautama had taught, thus Buddhist teaching could not be limited to the *tripitaka*. To illustrate this, one of the Mahayana legends has the Buddha telling the following story. While teaching one day, the Buddha, " took a handful of leaves from the forest floor and explained to his disciples that as the leaves in his hand were less than the total leaves of the forest, so were the teachings that he had given them openly less than the total amount of truth that could be imparted in secret."[193] Continuing with this image, one could say that the Mahayanists perceive themselves as simply "accumulating more leaves."[194] This move threw the gates wide open for new interpretation and creative thinking about how one attains enlightenment. Accompanying this opening of the canon was a change in the language of choice from

Pali, to *Sanskrit*. Sanskrit, the language of the Brahmin literati, became the universal language of choice for Buddhism in an increasingly multilingual Asia, and served as the original language for Mahayana and Tibetan texts. Once again, one can see an attempt to make Buddhism more accessible.

Secondly, Mahayana brought a radical alteration of how one views the Buddha himself, and once again, the consequences were deep and wide. Whereas the Theravadins saw the Buddha as *only* a human figure and teacher, the Mahayanists saw the Buddha as a divine-like being—some would even say eternal, with no beginning and no end—who brought us truth incarnate, but not the whole of truth. Moreover, they taught that Siddhartha Gautama was not the only one who fit such a category; there must be many others as well.[195] If there were, in reality, many of these divine-like beings who served as helpers in the universe, certainly they would be worthy of our veneration and respect.[196] This concept was a boon to the Buddhist missionary movement.

> When Buddhist missionaries entered a new country, they did not have to ask the natives to give up their old gods; they simply presented these gods as various incarnations of the Buddha, and their cults could continue. In the same way that Hinduism absorbed Buddhism by saying that Gautama was really an avatar of Vishnu, Buddhism absorbed many other religions by saying that their gods were really incarnations of the Buddha.[197]

Out of this innovation came another primary feature of Mahayana, the *Bodhisattva*, or "future Buddha:" one who achieves enlightenment, but then renounces nirvana to come back and teach others the way. Although the doctrine's roots lay in Theravada, in the soil of Mahayana the *Bodhisattva* concept grew to encompass not only a "future Buddha," but a savior-like figure of popular devotion.[198] A number of *Bodhisattvas* had names, each having a certain characteristic of Theravada teaching pertaining to the Buddha.[199] The most well known among these is one by the name of Avalokitesvara, the *Bodhisattva* of compassion.[200] (Interestingly, as this Buddha figure made its way across China to Japan, he took on feminine qualities, and eventually became female.[201])

Buddhism was not only a religious movement, but also a social reform movement. In essence, it was anti-Brahmin. Since it is opposed to caste, it has held a certain appeal for the Dalit in India, significantly so after the conversion of the famed Dr. Bhimrao Ramji Ambedkar, a former untouchable who became free India's first Minister of Law, and a framer of India's constitution.[202] Ambedkar first investigated Christianity and Islam, but saw Buddhism as an effective foundation for a more egalitarian society.[203] This anti-caste appeal in Buddhism is still evident today in large conversion movements such as the one led by Dalit leader, Ram Raj.[204]

In this counter-cultural sort of way, Buddhism attempted to unite the various strata of society. Although Buddhism expressed itself as a monastic movement, whereby the individual sought release from this world, the Buddhist layperson could also benefit without becoming a monk by serving instead as a benefactor of the monastery. By giving to the monks, one earned merit, positioning one's self for a better status in the next life.[205] In this way, the religious elite and the laity came together in a unified purpose and goal. Buddhism also held an immediate appeal for the laity in that the monastery was a place of education. The monks served as teachers, and the lower strata of society could now receive hope for bettering their existence through literacy and education. In this way too, the lower social strata and the educated elite could come together.

Today's picture might have been starkly different, however, were it not for the Indian monarch, Asoka (ruled 273-232 B.C.), heralded as one of India's greatest rulers. After his conversion to Buddhism, Asoka became a major patron of the religion, appointing those who would be responsible for propagating the faith among his own subjects, and sending missionary monks out into neighboring realms. Writings have frequently compared Asoka to Constantine as an advocate for the movement, but he exceeded Constantine in this respect, not only personally embracing and tolerating the religion, but actively and vigorously promoting it via fiat and promulgation from the throne. Like many rulers in history and the present time, Asoka also saw in religious ideology an opportunity to unite a people, and he decided to use Buddhism as just such a unifying force.[206]

The next step was expansion: at Asoka's orders, Buddhist followers carried their teachings to Ceylon (modern day Sri Lanka), Kashmir, and outlying areas as far away as Afghanistan. Ch'en comments,

> Due mainly to his efforts, Buddhism burst out of the confines of India to take its place in the mainstream of world culture. From Gāndhra and Kashmir, where the religion had reached during Aśoka times, it spread into Central Asia and

eventually to China and Japan; From Ceylon and southern India the religion leaped across the ocean in later centuries to what is now Burma, Indonesia, Thailand and Indo-China.[207]

Its first major move outside of India appears to have been through the northwest border and out into central Asia. Central Asia, the Tarim basin, was a choice route for the propagation of Buddhism, filled with various nomadic ethnic groups who acted as cultural transmitters.[208] The already established trade routes were a natural means of transporting the new teaching, and the Silk Road was the easiest and most strategic. According to Frank E. Reynolds, "What had been, only two centuries before, a small, non-conformist sect was elevated to the status of a potentially universal religion."[209]

As we step into the early history of Buddhism in China, the major forces which seem to be at work there are, remarkably, neither Indian nor Chinese, but central Asian.[210] In the first wave of missionaries to enter China, only three appear to be Indian. The first major translator is a Parthian of nobility, An Shi-kao (also written An Shigao). Two others who followed him were also from Central Asia: Chih Ch'ien, from the Yüe-chih (Scythia) and a Sogdian named K'ang Seng-hui.[211] Translation work commenced immediately, as great numbers of Buddhist scriptures and texts found their way into the region. A flood of translators followed An Shi-kao; however, since the abilities of these early Buddhist missionaries were primitive, most of their early translations were quite substandard.

While discussing Han period translations, Ch'en hypothesizes that the many similarities between Buddhism and Taoism appear to have influenced the choice of Buddhist texts for translation. For example, both the Chinese Buddhists and Taoists practiced breathing techniques; both emphasized concentration and meditation; and both worshiped without sacrifices. The curious thing about the translation of texts in the Han period is that we do not see much in the way of texts that deal with the fundamental doctrines of Buddhism (The Four Noble Truths, Nirvana, anatman, etc.). Instead, we see texts that exhibit similarities with Taoism—breathing techniques, concentration practices and the like. Ch'en considers it an open question whether this is because early translation assistants were Taoist in background and were interested in those texts, or whether early Chinese Buddhists themselves became interested in those texts for translation.[212] It would be interesting to pursue the latter possibility and ask why Chinese Buddhists would take interest in such texts. Would they be interested simply because there is a cultural connection to their religious past, or would there be an apologetic intentionality here similar to that of Paul on Mars Hill? Were these monks recognizing the potential in these texts as analogies for their Buddhist gospel? Also, like Paul, there seems to be an intentional lifting of these concepts to a plane not known before. While affirming certain aspects of the local religions, Buddhism also brought with it a higher level of philosophical sophistication that impressed its hosts.

Another feature of this period is that the question of doctrine seemed rather confusing, as there appears to have been a distribution of a great mixture of Theravada and Mahayana texts. Differentiating between the two schools seemed to be of little consequence in the thinking of these early monks.

We have referred to this *initial* thrust of Buddhism into China as having occurred in the Han Dynasty, roughly within the 200 B.C. to 200 A.D. period (the period of Hinayana's development). Was there anything about this period that might have influenced the acceptance of Buddhism? China had centralized its government for the most part, but the political tapestry was now beginning to unravel. With the weakening of the political system, old systems of thought that supported it, particularly those of Confucian origin, were losing credibility, making this an apt time for new thought to enter into the region. Although Buddhism had points of similarity with native Chinese religions, it was sufficiently different to be attractive. In fact, in many aspects of culture and ideology, India and China were *quite opposite*. According to Hu Shih,

> Never before had China seen a religion so rich in imagery, so beautiful and captivating in ritualism, and so bold in cosmology and metaphysical speculations. Like a poor beggar suddenly halting before a magnificent storehouse of precious stones of dazzling brilliancy and splendor, China was overwhelmed, boggled, and overjoyed. She begged and borrowed freely from this munificent giver.[213]

Simultaneously, China was expanding its influence into Central Asia much as India was doing under the Scythian Kushan Empire. Says James Huntly Grayson,

> These commercial and cultural ties and the conversion of the Kushan king Kanishka to Buddhism permitted the rapid

penetration of the Indian faith into the desert regions north of the Kushan Empire. Missionaries who went to the great oasis cities of Khotan, Kucha, Turfan, and Tun-huang helped to convert the inner regions of Asia to Buddhism by the first century Before Christ. The encounter between Indo-Buddhist civilisation [sic] and Chinese political power in Central Asia created the conditions by which Buddhism was able to seep back into the heartland of the empire itself.[214]

Utilizing the monastic model, it was easy (as Christians in Europe would also later discover) to first establish a monastery for the monks, and then move out from that central location to establish beachheads in outlying regions. Scholars have proposed various systems for analyzing this process. For example, James Huntly Grayson has discerned three phases: (1) contact and explication; (2) penetration, and; (3) expansion. Grayson's approach is adapted from earlier work by E. M. Pye and Ralph Linton.[215] Ralph Covell follows the pattern of Chinese academician Hu Shi: (1) mass borrowing; (2) resistance and persecution; (3) domestication; and (4) appropriation.[216] Regardless which model one chooses, there will always be stages through which a religion will be accepted or ultimately rejected.

In the early phase of Buddhism's entry into China, much went right. Though the monks put great emphasis on teaching, they employed a good deal more than academics in their method. In a stroke of brilliance, they brought in artisans, craftsmen and poets, influencing the culture as a whole. Their selected soil for planting this garden of culture/religion was the literate elite. Among China's educated, the seeds of Indian Buddhist culture found fertile ground for its ideology and artistic expressions.

In its encounter with Taoism, Buddhism provided an appealing setting for the philosophically minded Taoist. Whereas both Confucianism and Taoism taught a harmonization with one's world (though in starkly differing ways—in the milieu of personal relationships in the former, with nature in the latter[217]), Buddhism provided a higher and more complex form of religious teaching and ethics, which the Chinese found attractive and powerful. Taoism is a philosophy of "active-inactivity," a not-so-practical system that taught the adherent to abandon effort and simply to go with the flow of life. Its teachers, in fact, depicted life through the image of the "uncarved block." Added to this was a sense of rebellion in Taoism against the common way of life. Consequently, in its purer forms at least, Taoism appealed primarily to a philosophical and somewhat countercultural mind. With this understanding, it is not hard to see why the Buddhist monastery provided the Taoist with a natural setting in which to retreat from all the "activity" of the common world.

The Buddhist monk also found points of compatibility with the Confucian scholars who, while generally acknowledging a spiritual realm and a sort of Creator god, did not see this existence as particularly central or primary to the Confucian way. In fact, for Confucius the value of religious rites resided more in their ability to serve a social need over a particularly religious one. Confucianism has shown itself to be more of a philosophy or worldview than a religion in the sense of humans relating to gods.[218] In a similar vein, for the Buddhist, if gods did exist, they were not particularly helpful to us, but perhaps themselves in need of salvation. The Chinese also saw consequences in good and bad behavior and held to an immortality of the soul. Interestingly, explaining the concept of the soul was one area where the inability of early monks to articulate their religion clearly caused problems down the road. Though a central teaching of Buddhism is the *anatman* concept (the "non-soul"), the Chinese got the teaching wrong the first time around, and thought the Buddhists were actually *affirming* the existence and immortality of the soul.[219] This would surface at a later Asian Buddhist conference, where the Buddhist traditionalists would get into heated debate with the Chinese over this concept. It was, however, a temporary problem, as the Buddhists were able to speak to the issue from the perspective of the neverending cycle of the soul through karma and reincarnation.

Over time, the method of building upon similarities of thought gave way to a wider and more independent approach that incorporated not only doctrinal teaching but painting and sculpture, literature, and other artistic expressions.[220] In this manner, the Buddhists were able to present a high form of aesthetic that the Chinese found attractive, resulting in a further penetration of the religion into the mainstream of culture.

In the southern regions, the messengers employed a "slow penetration" method among the literate that relied heavily on a translation model. This was very much an appeal to the mind and the aesthetic sensibilities, which scholars have since dubbed, "gentry Buddhism." In the north, Buddhism spread in large part according to a "rapid conversion" method, utilizing miracles and magic that impressed the populace—a sort of "power encounter" approach, to use the phrase of Allan Tippet.[221] This method tended to have its greatest effect among the non-elite. Grayson refers to it as a "better shamanism."[222] This required that the monks take the worldview of the culture very seriously, and it worked only in cases where the proclaimer was culturally close to the people he was attempting to reach. In fact, Grayson maintains that in order for one to employ this method effectively, the proclaimer must be in the same cultural sphere as the receptor culture. A monk straight from India with no knowledge of the Chinese language or culture would not have been able to do this.[223] Grayson also maintains that this method tended to see cycles of acceptance and rejection, since it depended in part upon political favor. Consequently, it did not seem to result in the same kind of long-term stability as the slower penetration method which based itself upon translation and early resolution of conflicting values, both of which the rapid penetration method would skip over.[224]

One can think of any number of similar models in Christian history, such as that of Boniface, or Gregory Thaumaturgus (an appellation which means "miracle worker"), where missionaries employed such a "power encounter" method in the proclamation of the Gospel of Jesus Christ. In the case of the former, Boniface saw power encounter as an effective means at the start, but questioned the wisdom of its long-term practice. Nevertheless, the example of these early Buddhist monks taking the worldview of the culture very seriously and their having been culturally close to the people they were attempting to reach is certainly exemplary and deserving of serious consideration. This is valuable not only for the purpose of seeking rapid conversion, but even in tandem with the "slow penetration" method based upon speculative philosophy and translation. Perhaps there are elements in each of these methods that one could integrate for an even more effective means of proclamation.

Although the Buddhist missions employed varying methods, in all cases the Buddhist missionaries encountered the challenge of enculturation. Any type of missionary endeavor will inevitably meet with a "receptor" culture, which will have enculturated its people from childhood in how to perceive and behave in their world. As a missionary, one will come upon and have to cope with views of the gods, of the family, of work, etc., different from one's own. Newly imported concepts will have to be "clothed" with native trappings in forms that will feel familiar to the people. The missionary will need to search out what Don Richardson has termed "redemptive analogies" for these new teachings to cross over into the culture and be accepted.[225] According to Covell,

> The most significant way in which Buddhist views were related to the contemporary Chinese environment was by *go-i*, the "matching of concepts." In this method scholars placed groups of Buddhist ideas alongside a group of somewhat similar Chinese ideas—for example, the *wuchang* or five relationships with the five precepts of Buddhism, and the four elements of Buddhism with the five Chinese elements. The Buddhist precepts, for example are: do not kill, steal, commit adultery, lie or drink intoxicating beverages. The Confucian virtues are: human-heartedness, righteousness, propriety, knowledge, and trust.[226]

Right from the start, Buddhist messengers searched for these points of contact, and recruited from both the elite sectors of society and from the lower sectors through a monastic structure. As was also the case in India, converts from the elite found themselves moving into positions as Buddhist leaders and teachers, but the non-elite also found a place in the monastic community. Thus, these propagators of Buddhist faith gave proper emphasis to indigenization.

But the process went beyond simply dressing Buddhism up in Chinese clothing. Their message became inculturated or contextualized as it found a place among the Chinese, not only in core teachings promising enlightenment, but in its approach to art and beauty as well. Buddhism truly became a way of life, which led to a need for yet a new enculturation from a Buddhist perspective. A process would have to originate whereby future generations of Buddhists would view and interpret their surroundings via the Buddhist worldview.

Another feature of Chinese religion was also useful for Buddhism's gaining of acceptance: the practice of ancestor veneration. The Buddhists employed this concept in countering the charge that its monasticism was not in harmony with filial piety. Through ancestor veneration practices, one could still carry out, and affirm, the Confucian requirements to honor one's ancestors. Thus, again, Buddhist missionaries overcame a point of resistance by utilizing a form already in the culture.[227]

A primary point of resistance that Buddhism encountered was that which any religion or thought form seeking admittance into a new cultural environment comes upon, *viz.*, its very newness and its non-native status. Especially in the case of the Chinese, anything that was not ancient was not easily accepted.[228] However, one advantage that Buddhism had over the indigenous religions of Confucianism and Taoism is that it had a message of salvation that was both similar to that of Taoism and more distinct.[229]

Moreover, Buddhism found acceptance among the ruling elite. Rulers wanting to counteract the political power of Confucianism or Taoism saw in Buddhism a ready-made tool by which to do that. This counteracting role that fell to Buddhism, in many cases accelerated Buddhism's acceptance by the populace; but at other times, when Buddhism fell into disfavor with the changing of rulers, this adversarial position brought great difficulty. For example, in the north the populace consisted of non-native Chinese tribal groups. In that region, due to the nature of the foreign occupation of the Huns, an unfortunate sort of Caesaro-papism developed, where Buddhism became firmly wedded to the ruling establishment.[230] This development started out with great energy in the northern region of Korea (Koguryo) and proliferated more slowly in Korea's other two provinces. Momentum gained in Korea as political upheavals in China caused Buddhist workers to flee not only to the south in China (where "gentry Buddhism" developed amongst the intelligentsia), but also further north, which brought them into the Korean sphere.

Related to the issue of Buddhism's newness, another major problem for Buddhism (and Christianity, for that matter) in China was xenophobia. There was a natural and strong resistance among the Chinese toward anything foreign. Thus, Confucianism and Taoism always had a ready political tool at hand in their political tug of war with Buddhism when they saw a ruler in the court whom they could sway against this foreign religious competition.[231] Nationalism was one force that they could employ to restore their status in the court before the people. It is probably for this principal reason that Buddhism never became the dominant religious force in China, and in time waned considerably. What influence it has had has largely resulted from its being one element within an amalgamated religious system. This opportunity came to it especially with the rise of "neo-Taoism." (This term is unfortunate because "neo-Taoism" is actually a gathering of all religious thought in China into one major force, often referred to more correctly as "Dark Learning."[232]) Buddhism found itself in harmony with this emphasis on amalgamation, and embraced it. If not for such adaptation, Buddhism probably would not have been able to survive the centuries.²³³

Later, the Chinese emperor sent out Buddhist missionaries to the Korean court as an expression of favor (as did also the king of what is today Sri Lanka) giving Buddhism a still greater status in the eyes of the Korean receptor culture. It helped that Buddhism was a higher form of religious expression than what they had known thus far, but politics played a major role here as well. Such was also the case in Japan, as Korean rulers in turn sent Buddhist missionaries scriptures and artwork to the Japanese court as gifts.

However, before we proceed too far into the history of Buddhism in those two countries, let us return to the context of China, and sum up the major points of interest for our study. In doing this, it might be helpful to look at two previous studies and do a side by side comparison, and then draw some conclusions from that comparison. Let us begin with five points of interest highlighted by James Huntly Grayson. Grayson concludes that Buddhist missionaries had to confront a minimum of five types of inter-related factors before their teaching could exercise a major impact upon Chinese society. He lists those five as follows:

1. The contradictions between the new doctrine and the core values of the society. Before a position of significant influence could be attained, Buddhism had to resolve the contradictions between monasticism and filial piety;

2. The achievement of acceptance or toleration of the new doctrine by the ruling elite. Certainly, the continued presence of Buddhism throughout the late Han Dynasty must be attributed to the tolerance of this doctrine by the elite sector of society.

3. Linguistic or conceptual barriers which might impede the growth of the new doctrine. Before genuine missionary work could begin, Buddhists had to translate their scriptures into Chinese, and to find suitable terms to convey Indian concepts in Chinese thought patterns;²³⁴

4. Resolution of conflict between the new doctrine and other religions or philosophies present in the culture. Although Neo-Taoism was a factor in the acceptance of Buddhism during the initial phase of missionary endeavour, at a later stage Buddhism had to contend with Taoist hostility.

5. Political conditions predisposing the acceptance of the new doctrine throughout the culture. Clearly, it was the breakdown of the Han order which provided Buddhism with a unique situation for rapid growth. In northern China, at a later date, the political uses to which Buddhism might be put predisposed barbarian rulers to accept the new doctrine.[235]

From the observation of the above factors, Grayson has developed a three-stage general pattern for the growth and acceptance of any missionary religion in any culture: (1) Contact and explication; (2) Penetration; and (3) Expansion. Within this pattern, he includes two further patterns already mentioned: the Slow Penetration and Rapid Conversion Patterns. Once again, we must remember that according to Grayson's analysis, the Rapid Conversion pattern applies only to contacts within a single cultural sphere.[236] Grayson then outlines the course of development for this process as follows:

A new religion makes initial contact with the receptor culture, establishing a beach-head for further work. Once established, it proceeds to the task of more securely emplanting itself in the culture by explicating its doctrines, translating, if necessary, its texts into the language of the society, and resolving contradictions between itself and the core values of the society. Achievement of a state of penetration within the culture then becomes the foundation for the propagation of its teachings at all levels of the society. In this third phase, the missionary movement while continuing to work at some of the tasks from the first phase of its emplantation, will now encounter significant resistance to its teachings from the indigenous religious traditions of the society. The attack might be along the lines of "these new ideas were unknown to our ancestors", as in China. If the missionary movement is able to contend with these attacks successfully, we may expect that it will achieve a position of significant if not supreme influence within the society. If this latter subphase is attained, the missionary movement will have ceased to be such at all, as it will have become an indigenous cultural element of the society.[237]

Notice in the above paragraph that Grayson speaks of translation in terms of "if necessary," which would be a reference to the fact that the Rapid Conversion Pattern skipped over that phase in the history of Buddhist propagation in China. He also points out that a factor of major importance for the religion to be emplanted is for it to face and overcome the challenges or attacks thrown at it from the indigenous religions. Buddhism began in China by accommodating itself to Taoism to such an extent that people initially thought it merely to be a sect of Taoism; Taoism was a thought form that Hinayana could easily adapt, considering its claim to have magical powers over demons.[238] Later, as Buddhism gained sufficient strength to stand on its own, missionaries abandoned this approach in an attempt to avoid extreme syncretism and to preserve the core teachings of Buddhism. Ch'en comments that the writings of Mou-tzu may have encouraged Buddhists in this direction, since these writings strongly opposed Taoist doctrines. Buddhism had come to a place where it could assert its independence from Taoism.[239]

Next, let us examine Ralph Covell's list of factors for acceptance of Buddhism in China. At the close of a chapter on Buddhism in China, Covell asks the question, "...what are the factors that enabled a 'foreign faith' to become one of the three religions in China?"[240] He then responds to his question with the following list:

1. A relatively easy access route by land into China and zealous missionaries able to relate well to Chinese life within the overarching Asian milieu.

2. A Han China desperately needing revitalization and open to new ideas.

3. An available and acceptable role to be a "sect of Daoism," asserting no exclusive claims.

4. A "people movement to Buddha" of such mass proportion that the faith gained hold with minimal social dislocation.

5. A faith perceived by the Chinese as adequate to deal with incredible human misery and suffering. Part of this, of course, meant catering to Chinese religious views in what even non-Christians would label syncretism.

6. No external power base to pose as a threat to the Chinese state.

7. A flexible methodology adequate to exploit differing

opportunities in northern and southern China.

8. Penetration of Chinese life at all levels—linguistically, economically, religiously, socially, politically, artistically, and educationally—to overcome resistance and persecution and gain popular favor. Submitting to the state politically was of crucial importance.[241]

In reference to the first point, this is a major difference between Asian Indians reaching China with Buddhism, and Christians from the West reaching China with the gospel—the issue of access to the country. It was much easier to penetrate China from India than from the Christian West. On this point, early Buddhist missionaries had an advantage.

On the second point, we can see similarities with the gradual penetration of Christianity into the Roman Empire. As with Rome, where the empire was declining, the mythological gods also came into discredit. Roman citizens began to open themselves to other options for ethical, and eventually political, direction. So with the decline of the Han dynasty, the Confucian philosophy upon which the state's leadership was built also began to lose credibility. Covell quotes Arthur Wright as saying, "Buddhism could no more have established itself in the Empire of Han than Catholic Christianity could in the prosperous years of the Ch'ing dynasty."[242] It was only in the declining years of the Han period that Buddhism gained a foothold in China.

As Buddhism initially identified with its indigenous competition—Taoism—it was positioned to grow in strength until it could at last gain its own identity as the competition for both Confucianism and Taoism, and eventually be an equal partner in the amalgamation of religions in later times. Thus even today the three leaders—the Buddha, Lao-Tzu and Confucius—will be depicted as equals in temple art, and the Chinese people will worship at community temples where all three religions will be represented.

Buddhism also was able to see itself propagated through people movements, such as the Rapid Conversion phenomenon seen in the north. As the slower, but more stable, movement of the south gained the gentry elite through translation, speculative philosophy and high forms of art, the two movements were able to come together into a countrywide influence on society as a whole. Such flexibility prevented the imposition upon the north of methods successful in the south, and vice-versa. Success was dependent upon principle over method, upon using what was locally appropriate, rather than utilizing a means imposed from the outside. Here Christian missionaries can observe that the primary aspect of mission is not in the method, or the "how-to," as though one were looking for a model to duplicate in all settings. Instead, one needs to give attention to the principles that lie below the method, to making the message accessible and understandable to the people in relatable terms while carefully discerning the border between absorption and accommodation.

Both Covell and Grayson referred to the syncretistic approach that Buddhism had with Taoism, which was later abandoned. Had this approach not changed, rather than Buddhism *accommodating* itself to the culture, undoubtedly the culture would have *absorbed* Buddhism. In this regard, Christianity is by nature far less flexible than Buddhism and far more exclusivist in its core beliefs. This inability to compromise content along with form contributed to the Rites Controversy under the mission of the Jesuits.[243] The key question in the debate was one of accommodation versus syncretism. Can one draw the line in the same place in all situations? Buddhism solved this problem and avoided absorption by eventually disengaging with Taoism to the degree that Buddhism could stand on its own alongside Taoism and Confucianism as an equal player. At the same time, it was still properly flexible enough to be able to employ different methods of diffusion in the north and the south, as stated in Covell's point number seven above.

Moreover, history shows that Buddhism succeeded in penetrating all aspects of Chinese society: ethics, politics, economics, art and education. Under the topic of educational efforts, Covell comments,

> During the Tang dynasty, when Buddhism reached the height of its impact on Chinese life, it was the dominant faith at all levels of society. Its educational process was obviously very effective to have reached so many diversified groups of persons. Some of this influence came informally, through the life and work of well-known literary figures such as Bo Juyi (772-846). The monasteries were favorite places of recluse for poets, and they made extensive use of Buddhist technical terms, doctrines, practices, and allusions to Buddhist scriptures to create a favorable impression.[244]

A popular way of teaching the sutras to the public included the chanting of sutras from a high platform, followed by an explanation by an assistant, after which came a time of question and answer. During the Sui and Tang dynasties, monks gave lectures on the law utilizing the form of stories and parables, which they directed to specific needs of the audience. The most popular type of lecture form, used by those most skilled, included not only stories and parables, but anecdotes, miraculous tales and other forms that presented abstract truths in word pictures.[245]

Covell's eighth point is interesting, where he highlights the importance of submitting to the state. This was the most difficult adjustment for Buddhism in China, but proved also to be one of the most important aspects in Buddhism's shedding of its foreign skin. In India, the *sangha* was not responsible to the state. By definition, the *sangha* consisted of people who had withdrawn from society. If anything, Indian political rulers would defer to the monks, and the rulers may themselves become monks. The situation in China was vastly different. The Confucian concept of *li* demanded that the emperor's influence held sway at every level.[246] The ruler was to exercise benevolence; the subject was to give loyalty. Only as each member of society performed the duty for his or her level could there be harmony in the empire. This stark cultural difference precipitated an intense struggle between the Chinese *sangha* and the government officials that lasted for hundreds of years, resulting in the eventual surrender of the *sangha* to the state. Covell goes as far as to say, "Without its coming to terms with Chinese law and giving up the types of freedom it had known in India, Buddhism would never have been indigenized in China."[247] The importance of subjection to government authority has not waned in China, and is still of paramount importance today. Does this aspect of Buddhism's early success have anything to say to the twenty-first century Church ministering in Northeast Asia? To what extent can the Church submit to governing authorities without denying her Lord? In the past, local authorities often perceived the Church as a threat to local authorities because of the papacy in Rome and the Church's connection with foreign colonial powers. These kinds of obstacles were not an issue for Buddhism's acceptance in China. Nevertheless, Buddhism struggled for hundreds of years with the idea of submitting to the state before taking that step. And yet once Buddhism took that step, the obstacle of its "foreignness" soon dropped and Buddhism became Chinese.

How does the Pauline concept of submission to governing authorities (Romans 13) apply in such a light? What does this mean for the registered and underground churches of an atheistic China today? The level of freedoms under such a structure will depend in large part upon the attitude of local officials toward the Church. Would a more Confucian, more submissive attitude on the part of the Church lessen the degree of perceived threat in the mind of governing authorities, as it did with Buddhism long ago? It is probably not appropriate for someone in a Western democracy to attempt to answer such a question. Obviously, in the case of Buddhism, submission has not equaled silence, but submission has been beneficial in gaining the trust of authorities. In the words of Ch'en, for early Buddhists in China, submission meant that "The Buddhist monk became a Chinese subject, the monastic community a Chinese religious organization subject to the jurisdiction of the imperial bureaucracy. Buddhism had become Sinicized politically."[248] This kind of adaptation would continue as Buddhism made its way into regions of Korea and Japan.

Buddhism in Korea

We mentioned earlier that political upheavals in northern China propelled monks further south, and likely further north. The key incident that scholars point to most often in this regard is the sacking of the capital city of Lo-Yang in 311. At this time, Korea had firmly settled into the Iron Age, which proved to be a time of great openness toward outside influences, which would continue until roughly 300 A.D. in the northern part of the kingdom, and to 500 A.D. in the south. From the time of the Chinese occupation of the Korean peninsula (108 B.C.), China had exerted great influence on the region for centuries. During the fourth and fifth centuries A.D., Buddhism entered Korea from China, and came to dominate the religious scene.[249]

The religious form that Buddhism encountered was that of shamanism. As is the case in many early forms of religion, and religions rooted in Basic Religion concepts, the practitioner is concerned primarily about what the gods or spirits will do about daily needs: rain, healing, fertility, power in war, etc. In our discussion of Buddhism in China, we saw that especially in Hinayana form, and in the Rapid Conversion method, the missionaries addressed such issues in their magical and mystical approach to propagation.

Although there is some controversy over the exact date for Buddhism's entry into Korea, the traditional date is 372 A.D., when the Chinese Emperor Fu-ch'ien (of Former Chin), an ardent Buddhist believer, sent the missionary monk Sun-do to the capital of Koguryŭ. The emperor's intent was for Sun-do to deliver gifts and to preach the Buddhist message. The gifts included sutras, ritual implements, and Buddhist statuary. Interestingly, the emperor did not wait for the monk to be escorted to the palace, but went out to meet him at the gate of the capital, and personally accompanied him back to the palace. This would imply that there was level of relationship between these two rulers that gave added weight to the arrival of this missionary monk. Once the monk was established in the palace precincts, his work of evangelism began in earnest. No doubt, the influence of the Chinese court greatly added to the chances of Sun-do's success. With such imperial influence behind the visit, it would make the embracing of this religion much more politically and socially acceptable. Two years following the arrival of Sun-do, we read of a Korean monk returning from Northern Wei, where he had studied under a Buddhist scholar by the name of Hsu-an-chang. By 395, a large number of Buddhist texts arrived in Koguryŭ with a mysterious and magic-working monk from the Kuan-chun region of Chine (modern Shen-si), T'an-Shi, who remained for ten years.[250]

The building of temples quickly ensued with the coming of these missionaries. The following quotation from Grayson demonstrates the power of court favor in Korea. (The "r." in the parentheses below refers to "reign.")

> Temple building and evangelism were continued vigorously under the successors of King So-su-rim. His immediate successor, King Ko-guk-yang (r. 384 to 391), laid great stress on evangelism amongst the people, taking Buddhism out of the court circle and spreading its benefits amongst the ordinary citizens. Ko-guk-yang's successor, the great King Kwang-gae-t'o, turned Koguryŭ into a Buddhist state. Among other tangible results of his efforts, he ordered the construction of nine temples in and around the region of P'yŏngyang area, which was the southern capital.[251]

One can see the importance of favor with the rulers in the early work of Buddhist missions in Korea, starting with the Chinese emperors sending missionaries and gifts. One could call this early expression of Buddhism in Korea a "court cult," to express that this is where it had its start, and it is from the court that it gained its momentum, filtering down to the aristocracy, and eventually to the masses.

Another feature of Korean Buddhism's is evident in the waves of scholars that traveled from Korea to China and India to study and to bring back the expressions of various Buddhist sects. It is important to note in this regard, that the draw was not only Buddhism per se, but also Chinese culture. For example, after the fall of the state of **Koguryŭ**, the new state that eventually resulted from its ashes, Parhae, was rebuilt according to the Chinese model of T'ang, its neighbor to the east and south. T'ang influence included T'ang forms of government, art and city planning. Later, in the middle of the seventh century, an influential monk from the royal family, named Cha-jang, effectively promoted the T'ang style of dress and the acceptance of the T'ang calendar.[252]

There are many similarities in Buddhism's move to the southern tip of the Korean peninsula, to the state of Paekche. The ancient records say that in the first year of the reign of the fifteenth king of Paekche, King Ch'im-nyu (reigned 384-385), the Indian monk Mālānanda (Maranant'a) became the first recorded person to introduce Buddhism to that region in 384 A.D. (He had apparently been inspired to this mission through meeting a Korean official of the Paekche court while journeying in China.) In a fashion very similar to what we saw in **Koguryŭ**, the king went out to meet the monk, welcomed him to the court, worshiped him and listened to his teaching. The monk went on to win the populace with the endorsement of the king.[253] His enthusiastic reception by the royal court greatly aided the diffusion of Buddhism throughout the kingdom. Less than a year later, the king built a temple for the monk on Mount Han, and the first ten Korean natives were ordained as Buddhist monks.[254] Grayson sums up the chief characteristics of the early penetration of Buddhism to Paekche as follows:

> First, Buddhism was brought to Paekche at the instigation of a missionary monk, and was in part the result of a network of international relations which existed at that time. Second, as in **Koguryŭ**, it was recorded that the king went out to greet the monk as he entered the city, which would have been a most unusual mark of respect. Third, the monk did not travel alone, but must have been at the head of a small entourage. Fourth, Buddhism developed first, as in **Koguryŭ**, as a cult of the royal court, from where it then spread to the mass of the population. Fifth, the king built a special temple for the missionary as was done also in **Koguryŭ**.[255]

Following this incident, the records appear to be silent until the reign of a King Sŏng (reigned 523-553), when Paekche is to have achieved its highest point in cultural development. It is also the time of a particularly notable monk in the Buddhist history of Korea, Kyŏm-ik. He is important in part because here began a stream of Korean monks who journeyed to India over the next 200 years. An interesting fact about this monk is that he studied in particular the doctrines the Buddha laid down about the communal life of his mendicant followers, the *vinaya* texts. These doctrines of the *vinaya* became the dominant form of Buddhism in Paekche. He also brought back with him copies of the *Abhidharma-pitaka*, which is known to contain both Mahayana and Hinayana treatises.[256] Upon his return, King Sŏng placed him in charge of the Hungjung Temple, and appointed twenty-eight scholars to help him translate over seventy-two volumes of scriptures during his lifetime.[257]

Another great accomplishment of King Sŏng is his initiation of Buddhist missionary work in Japan. Paekche possessed great nautical skill, making it the "Phoenicia of medieval Asia."[258] In 545, as other rulers had done before him, he sent a Buddhist statue and some Sanskrit scriptures to the Japanese court. Seven years later, he had a bronze statue made and sent it along with some Buddhist sutras and a stone statue of Maitreya (the future coming Buddha) to the Japanese king. In a letter he sent with the gifts, he explained that he was recommending Buddhism, "because it was a doctrine superior to that of the teachings of Confucius, and because it had found acceptance in India, China, and Paekche."[259] In 554, King Sung dispatched Buddhist doctrinal specialists, psalmodists, iconographers, and architects to Japan.[260] On this point, Joseph Kitagawa remarks that this was not Japan's first contact with Buddhism, rather, during this era, government administrators in Japan were very dependant upon expatriate Chinese and Koreans and many of these officials were practicing Buddhists.[261] Masaharu Anesaki also comments upon this earlier influence in his *History of Japanese Religion*.

It was chiefly Korean Immigrants and some Chinese who introduced the various arts of civilization, and these artisans and scholars greatly contributed to the rise of the ruling family, in whose service most of them worked.[262] Kitagawa also refers to immigrants from China, due to the political turmoil at the turn of the fifth century, and puts the arrival of Korean scholars as early as 400 A.D.[263] More will be said about the introduction of Buddhism to Japan later in this chapter.

Our final comments on Buddhism's acceptance in Korea relate to the middle region of Shilla. Shilla was the victor in Korea's internal wars for supremacy in the seventh century, and therefore more was recorded about this state than the other two. Since Shilla emerged as the superior power, there is also a definite bias in what is recorded, as it is often those with power that write their own versions of history; Shilla's case is no exception.

Five men are involved in the initial introduction of Buddhism to this region, two of whom were martyred, due to fear of the new religion. Of the other three monks, one of them, Huk-ho-ja is interesting for his involvement in the healing of the daughter of King Nul-Chi (reign beginning in 514). The monk is said to have accomplished this healing by the use of incense and the taking of a vow. He apparently then disappeared before the king could express his favor, but seemed to return later under another name.[264] As we saw in previous cases, Buddhism begins with the favor of the court, as a "court cult." Also, its initial acceptance at court had little to do with the acceptance of Buddhist doctrine, but rested on the performance of a miraculous ceremony—a "better shamanism."[265] In like manner, Robert Evans Buswell, Jr., characterizes the Buddhism of Korea's early period by thaumaturgic practices and "a symbiotic relationship between the ecclesia and the state."[266]

Another indicator of Buddhism's acceptance at court is the taking of Buddhist reign names by Shilla's rulers, a phenomenon also apparent in the history of Paekche. Grayson comments as follows.

> The three kings before Pŏp-hūng [reign began in 514], in whose reign Buddhism was officially accepted, all had Buddhist names... He gives the kings as Cha-bi, So-ji, and Chi-jŏng. Certainly, Cha-bi's reign name would imply the Buddhist concept of compassion and Chi-jung's reign name likewise is clearly Buddhist, conveying the sense of one who witnesses to the Wisdom of the Buddha...the choice of reign names for these three kings is indicative of what must have been growing Buddhist influence at the royal court.[267]

Martyrdom again plays a significant role in Shilla in the story of a Buddhist believer who agreed with the Buddhist king concerning the building of a monastery. The story also illustrates the conflict between those who supported the new religion of Buddhism, and those who supported the indigenous religion. The king referenced in the following quote, Pŏp-hŭng, is also the first king to use the Chinese title, *wang*, rather than the Korean title, *maripkan*.[268]

King Pŏp-hŭng, who came to the throne in 514, was the first king who was avowedly Buddhist. However, as in Japan at a later date, there was a conflict between those who supported the new doctrine and those who supported the indigenous religion. In the *Haedong kosŭng-jŏn*, it is recorded that when the new king began his reign, he desired to propagate Buddhism in his realm but was opposed by a significant number of his ministers and court officials. It was at this point that the king and a young court official entered into a pact to force the issue. Pak Yŏm-ch'ok (503-527), also known as I-ch'a-don, was a Buddhist believer who secretly agreed with the king to send out an order for the construction of a monastery. When the ministers of the government discovered this order, they brought it to the attention of the king, who denied having issued it. I-ch'a-don, who had issued the order, was ordered to be executed for his usurpation of royal authority. Before his death, he foretold that a miracle would happen. The *Haedong kosŭng-jŏn* records that his head flew to the top of a mountain and that blood white as milk flowed from his neck. The occurrence of this miracle is said to explain the rapid acceptance of Buddhism in Shilla. The martyrdom of I-ch'a-don probably occurred in the year 529.[269]

In 554, the first Shilla monk, Ŭi-shin, returned from India with a large number of sutras. He was the builder of a major Buddhist institution, the Pŏpchu Temple. Two other important events followed: Hyon-gwang returned from Ch'ên, after studying *T'ien-t'ai* (*Tendai* in Japanese) under the Chinese monk, Jui-szu, becoming the first recorded teacher of *T'ien-t'ai* in Shilla. Secondly, it is also in this period that we first hear of the Hwarang Troop, an organization focusing on teaching youth moral virtues and patriotism. The Haedong *kosŭng-jŏn* records that these youths, "instructed each other in the Way and in righteousness, entertained each other with songs and music, or went sightseeing to famous mountains and rivers." Grayson comments that these activities seem more Taoist than Buddhist, but I do not believe that such activities necessarily communicate a Taoist-centered focus upon nature as our teacher. Rather than a seeking of the Tao, instruction in "the Way and in righteousness" is very compatible with Buddhism, and the other activities seem like very normal activities around which Asians in general still gather today, apart from any religious significance.[270]

Another king who comes upon the scene at this time is renowned for shaving his head and taking the vows of a monk: King Chin-hŭng, who then took the Buddhist name, Pŏp-hŭng. A number of pro-Buddhist characteristics mark his reign:

> In surveying his reign, we note that temple construction increased considerably, that it was increasingly common for monks to go to foreign lands to deepen their knowledge of Buddhism, that *sūtras* were brought back to Shilla presumably for translation, that relics were venerated, that certain state ceremonies were performed according to Buddhist practice, and that the king like his predecessor had seen his role to be that of the *wangsŏn*. It was the king's desire that the nation state should become a Buddhist state.[271]

The second king to follow Pŏp-hŭng, Chin-p'yŏng (reigned 579-632) was a promoter of Buddhist missionary work directed toward Japan. One monk in particular was prominent during his reign, Wŏn-gwang, who left to study in China in 589. He returned to Shilla ten years later at the request of the king, and set about explaining the nature of Buddhism to the royal court. In 608, King Chin-p'yŏng appointed him as a diplomatic envoy to the imperial court of Sui. Grayson gives the following account,

> In the year 613, the *Haedong kosŭng-jŏon* records that he held a Paekchwa-hoe or an Assembly of One Hundred Seats, which was the second to be held in Shila, and at which he expounded on the scriptures before a select assembly...It is also recorded in the *Haedong kosŭng-jŏon* that the king called Wŏn-gwang to his side during an illness. By reciting the sutras, it was believed that Wŏn-gwang had cured the king's illness. When he was nearing the end of his life, Wŏn-gwang was called again to the palace, and nearing the end of his life, was personally tended by the king until his death. He died in 631 and was buried with the rites which befitted a king.[272]

It was under this same king's reign that the occasional travel of a monk to India, "rose to become virtually a stream of scholarly monks who went to see the sacred sites of Buddhism."[273]

So when did Buddhism trickle down and begin to embrace the public? The records show that the greatest of all Shilla monks, Wŏn-hyo, was born in the thirty-ninth year of King Chin-p'yŏng (617). He had a strange experience while studying in China that shaped his later thought. One night a storm arose, forcing him and another monk into a cave for shelter. During the night, he became thirsty and found some rainwater gathered in what he thought to be a stone container. The next morning he discovered the container to be a human skull, and the cave to be a tomb. This caused Wŏn-hyo to become revolted to the point of nausea, which resulted in turn in his sudden enlightenment. The substance of that enlightenment was his learning that all things are relative, that everything is really in the mind. "We know what things are by what we perceive them to be."[274] Wŏn-hyo was unique in that he was not a member of any sect, nor did he feel that enlightenment was attainable by any one experience. In him, we see a non-doctrinal emphasis on ministry to the laity.

> Because he felt strongly that Buddhism must take root amongst the common people, he devoted the rest of his life to non-sectarian evangelism amongst the general populace. It is said that he would play a six-stringed instrument called the *kŏmun'go* in front of local shrines for the entertainment of the farmers, frequented wine shops, practiced meditation in the mountains, sang songs with a Buddhist import as he passed through the countryside, and in all ways lived a life which was little different from the ordinary man. Some of the songs which he composed became so widely known that even non-Buddhists were known to sing them.[275]

Another of his contributions was the writing of an important introduction to Mahayana Buddhism and another work which was a guide for members of the laity seeking the way to paradise.[276] Here we see a major emphasis in moving the influence of Buddhism to the general populace.

In summing up the movement in Shilla, Grayson gives a very detailed outline, suggesting the following stages:

1. Contact and General Rejection, 410 to 520;
2. Official Acceptance, 529 to 540;
3. Growth and Evangelism, 540 to 599;
4. Penetration; 599 to 631;
5. Popularization and the Growth of Doctrinal Sects; 631 to 742;
6. Growth of Non-Doctrinal Sects, 742 to 936.[277]

According to the above breakdown, it is recalled that initial contact of Buddhism with Korea penetrated the royal court, but there was resistance among the majority of the nobility. Neither was there acceptance yet by the population at large. In the second stage, Official Acceptance, Grayson includes the martyrdom of I-ch'a-don (although in the body of the chapter he dates him earlier, from 503 to 527), and takes in the reigns of kings Pŏp-hŭng and Chin-hŭng. This moved Buddhism from the practice of members of the royal family, to a blanket royal sanction. With this stage, we have the royalty adopting Buddhist names for their reign. Such endorsement made acceptance by all portions of Shilla society possible. This is significant because such sanction opened the door to a full-scale people movement. As we move into the period of Growth and Evangelism, we see the outgoing stream of monks to China and India, and the incoming stream of sutras and other teaching and artistic material with increased attention to evangelism. It also features the outward movement of mission work to Japan.[278] With the coming of the fourth stage, Penetration, we have Wŏn-gwang returning from Sui and launching a movement for training the elite youth of Shilla in the tenets of Buddhism and patriotism. He openly established Buddhism as a friend and ally of the state, not a threatening foe. He was able to see the potential for unleashing great power for the establishment of Buddhist ideals through tapping into the elite of the upcoming generation. This was an extremely wise move on his part—one that major political movements have recognized throughout history, and one that the Church would do well in consistently duplicating. In this fourth stage of penetration, Buddhism was able to become an integral component of Korean society. Buddhism marked major gains here; as Grayson put it, "from this period forward there was a dramatic change in the fortunes of the Indian religion."[279] In the fifth stage of Popularization and the Growth of Doctrinal Sects, Buddhism gains popularity with the masses, largely through the efforts of Wŏn-hyo, and we see the establishment of sects in Shilla according to the trends of T'ang.[280]

Buddhism secured a footing at all levels of society. Grayson offers some important analysis of this stage:

> First, Buddhism came to be seen not only as the dominant religious and philosophical mode of the state, but as its protector as well. Second, the effect of outside cultural influences were witnessed on the budding number of Shilla monks who went to T'ang and even India to study. Third, Buddhism adapted itself to the shamanistic substratum of Shilla's religious life as is evidenced by the association of the kings with the *Bodhisattvas*, and by the correlation of important Korean mountains with mountains sacred to various *Bodhisattvas*, such as Wu-t'ai Shan. It must have been in this period when the practice of associating shrines to the mountain god with Buddhist temples became firmly established. The growth of esoteric orders which used magical formulas and sacred diagrams...give further evidence for the accommodation of Buddhism with shamanism. By this point, Buddhism was no longer an important foreign doctrine, but an indigenous component of Shilla's life and society.[281]

Buswell affirms this analysis of what he calls, "a thoroughgoing amalgamation of the foreign religion and indigenous local cults. Autochthonous snake and dragon cults, for example, merged with the Mahayana belief in dragons as protectors of the Dharma..."[282]

With the sixth and final stage, we see a rise of non-doctrinal sects centered upon spontaneity and intuition. Such emphases were appealing in a time when government was going through a period of instability and society was in chaos. Here is an example of how religion adapts to the needs of the times or loses influence. Religion must, to some degree, answer the questions people are asking, and minister to their heartfelt needs. While on the one hand one wants to avoid total relativism, on the other hand, maintaining a rigidity that worked in previous generations will ultimately prove ineffective. This requires a sort of balancing act between total relativism and total irrelevancy.

Buddhism spoke to the times as it penetrated Northeast Asia. Nevertheless, in Korea, as in China, Buddhism had its highs and lows. In Korea, Buddhism had its zenith in the thirteenth century, but then went into a decline from which it never fully recovered, taking an almost fatal blow from pro-Confucian and anti-Buddhist political policy in the fifteenth century.[283] Here lies the danger of overdependence upon political power alliances.

Buddhism in Japan

Next, we will consider the object of Korea's Buddhist mission: Japan. When Buddhism came to Japan, it encountered a religious context more similar with shamanism in Korea than the Taoism or Confucianism that confronted missionaries in China. Religion in ancient Japan evidenced itself by distinct local cults and traditions, which gradually integrated under the Yamato court.[284] Scholars have at times spoken of indigenous Japanese religion as nature worship, or nature religion. However, although there is that element to it, it is more than that. What we today call Shinto is centered on the concept of *kami*. The word is notoriously difficult to define. Similar to the *mana* of the Melanesians, it takes in animate and inanimate beings, arousing a sense of awe. Masaharu Anesaki explains, "Any object or being which evoked a thrill of emotion, whether affectionate or awe-inspiring, appealing to the sense of mystery, might be regarded as a Kami and accorded due respect."[285] The *kami* include mythical gods, mountains, trees, and although at one time humans were also *kami*, that usage became more limited to the imperial family over time. Joseph Kitagawa is careful to point out that the mountains, trees, rocks and rivers did not merely symbolize or manifest the *kami*, but in the minds of the Japanese, these were *kami*. Kitagawa uses the example given by John Wilson to illustrate that when the ancient Egyptian said, "that the king was Horus, he did not mean that the king was playing the part of Horus, he meant that the king was Horus, that the god was effectively present in the king's body during the activity in question."[286] This, says Kitagawa, is different from Mircea Eliade's contention that, "Since man is *homo symbolicus*, and all his activities involve symbolism...it follows that all religious facts have a symbolic character...When a tree becomes a cult object, it is not as a *tree* that it is venerated, but as a *hierophany*, that is, a manifestation of the sacred."[287] However, in the case of Japan, one venerates a tree as a tree, a rock as a rock—symbols are not understood symbolically. Although their world may contain what we call symbols, there is here no recognition that symbols are a way of processing the world we experience, that "the world of perception and concept, is created out of the world of physical reality."[288]

Kami figured prominently in early social organization. Family clans, or *uji* (also called *ie* or *uchi*) each had their progenitor *kami*, and as clans and their chieftain grew in power and prestige (such as the Fujiwara, from which the imperial line came), so did the *uji-gami*, or *kami* of the clan. Each *uji* was a social, economic, political and religious unit.[289] There was no separation of church and state. The chieftain was both political leader and high priest, a fact which is depicted in the word *matsurigoto*, which means both "government" and "religious rites."[290] Thus, "the meaning of each being was sought not in itself, but in its mutual participation, continuity, and correspondence to and with others within the total monistic world of meaning."[291]

One could classify the world-view of Japan as monistic; the "world" for them was the world that the Japanese knew and experienced in their homeland, and they did not seek another. There was no hidden meaning behind Japan, nor any future and better world to long for—Japan was it. Kitagawa refers to this as a "one-dimensional meaning structure," and a "unitary world of meaning."[292] There seems to be a one-dimensional meaning structure in a three-dimensional universe: the plain of heaven (*Takama-no-hara*), the manifest world (*Utsu-shiyo*), and the nether-world (*Yo-motsu-kuni*). All of this added up to an ethnocentricity whereby the Japanese viewed themselves as the children of the gods, possessing a culture superior to any other. Kitagawa comments,

> In this connection, Nakamura astutely observes that although nationalism has been advocated by many thinkers in India, China, and the West, "their nationalism was theoretically concerned with the state in general, not with their particular states," whereas in Japan, "the particular state of Japan came to be the sole standard upon which all judgments were based." In short, Japanese religious tradition has rarely questioned the ancient Japanese principle that Japan was the world and that the nation, that is, the Japanese nation, was, "the measure of all things."[293]

Nichiren, founder of the Nichiren school of Buddhism maintained that in the phrase "the Buddha appeared to the world," from the Lotus sutra, "world" means Japan. Confucian scholars used their universal Confucian ethic to uphold Japan's claim to be a divine nation.[294] History served the same ends. Rather than viewing history objectively, history was a tool to serve the goals of the ruling powers. Kitagawa cites examples from two of the provincial and historical records, or *fudoki*, which begin this way,

> For example, the *Hitachi Fudoki* begins as follows: "When

asked about the traditions of the province and countries, the elders answered by saying, 'in ancient times…'" "In the Izumo Fudoki, the historical background of Izumo was explained in terms of myth: "Izumo was named after the words of the God Yatsu-kamizu Omizunu. The august Omizunu…spoke majestically, 'Clouds-rising Izumo is a narrow strip of young land. When the creator gods established the land of Izumo…'" The provincial officials who compiled those documents selected those folk stories and myths that were particularly relevant to the expanding imperial government rather than preserving the objectivity and integrity of the historical data as such.[295]

The better known *Nihongi* (Japan Chronicles) and *Kojiki* (Records of Ancient Matters) bring out this use of history even more clearly. The compilation of these records were ordered by the Emperor Temmu after he defeated a coalition of *uji* and usurped the throne. "In this situation, the new 'present' called for the new 'past,' rectifying the 'mistaken' facts and 'corrupt' documents, as stated in the preface to the *Kojiki*." An explanation of how they went about this helps us to understand how Buddhism served their cause.

Significantly, the chroniclers perceived two or three factors simultaneously on their horizon: (1) the cosmogonic and other "heavenly" myths that authenticated the genealogical backgrounds of the imperial *uji* (the Sun Line) and of other prominent *uji* which claimed the *kami* lineage; (2) mythohistorical accounts of activities and events connected with the forebears of the imperial and other prominent *uji* who, in accordance with the alleged mandate of the Sun deity, pacified the world, that is, Japan, and established the national community under the sacred king; and, in the case of the *Nihongi* (3) contemporary events that proved the legitimacy of Temmu's regime both in terms of the Shinto mythohistorical tradition and of the *Sūtra of the Sovereign Kings of the Golden Radiance* (*Konko myo saisho o gyo*). The latter explicated a Buddhist doctrine that a monarch is a son of divine being: (*Tenshi, devaputra*) "to whom has been given a mandate of Heaven and whom Heaven will protect."[296]

To accomplish such a feat, the chroniclers translated these three factors from a circular to a horizontal, spatial, and chronological format based upon the Chinese calendrical system, appropriating the Chinese dynastic model, which required positioning their age of the *kami* prior to the beginning of the Japanese nation.[297] This illustrates that Japan's rulers viewed Buddhism as an advanced form of culture that would serve political purposes, as well as religious. The cultural dynamic is of utmost importance in our understanding of Buddhism's place in Japan's history.

Since the tutelary *kami* of the imperial *uji* was the sun goddess, Amaterasu-Omikami, with the emperor considered her direct descendant, all religious duties, cultic functions and ceremonies served to buttress the myth, in turn preserving the divinity of the imperial family.[298] It is under this divinity that Japan would unite, a divinity symbolized yet today by the national flag, depicting a red sun on a white background. Such divine sanction was consistent with the "heavenly mandate" of Confucianism and, as pointed out above, Buddhism as well.

This, then, is the setting which confronted the early promulgators of Buddhism. Although we know the first informal influence of Buddhism dates back perhaps as far as the early fifth century, the date of 538 A.D. is a standard date given for Buddhism's official introduction to Japan in the early Asuka period (500-710). The *Nihonshoki* sets the official date at October 13, 552 A.D, which would be the 13th year of the reign of the 29th *Mikado* of Japan, the emperor Kimmei.[299] Buddhism came to Japan primarily via Korea, but later, intermittently from the sixth to the sixteenth century, Japan learned of Buddhism directly from China. Also, similar to much of Asia, although Mahayana is dominant, the kinds of Buddhism practiced in Japan take in both the Mahayana and the Theravada traditions, incorporating some of the earliest forms of Indian Buddhism, as well as some of the more contemporary expressions. Nearly every period and culture of Buddhism is present today in Japan.

According to the historian Shinsho Hanayama, the first encounter with Buddhism at the imperial level threw the court into a feud, or at least exacerbated a feud already present in the court. The emperor was to have asked his advisors how he should respond to Buddhism. The Soga clan, in charge of foreign affairs, and progressively inclined, advised its acceptance. The Mononobe clan was a warrior clan, and the Nakatomis were in charge of Shinto ritual, and thus more conservative, and apparently opposed the introduction of Buddhism.[300]

The emperor is to have then rejected both Shinto and Buddhism, and to have turned the Buddhist images and gifts over to the Sogas for private worship. This situation continued for forty to fifty years.[301]

The second emperor to follow Emperor Kimei, Emperor Yomei (31st Mikado) was the first to put his faith in Buddhism, but he died after reigning only a short time. A layman had to be made a priest for leading the court in prayer, and thus one named Kuratsukuri-no-Tasuna became the first layperson to become a priest in Japan. Emperor Yomei's younger sister followed him in reign as Empress Suiko. Her son was the famed Prince Shotoku, who would give Buddhism the boost that it needed for widespread acceptance.[302]

As we mentioned earlier, the acceptance of Buddhism was not only for its religious teachings, in fact, the religious benefits were often initially of secondary importance. That which came along with the Buddhist missions served as a strong incentive toward Buddhism's widespread appeal. As Anesaki comments, "It was quite natural that the display of ritual and the practice of medical arts were most effective in inducing a people like the Japanese of that time to receive civilization."[303] With Buddhism came also Chinese arts and medicine, writing, and astronomy, leading even the conservatives to a gradual acceptance of this foreign religion.

Early on, Buddhism found itself appealing to the court, but did not gain real momentum in Japan until the son of the Emperor Yomei, the Prince-Regent Shotoku, came to the throne at the age of nineteen. Supported by the progressive party, Shotoku embraced Buddhism whole-heartedly and made the promotion of Buddhism a major priority. Shotoku became the Japanese equivalent of India's Asoka. Cultivating relations with China, monks, and students accompanied envoys to the continent, and Chinese and Koreans were invited to Japan to spur the nation on to progress in religion and civilization. At this juncture in time, China had just become unified (590 A.D.) under the powerful Sui dynasty, and China herself was blossoming. Under such favorable conditions, Japan benefited from the introduction of new schools of Buddhism as they arose in neighboring China.[304] Shotoku himself embracing the Sanron school, which adhered to the transcendental idealist philosophy of Nagarjuna of second century India, became the "pioneer of philosophical thinking in Japan."[305] Utilizing Buddhism as the guiding principle for his reign, he also gave lectures in the palace and in the temples. Central to his lectures was the theme of universal salvation as described in the Lotus Sutra.³⁰⁶ In addition, he established a Buddhist institution, overlooking the port city of Osaka, which included a temple, an asylum, a hospital and a dispensary. The temple held departments for the study of Buddhist philosophy and sciences, and an order of monks who were trained in the arts and in ceremonies. The other institutions were the first of their kind in Japan and became models for ages to come.³⁰⁷ Skilled ruler that he was, Shotoku also developed Japan's first constitution (April 3, 604 A.D.), in which he promoted the unification of and harmonizing of the nation, based upon reverence for the Three Treasures: the Buddha, the Dharma (the Law, or Truth), and the Sangha (the Brotherhood).³⁰⁸ "According to *Nihonshoki*, all officials civil and military competed in erecting Buddhist temples. And these temples were built primarily to express gratitude toward mikados and ancestors."³⁰⁹

The extent to which the emperor and his family took these teachings to heart is evident even after his death. When the Soga clan attacked all those related to him in 643, they gave the Soga no resistance. All perished rather than be the cause of an increase in the number of deaths through armed struggle and so violate the Buddhist admonition against taking life.³¹⁰

Following this period of imperial favor and Chinese prestige, Buddhism next began to penetrate the lives of the common people. This came in the medieval era (the Kamakura period, 1185-1333 and the Muromachi period, 1336-1573). When political authority transferred from the aristocracy of the imperial court to the newly powerful military class, ushering in the age of feudalism.³¹¹ Again, we see a top-down movement, from the aristocracy to the common people. It was during this era that Zen (Ch'an in China) grew in prominence, with Zen priests going to and coming from China. Temples and stupas were constructed in sixty-six provinces and two islands to assist the propagation of Zen. The cultural impact was lasting, as these buildings stood in forests and near ponds, decorated with black and white pictures. Hanayama adds,

> And in a small-sized '*chashitsu*' or 'tea house' one sat saw, and felt the universe; in a little twig on had all the beauty of hundred flowers [sic]. This was the spirit of '*kado*', the Japanese flower-arrangement. It was no sheer arrangement of color and form in pleasing ways. There was more than what appealed to the eye. Here came out to be a way of life to sink in what is calm and serene, deep and graceful. The serene gardens of the *Tenryuji*, the *Saihoji*, and the

Ryuanji temple in Kyoto were all works of Zen priests of this age. They were the centers of culture of those days; they were not only well versed in the teaching of Zen Buddhism, but also their learning much helped to develop the philosophy of Confucianism of the Sung age. They wrote Buddhist books along with those on Chinese classics. They were proficient in Chinese poetry and literature, penmanship and painting...The knowledge of flower-arrangement and tea-ceremony gradually become part of the accomplishment of the populace. This goes down even to this day.[312]

Other forms of Buddhism that blossomed during this period were Nichiren and Shinran; but it was still Zen that wielded the greatest influence among the nobles and the *samurai*. Among the populace, the Pure Land sect offered a simple salvation by faith in Amida Butsu, and a promise of a future heavenly paradise. This unique form of Buddhism flies against the main tenets of Buddhism, for there is no striving for self-enlightenment, and no longing for extinction. Each of these three movements arose from within the Tendai orientation, later becoming independent schools in their own right. Noriyoshi Tamaru comments on these as follows:

> What they did, in effect, was to select, from the range of teachings included in the harmonizing approach of an earlier day, one particular motif and give it the sole place of honor. Pure Land Buddhism chose the way of salvation through faith in Amida Buddha; Zen, the way of concentrated meditation; and Nichiren Buddhism, the way of dedication to the truth of the Lotus Sutra. All three, in contrast to the synthesizing perspective of Tendai and Shingon, were selective, uncompromising and sectarian in outlook.[313]

Of these three movements, only Zen came to Japan as an innovation rooted in China. In Japan it took two forms: one for the high-ranking samurai class (Rinzai Zen), employing riddles and sayings of past Zen masters; and another for the lower-ranking provincial samurai and commoners (Sōtō Zen), based solely upon meditation in an upright lotus position (*zazen*). This latter form was introduced by Dōgen and took on indigenous folklore elements, thus taking on increased emphasis in funerary rites.

The other form of Buddhism to arise in the thirteenth century was Nichiren, which bears the name of its founder. Nichiren attributed the unrest and chaos of his day to impure forms of Buddhism, and like many cultic leaders of the West, set out to "purify" those forms. He focused all of his attention on the Lotus Sutra, pronouncing all other forms of Buddhism as faulty forms that would only lead one to hell. As can be imagined, his highly critical stance led to repeated persecution, as he opposed not only the conditions of Buddhism, but the decay of the state as well. He was exiled to the island of Sado, which effectively ended his impact on direct reform. Following the Meiji Restoration (1868), Nichiren had closely allied itself with the spirit of nationalism in Japan. More importantly, what Japan refers to as "New Religions" have sprung from Nichiren: Reijukai, Risshō Kōsei Kai, and Sōka Gakkai (a sect that has been able to gain impressive political influence, including its own political party).

In China, Pure Land Buddhism was a form of spiritual training that all sects used. However, in Japan it became a school in its own right. Pure Land began as a component of Mahayana, and appealed to the masses that lived in turbulent times with no assurance of what tomorrow would bring. The leading proponent of this salvation-by-faith form of Buddhism was Hōnen (1133-1212). Hōnen divided Japanese Buddhism into two categories: those who seek enlightenment through self-effort (*jiriki*), and those who seek to be reborn in the pure land, "the spiritual state of oneness with ultimate reality, through reliance on the mercy of Amida Buddha."[314] Hōnen obviously chose the latter, opting for reliance on the power of an other (*tariki*)—the mercy and compassion of Amida Buddha. This is an entirely revolutionary approach to Buddhism, since it calls upon one to abandon all the traditional forms of meditation, rituals, and the prescribed forms of attaining enlightenment. There was great appeal in this movement for a populace that was thrust into a feudal era, and for whom nothing was sure in life.

Pure Land Buddhism reached new levels under Hōnen's disciple, Shinran. Like his predecessors, Shinran selected one element of teaching and elevated it to prominence. In this case, he chose the element of compassion, and made it the centerpiece of "True Sect of the Pure Land" (*jōdo shin shū*. From this position, Shinran maintained a highly universalistic outlook, that Amida's compassionate intention of saving all people had already been accomplished. Consequently, there was no difference between the monastic life and life in the secular world. Much like the famed Protestant, Martin Luther, Shinran got married and raised a family to make the point that one could adhere to Buddhist ideals and still live in the secular world (*zaike bukkyō*). This form of Buddhism became immensely popular, especially in the farming communities, and it remains the largest single sect in Japan today.[315]

With the sixteenth century development of the shogunate in Japan, Hideyoshi Toyotomi, and later the Tokugawas, Buddhism was made the key factor in rallying the country to unity.[316] These shoguns pulled Japan out of a warring states period and into a unified nation by utilizing Buddhism as their operative tool. In order to maintain tight control over the populace, every family in Japan had to register at a local Buddhist temple, requiring the building of many new temples. Such registration also became a powerful instrument in the hands of rulers to stamp out Christianity (from 1587 until 1875), as registration at a local temple and the *gogumi,* or "five family group" system required mutual policing against the Christian religion.[317] The Buddhist temple system lent itself to political power and enjoyed great prestige and status, until the emperor Meiji (from 1868) in a spirit of nationalism decided to throw off Buddhism and reinstate Shinto as a state tool for the same ends.[318] Here, again, the downside of close political association was evident. And yet, as in China, Buddhism has managed to set itself somewhat comfortably alongside other local religious systems in an amalgamated construct.

This has not happened without a degree of setback, however. One often hears that the Japanese culture has a knack for importing items and remaking them into a uniquely Japanese product. In a sense, that happened with Buddhism also. When Buddhism met the competition of native Shinto, the Shinto priests said that their *kami* enlightened the Buddha, and all the Buddhist *Bodhisattvas* were simply the *kami* of Japan. The Buddhists countered that they knew the names of the Japanese *kami,* and that the Buddha had provided a way for the *kami* to achieve salvation. At best, however, the Buddha and the Bodhisattvas have become foreign counterparts to the *kami.*[319] Buddhism, however, went far beyond this charge/countercharge level of apologetics, to incorporating many local practices and ideologies into its system and, in some cases, it became just another polytheistic form with little content as far as the average lay-person was concerned. Kitagawa sees the downside of the Japanese transformation of Buddhism. As he points out, what may work well with foreign foods and technologies, does not always have a positive impact on thought forms or religious conviction.

> The so-called transforming genius of the Japanese people, however, had some serious drawbacks, too. In the main, it worked better with tangible material things and the external aspects of foreign culture and religion, but it was far more difficult for it to cope with thoughts, ideas, and religious beliefs from abroad. For example, within one century or so after the introduction of

Buddhism, the Japanese people learned and mastered the intricacies of Buddhist art, architecture and rituals. But it is not likely that many understood, or even paid attention to, the profound meaning of Buddhist doctrines. To be sure, a large number of Buddhist scriptures was introduced, and the government established bureaus for copying these scriptures. The court asked the clergy to recite appropriate scriptures for practical, mundane benefits in the same manner in which the native Shinto liturgical prayers (Norito) were recited to bring rain, relief from pestilence, safe childbirth, recovery from illness, and good fortune. And in return for these services, large estates were donated to Buddhist temples, and the clergy were showered with honors and favors by the court. But rarely were questions raised as to the meaning of the Buddha's teaching, except in a very general sense. To most people in Japan, copying the scriptures was in itself a meritorious act, and reciting them effectuated their magical potency. Therefore, it was not only unnecessary but it was better not to translate the scriptures into the Japanese language. There were, of course, some able Japanese monks who had studied Buddhist doctrines in China, but they constituted a tiny minority, numerically speaking.[320]

Kitagawa is perhaps being a little hard on his own people. One could rightly ask if this is not the condition to be found in many cultures, whether they be Buddhist, Muslim, Christian or any other religion. If one does not seek out the meaning or content of forms, but is satisfied with the form itself, it is easier to hold varying, and sometimes even conflicting systems harmoniously. In the Eastern milieu, it is perfectly acceptable to hold varied truth claims simultaneously. (This is the phenomenon of syncretism that both Buddhism and Christianity have tried to avoid—with varying degrees of success.) However, in such situations, people will accept some forms while rejecting others, depending upon how they understand the meaning and function of those forms. Thus, it can be dangerous to make blanket statements about content falling totally by the wayside. What may sometimes be happening is that one might sacrifice content for form in one instance, while totally rejecting content and form in another. For example, a Japanese friend of mine who had attended a church-related high school in his youth once explained to me his daily morning ritual. Just before heading off to work, he would pause before the household Buddhist altar to honor his ancestors, then he would pray before the household Shinto shrine to the Japanese *kami*, and finally he would say a quick prayer to Jesus, confident that all of his religious bases were now covered. When it came to discussion about baptism, however, he said that being a Christian was fine for his daughter or son, but as the eldest son in his family (*chonan*), he could not think of holding Christianity as the one true faith over the others. What would the relatives think? We discussed various ways that Christian forms and ceremonies could meet his Buddhist and Shinto needs, but the threat of social displeasure held him back. To accept baptism would imply to others that he had accepted an exclusivist religion and rejected all that it meant to be Japanese, primarily, ancestor worship. In some ways, he was like the teacher of the law in Mark 12:34, to whom Jesus said, "You are not far from the kingdom of God," and yet he was never willing to stand openly as a "Japanese Christian," even after publicly attending the baptism of his daughter, daughter-in-law and grandchildren. Did he know that in reality, being a Christian had to mean more than simply adding another god shelf in his home among others? It's hard to say, and yet it seems apparent that beyond any religious comfort that these god-shelves might have given him, they were a form of social identity, and the accepted social identity of being Japanese did not allow for being a baptized, confessing Christian. In such a setting, one's prior enculturation can be an extremely powerful obstacle to the appropriation of the gospel, and there seems to be no one simple tool for removing it. Once a person becomes a disciple of Jesus Christ in such a setting, for them to re-enculturate is a lifelong process. As Shusaku Endo, the famed writer of the novel, *Silence*, wrote, "Christianity is, for the Japanese, a Western suit that never quite fits."[321] Endo could never bring himself to "take the suit off," but he never could feel totally comfortable with it either. Endo is certainly not alone in his sentiment. My friend was correct in perceiving Christianity to be an exclusivist religion. The God of the Bible permits no rivals. The nagging question is how to overcome the other perception that many in Japan hold, that to become a Christian means to cease being Japanese, and how to overcome it without succumbing to the dangers of syncretism.[322] The problem of exclusivity would likely become less of a problem if being a Christian and being Japanese were not perceived as an oxymoron, for the previously mentioned Sōka Gakkai sect of Nichiren Buddhism is also fairly exclusivist, and yet holds a powerful position in Japanese society. But, we will save further discussion of this for the final chapter.

Chapter Summary

It is interesting that in each of the above cases of Buddhist missionary endeavor outside of India it took about 300 years for Buddhism to take firm root in the culture, even if in most cases it did not become a dominant religious expression. Beginning with translation, sometimes using "power encounters," and moving into cultural art forms, it generally found momentum once it connected with the power elite within the culture (as we saw even in India, and later with Christianity in the time of Constantine). It then went through political upheavals and manipulations eventually moving down into the populace at large.

Also, in each case there are patterns of ebb and flow, favor and disfavor, depending again upon the sway of political powers. Buddhism seemed to survive through providing forms for people to address the rites of passage in life—providing places and rituals to celebrate and to mourn, and to petition the gods and the ancestors.

So what remains as key factors in all three religions for the acceptance of Buddhism? What things were favorable to its spread? It is apparent, first of all, that there was imperial favor behind its outward movement. First in India, we saw Asoka propelling Buddhism outwardly in all directions. Some of Buddhism's spread was due to the natural movement of merchants and seamen traveling the Silk Road and the sea routes to various ports along Asia's coastline. But the stamp of royal acceptance and favor played a large role in Buddhism's initial phases of penetration to regions beyond India's borders. Just as important, Buddhism had the advantage of not having to give allegiance to an outside authority. Thus, it posed no threat to local powers. Secondly, Buddhism saw the need to translate. Translation is, as Lamin Sanneh is quick to point out, a form of incarnation. It demonstrates the willingness to learn the culture and to listen. Buddhism listened, as well as spoke. It was able to address both the deep levels of human suffering, as well as the ultimate joys of life. Thirdly, Buddhism seemed to fill a need in societies that were experiencing measures of instability, and looking for direction or a unifying factor. Buddhism was often a tool for unification. Fourthly, in each case there was opposition from local religions, due to the discrepancies that became apparent upon comparison. There were also political loyalties to the indigenous religions that had to be overcome. Buddhism had to demonstrate that it was either equal or in some ways superior to the locally established faiths. It had to discover the differences, and then strategize as to how to overcome those differences. In the case of

China, Buddhism actually became a sect of Taoism for a time in order to gain acceptance. It did not assert its points of exclusivity at the outset, but waited to gain strength enough to stand on its own. Fifthly, adaptability which allowed Buddhism to employ varying methods—depending upon the local situation—made it possible for missionaries to utilize the momentum of locally driven movements. In one area, there was the method of the exercise of spiritual power, in others where the audience was more educated, there was translation and the study of sacred texts. In each region, there was also the possibility for localized interpretation and expression. Sixthly, it is inspiring to see the level of sophistication that Buddhism was able to demonstrate in its artistic expression. Part of this was a cultural factor; becoming a vehicle for bringing the best from Indian and Chinese civilizations to their host cultures was definitely a plus for the religion. And yet, even in these cultural trappings Buddhism was able to communicate the heart and soul of its religious message. Finally, Grayson and Covell pointed out the importance of people movements. Buddhism was not satisfied with a one-by-one approach to evangelism, and it did not separate its converts from society at large, but rather sought to bring in any willing to come, regardless of their level of understanding, or even their motivation. A high level of orthodoxy was not set up as a port of entry. Rather, it was understood that in bringing in masses of people, there will be some who rise to become teachers and leaders of those masses. Basically many obstacles as possible were removed and this sometimes posed a problem for Buddhism, as its leaders had to address extreme forms of syncretism. Even today, Buddhist scholars lament that in places like Japan, Buddhism has been reduced to a funerary service, and a vehicle for ancestor worship. The core values and teachings of Buddhism get lost in the popular expressions or forms.

The story of Buddhism in Northeast Asia is not a glowing success story, and yet it found a footing and survived as an important player in the religious sphere through indigenization, and continued to spread across Northeast Asia. As a partner among others in the region, it can serve to instruct us in some of the factors that religions face as they work to gain acceptance among people groups. Buddhism today is still struggling in this region to maintain a level of relevancy, and to hold its place as a viable expression of religious faith among its peoples. In the next chapter, we will move on to explore the mission movements of Christianity in Northeast Asia, and we will attempt to draw some comparisons between the movements of Christianity and Buddhism.

CHAPTER FOUR

Early Christian Missions in Northeast Asia

Diligently seek to encourage and attract the natives of said Indies to all peace and quiet, that they may willingly serve us and be under our dominion and government, and above all that they may be converted to our holy catholic faith.
Isabella and Ferdinand[323]

As we pointed out in the first chapter, John M. L. Young has maintained that by 800 A.D. there were already more Christians east of Damascus than west.[324] If Young is even close to being correct, this is a remarkable statement. By the year 1000, the Church of the East was dominant between the Caspian Sea and the borders of China. Philip Jenkins describes the Nestorian Christians as the "Most spectacular among the growing churches" in medieval times.[325] He continues, "From their bases in Syria and Persia, Nestorian missionaries penetrated deeply into Central Asia and China by the seventh century...The Nestorians and their 'luminous doctrine' were welcomed at the imperial court, and in 638, a church was erected in the capital of Ch'ang-an, then perhaps the largest city in the world."[326] Yet, surprisingly, there is comparatively little that is available in print that would tell us the story of this amazing Christian movement that Alphonse Mingana dubbed, "the greatest missionary Church the world has ever produced."[327]

In this chapter, we will examine this and other early missions movements in Northeast Asia. However, different from the last chapter, where we proceeded according to region, in this chapter our investigation of the introduction of the gospel to this area will progress according to groups, including the work of Nestorians, Roman Catholics, and Protestants in the region. Similar to the previous chapter of Buddhist history, we must limit ourselves to the highlights, and refer the reader to authoritative works on the subject for further details.

As one considers the missions of the Church of the East, a number of questions come to mind: the first being the seemingly odd nature of this movement, in that Rome connected it with the condemned "heretic," Nestorius. Secondly, if it was a truly heretical church, how does one reconcile heresy with such a significant missions outreach? And if it was not heretical, we still want to know the sociological and theological factors at work that fueled this great missionary church.

A number of circumstances went into molding this church into one that would have great capacity for carrying the gospel to the East. For one, its people knew the meaning of *martvria*. These Syrian Christians experienced continual waves of persecution, first from the Romans, then from the Parthians, and then again from the Romans depending on who suspected them of what.[328] When Rome was pagan, the Christians of the East suffered; when Rome was Christian, the Christians of the East suffered at the hands of Parthians and any who resented Rome.

Another factor that influenced the missionary nature of the Church of the East was its asceticism, shaped in part by Tatian, who had been a pupil of Justin Martyr. Tatian is important in the history of the Church of the East not only for the *Diatessaron*, a sort of harmony of the Gospels which he compiled for the Syrian church, but also for his ascetic influence on the Church.[329] Critics in the Western church, such as Jerome, wrote Tatian off as a heretic for his ascetic views.

> Tatian...the very violent heresiarch of the Encratites, employs an argument of this sort: "If anyone sows to the flesh, of the flesh he shall reap corruption"; but he sows to the flesh who is joined to a woman; therefore he who takes a wife and sows in the flesh, of the flesh he shall reap corruption.[330]

In Tatian's address to the Greeks there are hints that he regards the world of matter as evil, for example, "Matter desired to exercise lordship over the soul and gave laws of death to man."[331] Tatian's influence stamped a stern character on the eastern Syrian and northern Persian churches for some time to come.

The topic of asceticism is especially interesting when considering the missionary character of the Church of the East. Comparing the asceticism of Egypt to that of the Syrian Church, Samuel Moffett attempts to draw a distinction between these ascetics, claiming that while those in Egypt were isolationists, the Syrian monks were driven to be mobile evangelists. This may be a bit oversimplified, but in the case of the ascetics of the Church of the East, asceticism did indeed serve to drive them out into the world in mission.[332] In the documents of this early church, *the call to ascetic self-denial is most always associated with the call to go out and witness to the gospel.* Says Moffett,

> This seems to have been the most striking difference between Syrian and Egyptian saint-ascetics. Egypt, more solidly agricultural, valued stability and tended to withdraw from outside contacts and movements. Its saints ignored the world and retreated to their caves and cells. Syria, on the other hand, with its travel and trading traditions, stressed mobility and outreach. Its ascetics became wandering missionaries, healing the sick, feeding the poor, and preaching the gospel as they moved from place to place.[333]

Again, one could make too much of this contrast; we know that Egyptian monks also did evangelism, but the depiction of the distinctly missionary nature of the Eastern monks holds true. For example, a story about the early missionary Addai, credited with the founding of the Church of Edessa, illustrates this point. The story says that he refused to receive silver and gold from the king, having forsaken the riches of this world "because without purses and without scrips, bearing the cross upon our shoulders, we were commanded to preach the Gospel in the whole creation."[334] And preach it they did. According to Moffett, before the end of the Parthian dynasty (225 A.D.), the Christian faith had not only taken root in Persia, but also in the steppes of Central Asia. At the end of the second century there were Christians living as far to the east as Bactria (what is today northern Afghanistan), among the Turkic tribes of Asia, the Hindu Kush, Armenia, and on to the Persian Gulf. A monument erected perhaps as early as the middle of the second century records the remarks of a Christian bishop as saying; "I saw the Syrian plain and all the cities, [even] Nisibis, having crossed the Euphrates. Everywhere I found people with whom to speak (i.e. Christians)."[335] Arbela of Adiabene was perhaps an even stronger center for missionary outreach than Edessa. Both Arbela and Edessa were well known for their Christian schools, *which were for the most part missionary Bible training centers.*[336]

This brings us to the discussion of another major factor for the rapid growth of the Church of the East: the monastic system. The monastic system combined with schools for a biblical education of the children and youth of the Christian community, considering such education as vital to the survival of the church. Every bishop maintained a school, run by the chorepiscopus, where the Bible was the main textbook. According to W. A. Wigram, "The course was purely theological, the sole textbooks being the Scriptures, and more particularly the Psalms....The Church services also formed a part of the regular course; and no doubt all the approved theological works of the Church were to be found in the library...The college in Sabr-Ishu's day contained eight hundred pupils."[337] Their historian, G. D. Malech, claimed that over 2,000 books, epistles, and letters by prominent leaders were circulating among these Christians.[338] John Stewart observed, "Many of the pupils knew the whole Psalter by heart and candidates for ordination were expected to repeat the whole...The sons of Christians were expected to study the Psalms, the New Testament and to attend lectures, before entering on a business career."[339] They apparently thought of "vocation" in its original sense of Divine calling, and considered the application of the Scriptures to be essential for *any* calling. Moreover, the Church of the East exhibited a more literal view of biblical interpretation, and shied away from the allegorical approach, which had been popular with other groups. The schools were primarily for Christians; for non-Christians there were government schools run by the Magi. Rabbans or monks served as teachers for the schools, and the students were under monastic rule.[340]

As these Syrian missionaries went out they took their love of education with them, giving the Turks, the Uigurs, the Mongols and the Manchus alphabets derived from the Syriac. In the fifth century the monastic system spread rapidly through Persia, to the extent that it was said, "the country of the east was filled with monasteries and convents and habitations of monks seeking to spread abroad the knowledge of Christ as Savior and King."[341] The Christians of Persia had learned not only to survive a difficult existence without a protectorate, but driven by the testimony of the martyrs and inspiration of its monks, they were a powerful force for mission. The testing, however, was not over. More would follow, politically and doctrinally, to push the Church of the East farther from the West.

In 410,[342] a council called the Synod of Isaac, met with about forty bishops present in Seleucia-Cstesiphon, on the lower Tigris, under the city's chief bishop (given the title Catholicos). They adopted the Nicene Creed and defined the boundaries of some of their seas.[343] (The church at this time was under the patriarch of Antioch, first established to fend off the Judaistic influences of Jerusalem.) The peace-minded Persian king, Yasdegerd I died in 420 and again persecution of the church broke out, as did war with Rome, with peace restored in 422. The effect on the church this time, however, was a strong conviction of the need to make a clean break with Rome and thus to escape future persecution over political loyalties.[344]

A council met again in 424, this time in Markabata with thirty-one bishops in attendance. They declared independence from the patriarch in Antioch and granted the Catholicos still greater authority, in that "no appeal should be made from his decrees to 'western patriarchs.'"[345] W. A. Wigram comments, "[It] did as much as a Council could do to set an Oriental papacy over itself."[346] Here we see the beginning of a major crack in the structure of the organizational unity of the Church. Clearly, momentum was building as the churches of the East and West grew further and further apart from each other. From the Eastern point of view, the politics of the West caused the schism long before there was any "Nestorian" controversy.[347] Political issues had been out in the open for some time. Seats of power were coveted.

Politics were not restricted to organization and administration, however. Doctrinal schisms followed. Henophysitism (also known pejoratively as Monophysitism) came to Edessa and covered upper Mesopotamia. The church then divided itself completely from the West, and the teachers with views akin to Nestorius moved to Nisibis, which had been the chief center for the training of the clergy of the Persian (or Assyrian) church.[348] Thereafter, this group considered the Catholic Church to be heretical, and considered themselves a separate entity—the Church of the East.[349] What began as a crack in their unity would now become a complete break.

A landmark event leading up to this condition took place at the Council of Ephesus in 431, which centered on two people—one being the person of Nestorius, formerly a monk from Antioch and later appointed as bishop of Constantinople. Secondly, there was Cyril of Alexandria, a powerful figure in Alexandria, which was the fortress of orthodoxy in its day. Doctrinally, the problems revolved around two ways of defining the natures of Christ—henophysitism and dyophysitism.[350] Did Jesus have one nature, or two? This controversy moved beyond the *homoiousios* vs. *homoousios* debate, and concerned the *physis* of Christ.

Synods in both Rome and Alexandria came out against Nestorius' position in 430 and deposed Nestorius, falsely accusing him of denying the deity of Christ. The emperor called an ecumenical council at Ephesus for the following year. Without delving into the political details, both Cyril and Nestorius ended up condemned by opposing councils in the debate; however, Cyril bribed the emperor's advisor and grand chamberlain, running his church of Alexandria into a debt equivalent today to around three million dollars. Nestorius, on the other hand, quietly accepted the decree and went into exile to his old monastery near Antioch, and then, because of hardened opposition, on to Petra in Arabia. "Finally, so greatly was his influence feared, he was moved far out into the Egyptian desert. There he died about 451—to the Western church a heretic, to the Persian church a hero and a martyr, but to himself neither a heretic nor a hero."[351] Moffett records words written by Nestorius near the end of his life.

> Earthly things have little interest for me. I have died to the world and live for Him...As for Nestorius—let him be anathema!... And would God that all men by anathematizing me might attain to reconciliation with God...Farewell desert, my friend...and [farewell] exile, my mother, who after my death shall keep my body until the resurrection...Amen.[352]

The Church of the East to this day has not accepted the results of the embarrassing Council of Ephesus in 431.

In the following years we see those of henophysite persuasion (loyal to Antioch) and those of dyophysite persuasion in serious conflict, and the Church of the East becoming sharply divided into the Syrian Church of the West, and the East (sometimes called the Assyrian Church of the East). By the end of the fifth century the henophysites (also called Jacobites after the Syrian Jacobus Baradaeus) had gained the upper hand in Edessa, and the Nestorians had fled to Nisibis in Persia, Kurdistan, and upper Mesopotamia under the protection of Persian rule. Emperor Zeno (474-491) expelled all the Nestorians from his realm and closed the school at Edessa, in effect purifying Edessa from Nestorian doctrine, a decision confirmed by the fifth Ecumenical Council of Constantinople in 553.[353]

The effect of this persecution was much the same as we see in the Book of Acts: as the believers fled the persecution in Jerusalem they took their zeal and their message with them. Although there are records of Christianity being in Arabia before Nestorianism existed, Nestorian thought is said to have come to that region because of the Sassanid Christian persecutions during the reign of Shapur II (310-379). During the fifth century, there were six bishops in Arabia, with the bishop of Hirah owing ecclesiastical allegiance to the Nestorian metropolitan of Kashkar. Monasteries and schools existed there in several places. Arab Christians were usually followers of the Church of the East, though there were some who affiliated with the Western (Henophysite) Church of Syria.

By 424 A.D., missionaries were planting churches northwards in Merv, Nishapur, and Herat, south of the Oxus river, each place having its own bishop. The monks taught the converts to read, and helped them improve their vegetable growing methods. The Nestorians taught much about the importance of fruits and vegetable to one's health, and they became famous throughout the Orient for the medicinal uses of a fruit sherbet and rhubarb.

Around 498 the tolerant Kavadh I (488-531) was ousted from the throne of Persia by Kjamasp (496-498) and fled to Turkestan "with Nestorians in his retinue."[354] This group included a bishop, four presbyters, and two laymen who set out to evangelize the Turks, and with considerable success. As was the Nestorian custom in doing missions, their holistic strategy included the use of physicians, scribes, and skilled artisans, and they succeeded in simultaneously bringing such knowledge to the cultures they reached.[355] The Nestorians were renowned for their skills in medicine. In 781, an unnamed king of the Turks wrote to Patriarch Timothy (778-820) asking him to appoint a metropolitan to his people, who had also become Christians with him.

The Nestorian evangelists pushed on to the region of the Tartars and ministered among the Keraits, the Uigurs, the Naimans, and the Merkites into the tenth and eleventh centuries. About 1077 'Abdishu, metropolitan of Marw in Khurasan, wrote to the catholicos to inform him of the miraculous conversion of a king of the Keraits along with 200,000 of his people to Christianity. Marco Polo (1265-1323) saw a church at the Kerait capital of Karakorum, and we begin to hear about the vast Christian kingdom of the legendary "Prester John" in Central Asia in the twelfth and thirteenth centuries. Both king and priest, Prester John also had the titles of "Unc Khan" or "Owang Khan." It is suggested that "Owang" is similar to "Joannes" and it is sometimes even identified as Jenghiz Kan, who was not as hostile to Christians as Timur Lane (also known as Tamerlane).[356]

Most of our knowledge of the history of Nestorian Christianity in China comes from the famous Nestorian Monument, discovered by a Jesuit priest in 1625 a though it actually dates from the year 781. This stone tells us that in 635 someone identified as A-lo-pen arrived in the capital of the great T'ai Tsung (Chang An, present day Xian), bringing with him the "luminous religion of Ta-ch'in' (Syria). He was well received by the emperor, who himself studied the religion and gave orders for its dissemination. In spite of Buddhist opposition, the church survived for more than 200 years.[357]

The Christianity of China appears to have been largely monastic, much like the Buddhists of the day. Christian books translated into Chinese suggest that the monks took the trouble to learn the language and to make themselves at home in their new surroundings. The question here is how far did their influence extend beyond the walls of the monastery?

> Their task was completely different from that of their fellow monks in the wastes and forests of Central Europe. There the monk was the only literate man, bringing knowledge and also better methods of agriculture to an essentially simple population. Here he dwelt in the midst of a highly civilized people, in constant rivalry with other religious systems which were perhaps more congenial to the inhabitants of the land.[358]

Trouble came in 845 when Emperor Wu Tsung, an ardent Daoist, set out to destroy all forms of monasticism, dissolving the monasteries, and ordering the monks to return to private life. This applied to Buddhist monks as well as Nestorian. Neither Buddhism nor the Church ever recovered from this act, and from this time on the church dwindled rapidly.[359] In 987, a monk sent with five others to investigate the state of the church in China returned reporting that he had found no trace of Christians in the empire.[360] The church's disappearance seems as amazing as its growth (though it does not seem to disappear entirely until the Middle Ages). One cannot help asking the question, why with the destruction of monastic life does the whole regional church go into rapid decline? Were the local churches not equipped to stand with their own clergy? Had they not grounded the Christians in the faith? Were there other factors as well?

The church made fresh gains again in the eleventh century. This has been termed by some as the "Second Nestorian Wave."[361] The prince of the Keraits, a Turkish people in Central Asia, asked for baptism. In the thirteenth century almost the whole people group was professing Christians, consisting of over 400,000 families.[362] Here is another example of openness to a religion following the sanction of rulers. The Onguts and the Uigars also, living along the northern bend of the Yellow River, were largely converted. Probably over 100 Syrian missionaries were active in China during this time.

What caused the demise of the Nestorian work in these areas? Some have pointed to a lack of high standards in faith and morals. Some point to heretical notions and compromises of truth that undermined the faith. Yet it appears that, considering the difficulties that missionaries of more recent centuries have had in Asia, there certainly must be more to consider. Neill points out a number of great obstacles in the way of the church that contributed to its demise. Isolation from Christian regions is one obstacle. Unlike the case of Buddhist missions, Christian reinforcements had great difficulty in arriving. Mountain ranges, cold climates, and disease all took their toll. There was also the steady instability with raiding bands of barbarians criss-crossing the region, and one ruler after another taking his place. People would convert only to meet with slaughter in the next raid. One tyrant stands above all others: Tamerlane (also Timur Lane or Timur-i-Leng). Neill comments,

> We have noted the universal panic caused by the first incursions of the Mongols in the years leading up to 1241, and the widespread annihilation of the missions for which they were responsible. Gradually the Mongols were brought under the influence of civilization, and both the land and sea routes to the far east were again opened. But hardly had the missionaries had time to enter in and consolidate their position when the last and worst of all the medieval disasters broke upon them like a flood. Tamerlane (Timur-i-Leng) was not, like the first Mongols, a primitive and illiterate barbarian; he was a civilized sovereign, who maintained a splendid court and had a wide knowledge of the world. Yet he was the most cruel and destructive of all the medieval conquerors...By the time of his death at Samarkand in 1405, the work of destruction had been completed. Everything of Western and Christian civilization had been swept away...when

travel again became possible, from the Christian point of view everything had to be begun afresh.[363]

What began with rapid momentum, and survived with tenacity in the Middle East, appeared wiped clean further east. As Jesus said, the servant is not above the Master; people persecuted Him, and they will also persecute His Church. As the Book of Acts records it, we must enter the Kingdom through many tribulations (Acts 14:22). On this point, William Frazier refers us to the Roman Catholic ritual that completes the sending ceremony in missionary communities: The equipping of new missionaries with a cross or crucifix. Frazier writes,

> Somewhere beneath the layers of meaning that have attached themselves to this practice from the days of Francis Xavier to our own is the simple truth enunciated by Justin and Tertullian: the way faithful Christians die is the most contagious aspect of what being a Christian means. The missionary cross or crucifix is no mere ornament depicting Christianity in general. Rather, it is a vigorous commentary on what gives the gospel its universal appeal. Those who receive it receive not only a symbol of their mission, but a handbook on how to carry it out.[364]

This risk comes when the Church takes up the cross; but it will never be in vain. Success in God's economy is certainly not measured by the degree to which we escape its shadow.

In looking at the history of this fascinating branch of the church, one can see some of the struggle of the Christian faith revealing itself in a broad spectrum of activity—ranging from the dirtiest and deadliest of politics—to the most glorious expressions of zeal for the gospel and the evangelization of the world. Clearly, there is much one can glean from the history of the Church of the East.

We can see examples of how power works in the Church. Much of the ado made over Nestorius' theological position often appeared to be highly contrived political slander. Though he lacked in appreciation of the *communicatio idiomatum*, it is doubtful that he was actually a heretic.[365] Certainly showing theological weakness, he seemed to be trying to steer a personal course between Arianism on the one hand, and Apollinarianism on the other.[366] Apart from his theological problems, he was also involved in a type of "cross-cultural communication" and did not do well at it. More attention to "people skills," as advised by his mentor, Theodore of Mopsuestia (350-428), would have saved both him and the Church a great deal of pain.[367] Nestorius clearly played into the hands of those who sought his undoing.

One might also learn something from the evangelistic method of the Nestorians. When they went into a region with the gospel, they came in with a holistic approach. They employed such things as education, translation, medicine, and farming methods to complement the message. Nevertheless, in more advanced societies with similar skills and knowledge, such as that of the Chinese, such a method proved to be a challenge even for the great skill of the Nestorians. Secondly, the fact that the type of Christianity practiced in China did not move much beyond the monastic model, did not do well beyond the walls, may have something to say to us. Much that they did, they did correctly—such as the learning of the language and the study of the culture—and this is laudable.[368] The whole missiological history of the Church of the East merits more work.

Moreover, as was the case with all churches of the Asian region, the challenges posed by Islam proved daunting. We are still learning about what it will take to have fruitful conversation and understanding with this group. Nevertheless, Nestorians were often the advisors and counselors to Caliphs, and their religious freedom in Muslim lands grew even greater when the Il Kahns were in power. The Christian encounter with Islam opens up a whole new area of study in regards to the history of the Assyrian Church of the East. Did the presence of Islam affect the way the Church taught Christology? Were there influences back and forth? What did the encounter produce on both sides? Regrettably, there is not space to cover these topics here.

The Church of the East in many ways suffered because of its position in the power struggles of East, West and South patriarchates. As is often the case, lust for power held evil consequences. Nevertheless, the Church of the East stayed committed to their high view of Scripture and bound themselves to the Word of God as their authoritative norm. This commitment propelled them to joyful obedience to the Great Commission wherever they located themselves. Seeing the power of God revealed through the Scriptures, and His love revealed in the life of Christ and His church, they brought a holistic approach to their witness that brought them as far as India, Cathay, and even perhaps Japan—though in that case probably only informally. We have here a truly remarkable history.

To return to the questions asked at the outset of this chapter: What was the nature of this movement that came to be identified with a condemned heretic, Nestorius? Secondly, if it was a truly heretical church, how does one reconcile heresy with such a significant missions outreach? What were the sociological and theological factors at work that fueled this great missionary church?

We have shown that for the Church of the East, the Bible was given a prominent place in the practice of their faith. This carried over into their mission work as well. The emperor ordered Alopen, the famous early missionary, to retreat to his library and begin Bible translation. Adam, an eighth century missionary, was famed for his knowledge of Chinese language and literature, and has been linked to a number of Bible translations or paraphrases in the bibliography of a tenth century document entitled *The Book of the Honored Ones*. Moffett derives from this source that there probably were at least the following in existence: the Gospels, the book of Acts, Paul's Epistles, the Psalter and "less certainly, parts of the Pentateuch and Isaiah."[369]

Another important feature of this early church was its ecclesiology. Taking into account that the Church of the East was outside of the Christianized Roman Empire, we immediately see a great degree of difference in what it meant for the Church of the East to be the Church. There was no protectorate for them; the believers in this realm were practicing their faith in a theologically hostile environment, much like the Christians of Rome did in pre-Constantine times. Martyrdom was still an inspiration to them, and persecution moved people about. In identifying with the faith there was still a stigma that tended to embolden one, and already knowing and feeling this made it less daunting to go to "tough places" with the gospel.

We have already discussed some of the political intrigues that figured highly in the claims that Nestorius was committing heresy. Though Nestorius had shortcomings in his Christology, the way the Church handled (or rather mishandled) these shortcomings proved far more significant than the doctrines in and of themselves. But the question asked here refers to what affect, if any, did this whole heresy trial milieu have on the mission of the church? Probably not all that much if we isolate this one factor. Moffett points out that scarcely any evidence of the "Nestorian heresy" is found in the Chinese documents from this period.[370] Nevertheless, together with other elements, it did play a major role in separating the Church of the

East from the West, and in pushing the Church farther East in missions. We might call this the schism factor. Certainly, heresy has something to do with schism, but again the degree of heresy or doctrinal difference does not need to be all that great in order for schism to take place. Moreover, more than the heresy itself, it is the alienation that comes from it that moves people physically.

Walter Sundberg has pointed to this connection of heresy in regards to various groups and their large impact upon mission. "What has struck me is the persistent pattern of connection between mission and heresy or marginal groups: Arians, Nestorians, Jesuits, Methodists and Baptists, Pentecostalists today."[371] In this sentence, Sundberg also goes beyond the heresy question to include marginalization. A classic example of this would be the Pietistic movement and the resulting Moravian community and large-scale missions effort.

Thus, in this marginalization could be included not only heresy, but persecution, revival, reform and any factor that would contribute to the separation of a minority from the majority. In the case of the Church of the East, a number of these elements were present. However, one must be careful not to make a hard and fast rule out of such a proposition. For example, in the Reformation, it was several hundred years before that movement gave birth to any real mission dynamic. That lack of mission was one of the evidences given by the Roman Catholic Church as to why the Protestants could not possibly represent the true church—they had no missions structure. There were of course sociological as well as theological factors that contributed to that sad state of affairs, such as the Thirty Years War and a belief that the Great Commission was binding only on the apostles. Under different conditions, we might have seen a different scenario.

Ralph Winter has spoken of a similar paradigm when he describes his theory about modalities and sodalities. When he speaks of modalities he is speaking about the established, nurturing church body that ministers to all kinds of people with all kinds of needs. The sodalities are then movements and institutions that are brought to reality by a healthy modality that produces someone, or a group of people with a fiery vision for a new movement of God that cannot really be facilitated within the present system. An example of a sodality could range from something like a seminary to a large faith mission like Youth With a Mission. The people of the Church will often marginalize those who rise up with vision, precisely because they are saying something new or different, and church leaders may perceive them as a threat to the established body. The interesting point is that this will not happen in an anemic church environment. Such "sodalities" are actually a sign of health, and point to the God-given ability of the Church to reproduce herself.

Could there be a connection between these theories of Sundberg and Winter? Is there perhaps a common link, which, though not directing us to any specific point in and of itself as the cause of missionary zeal and effectiveness, might, instead, guide us to a different understanding of what God is up to, and help us to understand better the often-resultant marginalization of the individual or group? One would have to explore a complex combination of factors, but the outcome of such a study may say something about parts of the Body of Christ, like the Church of the East, who choose to go their own way, and are, either in consequence or by design, used by God in great ways.

As we proceed to discuss the work of the Jesuits in the next portion of this chapter, it is interesting to note that when the Portuguese arrived in south India, they discovered the presence of about 100,000 "Christians of St. Thomas." According to Neill, this simply refers to Christians who had ties with the Nestorian Church in Mesopotamia. This group of Christians had been established for so long that they were no longer regarded as foreign in any way. Had it not been for probable contact with Mesopotamia[372] and the continued use of Syriac in their worship, they probably would have been absorbed back into Hinduism.[373]

Following the Nestorians, and preceding the Jesuits, there is a short, one-hundred year history of Franciscan presence in China. This comes in response to a great Council of the Church at Lyons in 1245. Invoked by Innocent IV with the blessing of the Emperor, its primary purpose was to address the imminent threat from the east of the "Golden Horde" to the safety of Europe. Cary-Elwes explains,

> The Golden Horde of Ghenghis Khan's successor, under the nominal command of Batu, grandson of Ghenghis, and Subotai the Mongol general, was advancing across the plains of Poland and Hungary. At that hour, Christendom's very existence seemed at stake. The Mongol victories both east in China and west in Europe had indeed been spectacular. The conquerors had taken Peking; Persian had been laid waste. Gibbon well remarks: "five centuries have been insufficient to repair the ravages of four years."[374]

The work of the Franciscans during this time involves visits to the Khans and Christians who lived under their rule. One comment that is repeated by Franciscans, that is of interest to our topic, is their criticisms of the Nestorian Christians who remained in China. There are many accusations of immorality, accounts of their drunkenness, and their frustrations with what they considered obstacles posed to witness because of the lifestyles of those who appeared to be descendants of the earlier Nestorian churches.[375] We also see the frustration of the Khans at the letters received from the Pope exhorting him and his people to convert. The response to the Pope consisted of their claim to be Christians already, and the Khan's judgment on the disobedience of Western Christians toward God and Ghenghis Khan. Coupled with this was their dismay at the perceived spiritual arrogance of the Church in the West. For example, as seen in the words of Güyük Khan in a letter to the Pope: "But you, inhabitants of the West, believe that you only are Christians, and despise others; but how do you know upon whom He may choose to bestow His favor?"[376] Looking at the unimaginable brutality and cruelty of the Khans, it is hard to see anything Godly about their behavior, and yet they truly seemed to believe that they, and not the Popes, were God's Vicars on Earth, and that the world needed to obey them. At the same time, it was under the reign of the Khans, especially Genghis Kahn, that the Church of the East enjoyed its greatest religious freedom, since even in Muslim lands the Khans insisted that Christians be treated favorably. It was also with the demise of the last Khan in 1294, due to the Ming revolution and subsequent persecution of the Church, and the rule of Tamerlane that followed, that Christians would almost entirely disappear. Not until the coming of Mao Tse Tung and his execution of forty-five million would the world see such human slaughter. However, the future of the Kingdom is not determined by human will.

The Jesuits: Accommodation

Another "marginalized" group mentioned in Walter Sundberg's comment is the Jesuits. In the work of the Jesuits in Northeast Asia, there are some rich examples of a developing effort to adapt the gospel to a host culture. The forming of the Jesuits, or the Society of Jesus, may be one of the most important events in the missionary history of the Roman Catholic Church. In 1534, Ignatius Loyola gathered around himself six friends in Paris, and with them formed the core of his new "militia of Christ."[377] Members of this new order were bound to the most rigid of vows and were completely subject to the Pope alone. They were dedicated to the re-conversion of those perceived to be heretics and to the conversion of pagans to the Catholic faith. In the words of Stephen Neill, "...within the next hundred years Jesuits were to lay their bones in almost every country of the known world and on the shores of every sea."[378] By the time of Loyola's death, only 16 years after forming the order, the Jesuits numbered close to a thousand.

One of the first to connect with Loyola was the Basque, Francis Xavier (1506-1552), who was to become the most famous of Roman Catholic missionaries, and one of the most well known missionaries of all time. "To a passionate but disciplined nature, profound devotion, and an eager longing for the salvation of souls, Xavier added the wide outlook of the statesman and the capacity of the strategist for organization on a large scale."[379] Xavier went to India with great powers in hand, not as an ordinary missionary, but as the Papal Nuncio, and as a representative of the king of Portugal with the right to correspond directly with the king.[380]

Xavier's first stop was Goa (May, 1542), a city that had grown to look like any southern European city with many churches and mosques. Goa was a bishopric with the entire east coast of Africa under its jurisdiction. The conditions in Goa were deplorable, as European immigrants took from the culture all they could, but gave little back in return. As those men who came without women took Indian women and had offspring whom they then neglected, the society of Goa, "...tended to manifest the worst characteristics of both races."[381] Xavier set about to evangelize the debauched Portuguese masses, but saw little success. It was then that he lit upon a method that would come to characterize his work. He would go out into the streets ringing a bell, gathering around him a group of children, whom he would teach to recite the Lord's Prayer, Creed and Ten Commandments. He would subsequently exhort them to go home and teach their parents. "Little by little, Xavier gained the respect of the adults, who eventually flocked to hear him preach. Then followed scenes of mass penance reminiscent of Florence in Savonarola's time."[382]

Goa is an example of one of many fortified cities that the Portuguese had taken and established for controlling trade. This point in history puts us into the Counter Reformation, and the period of Iberian colonialism. The Spanish-born Pope Alexander VI had allied himself with Ferdinand and Isabella of Spain and with Prince Henry ("Henry the Navigator") of Portugal in their twin quest of repelling Islam and accumulating wealth.[383]

The consequent colonial expansion of Spain and Portugal gave renewed energy to Catholic missionary work, and Catholicism would now enjoy its most rapid period of expansion. It had only been a half-century prior to Xavier's arrival that Vasco da Gama sailed around the Cape of Good Hope, in 1487. Since then he had sailed down the east coast of Africa, crossed the Indian Ocean and returned to Europe, proving that the West could secure commercial links with India without their having to pass through Muslim territory.[384] This activity marked the beginning of the period of "Colonial Christianity." When Francis Xavier entered India, Portugal was already losing interest in Africa, and turning its gaze to the "Far East."

Xavier inherited a very thorny task with the Portuguese in Goa, but he had not come to work among the Portuguese. Furthermore, the westernized city's population, which included a mix of Muslims and Jews, was not to his liking. Upon seeing that he had apparently failed to make any real impact on the city, he implored the king of Portugal to commence an Inquisition and force Catholic dogma and morals upon the people.

Before the making of any such arrangements, Xavier decided to move on. He was yet determined to reach out to those who had not yet heard the gospel of Jesus Christ. After five months in Goa, he set out for the so-called Fishery coast to work among people employed in the pearl fisheries, taking with him two young clergymen who knew the local language. About six years prior, in 1536, the entire caste of the Bharathas (Paravas), a fishing people group on the Coromandel Coast numbering about 10,000 had received baptism. Harassed by Muslim raiders from the north, and being poor, illiterate, and helpless, they turned to the Portuguese for help, and received it for a time. The price for this protection was baptism *en masse*, after which their benefactors abandoned them for six years with no instruction or pastoral care. When Xavier asked them what they knew, they answered that they did not know, for they did not understand Portuguese.[385] This group would be Xavier's assignment for three years. His work included a highly flawed translation of the Lord's Prayer, the Creed, and the Ten Commandments. As he had done in Goa, he focused his efforts on children and youth, going into the streets and ringing a bell. And again, as children gathered he would take them to a church, where he would teach them the Lord's Prayer, the Creed, and Commandments, sending them home to teach their parents. The Sunday service consisted of these elements in a kind of litany.[386] Requests then began to come in for Xavier to preach and teach in neighboring villages. Unable to meet all the demands, he then trained some of his converts to go about preaching and baptizing.[387]

In spite of the difficulties of language, caste and the lack of education among the Paravas, by the end of the century the Jesuits had gathered this group into sixteen large villages, each village having a Jesuit father as resident priest. Education never did make great gains, but discipline was enforced and the work remains today. "The villager who crosses the sandhills of Manappḍu today, expecting to enter a village of huts, is astonished to find himself in a city of palaces dominated by two gigantic churches."[388]

The fruit of Xavier's work was largely among those of the lower castes. Since Christians met together for taking communion, lower caste converts saw conversion as a means to be equal with the Portuguese. This was appealing to those of the lower strata of society, but it had an opposite effect upon those of the higher castes; They came to see conversion to Christianity as subversive. Martyrdom followed with Xavier himself coming under attack and causing him to seek military protection for his flock. "Such military action was ruled out by the Portuguese authorities, not out of pacifist ideals, but rather because it would interrupt trade."[389]

Xavier then moved on to Southeast Asia in 1545, working for a time in Malacca, but his heart longed to preach the gospel also in Japan. The West had little knowledge of Japan at the time, only the writings of Marco Polo really, and what was available was largely mythological. For example, there was a legend of a palace in "Chipangu" that was floored with slabs of gold two fingers thick. It is from this appellation, Chipangu, that we get the name, Japan.[390]

The first Western contact with Japan took place when some Portuguese sailors became shipwrecked on Tanegashima, an island off the coast of Kyushu, in either 1542 or 1543. In 1548, an escaped criminal named Yajiro (Anjiro), an escaped murderer, made his way to Goa. It was there that Yajiro and Xavier met and Xavier heard the ways of Japan. Filled with desire to minister in Japan, Xavier finally arrived there on August 15, 1549 at the port of Kagoshima accompanied by two other Jesuits, Yajiro and his Japanese attendants. As it turned out, Yajiro performed far below Xavier's expectations. Says Neill, "...he had very little knowledge of his own country; he was not a highly educated man; his efforts at the translation of Christian terms into Japanese was to lead the missionaries into errors, which there were later sorely to rue, and his character was far from being altogether admirable."[391] Rather than being a helper, he turned out to be a detriment. Nevertheless, the work prospered in spite of these setbacks.

At this time, Japan was in a period of political disorder with no central authority, divided up among two hundred and fifty *daimyo* (feudal lords). The country was still open to the foreigner, since the Japanese were eager for trade, especially trade in guns. Also, Buddhism was in discredit at the time, and Oda Nobunaga (1568-1600) saw the feuding monasteries as a hindrance to his efforts to unite the country. For reasons such as this, Nobunaga came to resist Buddhism, and support Christianity.[392]

One of the biggest challenges to Christian evangelism was finding Japanese terms to express Christian concepts, such as a word for "sin," or even the concept of "God." Yajiro had chosen inappropriate Buddhist terms, which ended up hindering the work. To overcome this obstacle, they took a bit of a short cut and introduced Portuguese terms into the Japanese language. However, his choice of *Deus* for God backfired, as the Japanese pronounced this as *Dai-uso*, or "the Big Lie."

Around the middle of January, 1551, Xavier journeyed to Kyoto in hopes of seeing the emperor and the shogun. Xavier concluded that it would be useless to try to reach the emperor or the shogun (Nobunaga). But he felt it would be equally wrong to only go for the lower classes, and thus he settled upon focusing on the daimyo, who when converted would be able to bring in their whole realm of subjects.

Xavier saw the Japanese as an intelligent and able people, and therefore called for the sending of the highest quality missionaries to Japan. Rome wished to reserve Japan for the Jesuits, but was unable to do so. (In the 1580's and even more in the 1590's the Franciscans and Dominicans also came, although they worked among the lower classes.) In 1588, Rome made Japan a bishopric.

According to Neill, Xavier's early contacts with the Japanese encouraged a change in his understanding of the nature of Christian missionary work in such a degree that the whole future of the enterprise would feel its effects. In a very real sense, he underwent a paradigmatic shift in this regard. Neill comments as follows:

> In earlier years he had been inclined to accept uncritically the doctrine of the *tabula rasa*—the view that in non-Christian life and systems there is nothing on which the missionary can build, and that everything must simply be leveled to the ground before

anything Christian can be built up. This was the general view of the Spanish missionaries in Latin America and the West Indies; in his dealings with the simple and illiterate fishers in South India, Xavier had seen no reason to modify it. But now that he was confronted by a civilization with so many elements of nobility in it, he saw that, while the Gospel must transform and refine and recreate, it need not necessarily reject as worthless everything that has come before. This new idea was to be fruitful in results—and also in controversies.[393]

As we mentioned in the second chapter, this *tabula rasa* approach, the need to "reject as worthless everything that has come before [the gospel]", would reappear later under colonialism in the "era of non-contextualization." But getting free from it at this point in history would require a hard-fought battle, which we will discuss here shortly.

The influx of missionaries accelerated rapidly with the first converts coming from the poorer classes. Then in 1563, Xavier's hope began to materialize as the conversion of *daimyos* commenced. The first *daimyo* to receive baptism was Sumitada Omura. Omura remained faithful and active all of his life; his example inspired others to follow. Oftentimes, the conversion of a daimyo resulted in the conversion of the majority of his subjects. Says Neill,

> This did not always take place immediately; in 1571 Sumitada had only 5,600 Christian subjects, but then the mass movement set in, and by 1575 the whole population of the region—amounting in all to more than 50,000—had become Christian. Of the depth and sincerity of these conversions it is hard to judge. As in the case of other mass movements there were no doubt many weaknesses and shadows, but unquestionably there was in Japan an élite of convinced and devoted Christians.[394]

Although Xavier did not try for the imperial family, he did seek to reach those who would have great influence over large populations, and this, like we saw in the case of Buddhism, eventually resulted in a mass movement.

In 1579, another famed Jesuit comes upon the scene, one who will also be greatly influential in China, Alessandro Valignano (1539-1606). An Italian Jesuit, Valignano became Visitor of all the eastern regions.

Neill underscores three ways in which Valignano left his imprint upon missions work in Japan. The first way relates to his strong view that it is imperative for missionaries and Christians to adapt to local customs and prejudice. For example, should a missionary adopt cotton or silk dress? The Superior of the Mission (from 1570-1581), Francis Cabral, felt strongly that cotton should be used since it was more in accord with the value of poverty—a natural assumption for a monastic order. However, the genius of Valignano opted for silk.[395] Columba Cary-Elwes shows how Xavier demonstrated the wisdom of Valignano's conviction.

> He made two excursions through Japan. The first he performed in poverty, dressed in his Western ecclesiastical clothes. He found that thus attired, he could not impress the Japanese, who despised him for his poverty, and suspected him for his foreign appearance. Knowing that such externals were not essential, he decided that on his second expedition he would wear Japanese dress. He therefore donned silk, the clothes of a Japanese sage. At one bound he had leapt the barriers of contempt and suspicion, and could now get in touch with the human beings whom he wanted to convert. His justification for this change of dress was the cry of St. Paul that he would be "all things to all men." What did it matter wearing silk? Holiness did not consist in a garment, but in striving to do the will of God and loving one's neighbour.[396]

The second imprint left by Valignano upon missions in Japan was his decision that select young men travel to Europe to see the glories of the Christian world for themselves. In 1582, four young men from noble families accompanied Valignano and another Jesuit to Europe and were received by King Philip of Spain and Pope Gregory the XIII.[397] The third imprint of Valignano involved his conviction to ordain Japanese priests. He was opposed by the more conservative Cabral who, ironically, feared that Japanese priests would become unbearably arrogant.[398] Thankfully, Valignano won the debate, a seminary was opened, and in the year 1593, eighty-seven students with five novices were in training, most of them later serving as *dojuku*, or catechists of a high order, "but none had yet been ordained to the priesthood, for the simple reason that there was no bishop in Japan."[399] Two men had previously been appointed as bishops for Japan, but had died before they had opportunity to exercise their office. Finally in September of 1601, a suffragan bishop was able to carry out the first Japanese ordination. This involved one secular and two Jesuits; the secular died as a martyr in 1622.[400]

At this point, it might be good to briefly explore the difference between Cabral and Valignano. We saw above that Cabral advocated a "cotton" approach to mission in Japan, whereas Valignano opted for a "silk" approach. Lamin Sanneh actually sees the tenure of these two Superiors as two distinct phases of mission in the early Roman Catholic period. Cabral's policies, shaped by his approach to acculturation, represent the first phase. Sanneh characterizes Cabral's method as a "dogged attempt to impose European culture on the Japanese as the price for membership in the church."[401] Cabral was a firm believer in the cultural mission of Europe. He held everything about Japanese culture in contempt, and saw the culture as a threat to the Church. This forced Cabral into contradictions regarding his mission to Japan. The purpose of the mission was to make converts to the Church and to the ranks of the Jesuit order. However, according to Cabral, the Japanese were "too inclined to learning and to novelties to be trustworthy, and the missionary could never take them at face value, so full of cunning and insincerity were they. Those Japanese who entered the Society of Jesus were consequently subject to ridicule, treated badly, and pushed to low positions. If all that was designed to strike at the self-esteem of Japanese Christians, it could not have succeeded more."[402] Moreover, Cabral despised the language, although he later saw the necessity of learning it, set up a language-school and required its study.

What Sanneh terms the second phase, that of Valignano, could hardly have been more dissimilar. The very things about Japan that Cabral viewed as despicable and a threat to the order, Valignano saw as praiseworthy, and worthy of accommodation. To flout Japanese custom would only result in setbacks for the mission. Utilizing his concept of translation in missions work, Sanneh remarks on Valignano's views,

> Christian mission, he felt instinctively, was vernacular in essence, and was thus inherently tolerant of all cultures. Our very difference from others is reason for respecting them as unique bearers of God's universal aim for the human race, not grounds for elevating our own cultural accomplishments as normative for them.[403]

Valignano saw European and Japanese cultures as differing not merely on the surface, but *in their very essence*. Thus, those coming to Japan to do missions work had to not only adapt, but had to basically start from scratch and learn appropriate behavior all over again. He went as far as to require the making of a manual based on the behavior of the *bonzes*, or Buddhist monks, in order to standardize the behavior of the missionaries before the eyes of the Japanese, so as not to give offense.[404] In fact, he so admired Japanese culture that he argued for European exposure to Japanese culture in the belief that such an exchange could only help to refine the uncouth Europeans.[405] Also unlike Cabral, he insisted upon a strong emphasis on the vernacular, even introducing the use of movable type to facilitate a literature ministry. Sanneh continues,

> He was adamant that Christian mission was not the cultural diffusion of Europe. Similarly, it is not necessary to prove the soundness of his method by the successful planting of the church in Japan. As it was, the church was rejected. What is important for our purposes is that Valignano believed, and rightly so, that Christianity should be at home in all cultures, and that cross-cultural exposure would help to mitigate Europe's cultural arrogance. Such an eventuality would be a positive gain for the march of God's kingdom. Thus, in his case too, we see a missionary in radical tension with his own culture, receiving from the feedback of mission a deepened sense of mistrust in the normative application of Western cultural patterns in the rest of the world...and in the bitter dispute between Valignano and Cabral, we catch more than a few echoes of Saint Paul's struggles with Saint Peter.[406]

Xavier obviously fits into this second phase of Valignano. Xavier had learned to listen to his surroundings and one of the things he discovered in his relationship with the Japanese was the power of Chinese culture upon Japan. This led to the final venture of the short remainder of his life. Since he saw Japan as an eager recipient of Chinese cultural imports, it made perfect sense to Xavier that the key to the acceptance of the Christian faith in Japan was the conversion of China. If China were Christian, Japan would not be far behind. Thus he returned to Goa after twenty-seven months in Japan, to make preparations for entering China. This was never to be, however, as he contracted a fever and died on a island just off the coast of China, only ten years after his missionary career had begun. The work of China would fall to another generation of missionary, characterized by Matteo Ricci.

Xavier was in Japan for only twenty-seven months, but he saw an amazing response during that brief period. In 1582, there were about 200 churches and about 150,000 Christians. By 1590, the number of converts had jumped to 240,000 and by the turn of the century, they numbered 500,000.

In assessing the work of Xavier in Japan, we see patterns of accommodation that would characterize Jesuit missionary work for some time to come. They did not consider culture a complete evil to be eradicated, but rather something to utilize in communicating the Good News of Jesus Christ. At the same time, while there was a willingness to accommodate culturally, there was a healthy resistance to accommodating the religion itself. Discerning the difference is not always so easy, as evidenced by the fact that other orders in China and India accused the Jesuits of accommodating the gospel as well as culture, leading to the Rites Controversy. The Church has seen throughout history that one person's heresy is another person's contextualized truth. The answer to this problem will not suit every missionary, but each must seek it out within the context of our discussion in chapter 2.

In the case of Xavier, we can commend much. Although his initial idea of reaching the emperor and shogun turned out to be a less than workable idea, he was able to secure the favor of two powerful daimyo (of Yamaguchi and Bungo), one of whom became the first stronghold of missions in Japan. His converts included Samurai, Buddhist priests, and the common people. When he left, he entrusted his work to two capable missionaries, Cosme de Torres and Brother Juan Fernandez, who also saw great gains during their tenure under the protection of the daimyo of Bungo, Toshishige Otomo.[407]

Churches, colleges, hospitals and leprosariums followed preaching and education. In the first ten years, progress was steady, despite Buddhist opposition and persecutions. Several thousands received baptism, largely in western Japan.[408] Noble families also converted, such as the Takayamas, who received the faith and endured half a century of hardship (including their eventual banishment to Manila in 1614 under Hideyoshi.)[409]

A missionary by the name of Vilela worked in the capital when times were at their worst, and saw a great change for the better when Nobunaga came with a great army that put an end to the chaos. This marked another boost to missions in Japan, as Nobunaga favored the Kirishitan, "and nearly ten years of his rule brought a thriving period of Kirishitan propaganda, when Jesuit missionaries numbered 80 in 20 stations and several educational centres, with 200 churches and 150,000 converts."[410] Nobunaga, although never counting himself a Kirishitan, even had a seminary in his castle of Azuchi, with some of his own sons counted among the baptized graduates. The greatest number of converts was in these first years of the seventeenth century, with percentages that have never seen equals since. Anesaki gives the figure for 1605 at 750,000, which would have been 4% of the whole population, although the north and east were largely untouched at that time. In recent decades, the percentage given for all Christians in Japan hovers around 2%.

All of this came to a close with the shogun that followed Nobunaga, Toyotomi Hideyoshi, who learned of the allegiance of the Japan church to their foreign Pope. After seemingly tolerating the Christians and befriending Valignano, he suddenly issued an edict of exile for all missionaries. Reports had come to him of Portuguese "Christian" behavior that was shocking even to the "pagan."[411] The Jesuit Vice-Provincial, Coelho, protested these charges, but did not prevail. There was also a perceived threat that such a foreign allegiance might threaten the hard-earned peace and unity of the nation. This issue of a foreign allegiance was an obstacle that the Buddhist missionaries never had to encounter. In 1587, Hideyoshi promulgated his infamous edict against the Kirishitan missions. Just as strangely, most of this edict was never enforced. The most conspicuous victim turned out to be the most well-respected of nobles, Ukon Takayama, mentioned above. However, just having the edict on the books meant that local senior officials could make use of it in whenever its purposes suited them; this resulted in a great deal of uncertainty for programs necessary to the future of the church.[412] The vacillation of Hideyoshi has been a subject of debate for quite some time. Moffett comments as follows:

> Many reasons have been advanced for the extraordinary vacillations in Hideyoshi's attitude to the church in this period, but one important reason for his distrust of the Christians was undoubtedly his fear that the Jesuit mission was the vanguard of Portuguese imperialist expansion, which could threaten Japan. Perhaps equally responsible for his lack of zeal in implementing

the edicts was the awareness that persecution of Christians could endanger Japan's trade with the West and invite military retaliation.

Whatever the reasons, the next ten or eleven years, from 1587 to 1598, were not the end of the mission, though the edicts did indeed mark the end of the period of euphoria. These years have been called "the period of restricted toleration." Hideyoshi completed the unification of Japan, disregarded his own edict and, with one conspicuous exception, the Nagasaki martyrdoms of 1597, left the Christians relatively free to organize and expand the church.[413]

The next important event in the mission to Japan was the opening of the work to the Franciscans. The Franciscans brought with them a strategy different from the Jesuits. While the Jesuits excelled at working with the nobility, though not disregarding the poor, the Franciscans focused their efforts on the sick, the poor, and the neglected. Unfortunately, these differences produced a rivalry between the factions that sometimes evidenced itself in public, resulting in a setback for the work. The Franciscans came not from Portugal, but from Spain, which added to the tensions in Japan. Japanese Buddhists warned Hideyoshi that this combination of factors—rivalry between missionary factions and the twin military aggression of Spain and Portugal—were a threat. An incident in 1596 supplied the fuse and the light to the powder keg—the running aground of the *San Felipe*. Moffett continues,

> This Spanish galleon, bound for Acapulco from Manila, had run aground on the Japanese island of Shikoku in 1596. It was loaded with guns, ammunition, seven missionaries, goods worth a king's ransom, and (if the report quickly carried to Hideyoshi were true, which it undoubtedly was not), a fool of a pilot who threatened that if the Japanese seized the cargo, Spain would retaliate immediately with its irresistible worldwide military might. It is difficult to believe the rumor being circulated at the same time that the pilot had also declared that Franciscan missionaries in Japan were preparing the way for just such a Spanish conquest as in Mexico, Peru, and the Philippines.[414]

A bloody martyrdom ensued with Hideyoshi ordering the arrest, mutilation, and crucifixion of six Franciscans, three Japanese Jesuits, and fifteen Japanese Christians from the Franciscan hospital in Kyoto. Two others volunteered to join them, bringing the number to twenty-six. In the number were three boys: twelve, thirteen and fifteen years of age. The boys raised their heads to sing, "O Children, Praise the Lord." Then all the martyrs were pierced with lances to speed their deaths, and they died. The bodies continued to hang, however, for nine months.[415]

Less than a year later, Hideyoshi died, hoping that his son, Hideyori, would replace him. The powerful daimyo Ieyasu Tokugawa saw an opportunity, however, and seized the throne. Calm came to the mission for more than a decade, and the work extended for the first time to the Edo (now Tokyo) area, building the first church there in 1599. This period marked a shift in Jesuit practice, influenced by the martyrdoms, where the missionaries avoided mass baptisms, opting not for "quantity but quality," as one missionary wrote to his superior in 1607."[416] The next wave of persecution, however, was just around the corner.

During the Hideyoshi years, the famed Christian daimyo, Yukinaga Konishi, hero of the Korean War, was seeing explosive growth in his domain at more than twenty-five thousand baptisms a year. In the civil war that broke out in 1600 between the forces loyal to Hideyoshi and those loyal to Tokugawa, Konishi had stood with the Hideyoshi loyalists, and lost. Konishi was consequently beheaded, and his territory was turned over to the Buddhist general, striking fear into the hearts of Christians across the land. Ieyasu, fearing the growing power of Christian daimyos more than the military threat of the West forbade further conversions of daimyos to Christianity. After that, only one ruling noble converted and received baptism—in secret.[417]

The first Protestants arrived in 1600, but not as missionaries. The Dutch "red-haired barbarians" displaced the Portuguese and Spaniards in sea trade. The loss of a trade monopoly hurt the Catholic missions who were financially dependent upon it, but it also removed the fear of Iberian military expansion, leaving the churches vulnerable to the Tokugawa government. Born out of a major global struggle for trade in what could be termed "the three S's"—spices, sugar and slavery—the Dutch were able to get a toehold in the Nagasaki harbor for almost two hundred years. Remarkably, during that whole time, not a single Protestant church resulted from their presence.[418] The Christian mission in Japan encountered still another setback, but greater testing awaited them. The unification of Japan produced a sense of nationalistic pride, and strengthened the national religion, Shinto. Buddhism was able to ride on the coat tails of this sentiment.

What has been described as "the beginning of the end" for Japanese Christianity began in the year 1614. Moffett, however, dates it two years earlier, to the destruction of the Franciscan church in Tokyo; and the daimyo of Arima, to the southwest, was executed as a result of a bribery scandal. His son immediately apostatized and became obsessed with persecuting Christians, until he was opposed by an outpouring of public support for the Christians. This only led, in turn, to deeper suspicion by the government of the dangers of Christianity to the hard-won unity of the nation. Two years hence, Ieyasu Tokugawa issued a stronger anti-Christian edict that marked the beginning of an ever-growing wave of persecution that can only rightly be called demonically-horrific in its proportions. Moffett describes Ieyasu Tokugawa's reasoning as follows: "Christianity, he charged, opposes all three of Japan's great religions: Buddhism, Shinto ('the [way of the] gods'), and Confucianism ("benevolence and right doing"). It threatens Japan's possession of its own land, and it aims to overthrow the country's national government."[419] This insight into Tokugawa's thinking lets us know that there was a combination of social factors that stood as obstacles to the *kerygma* in Japan. There was, of course, the issue of an allegiance to foreign powers, but coupled with that was a perceived threat from the Christian *daimyos*, and their Christian subjects. There was felt a need on the part of the nation's rulers to make a lesson of these people of the foreign religion, forgetting that at one time Buddhism was also a foreign import that had recently been in the position of *nakama hazure* ("outsider"). Buddhism had only been able to gain favor as Christianity came more into disfavor. Moffett continues in quoting Ieyasu Tokugawa,

> The Christian band have come to Japan not only sending their merchant vessels to exchange commodities, but also longing to disseminate an evil law, to overthrow right doctrine, so they may change the government of the country, and obtain possession of the land.
>
> Japan is the country of the gods and Buddha...The principles of benevolence and right doing are held to be of prime importance... Quickly cast out the evil law and spread our true Law more and more...Let Heaven and the Four Seas hear this and obey."[420]

Buddhism is reckoned here as a part of Japan's identity. But again, as we've seen before, a religion can fall in and out of favor with governments. Nevertheless, the time of any favor toward the Christian faith had now drawn to a close, and the fires of persecution were only to burn hotter and hotter. Moffett is absolutely correct in choosing to understate the conditions of this persecution, because, as he wrote,

> In describing the horrors of the next thirty years, during which the entire Christian population was systematically burned, strangled, starved, tortured, or driven underground, it is better to understate rather than exaggerate. The record needs no embellishment. The third shogun, Ieyasu's grandson Iemitsu (1623-1651), was more merciless than his grandfather and more brutal than his father. Under Ieyasu, noted one Japanese historian, the foreign missionaries were expelled but not one was killed, under Hidetada, they were killed but not tortured; but the sadistic Iemitsu enjoyed watching to see whether their torture would end in recantation or death.[421]

The suffering of this church was unspeakable. Their torturers even devised surgical methods to prolong the agony and forestall the death of their victims. The novel by Shusaku Endo brilliantly captures the era, and the theological questions that arise in such times. Where is God to be found in the suffering of His people? The title of Endo's book, *Silence*, is what many have experienced from God in times of adversity. And yet we find the answer in this: "Because he himself suffered when he was tempted, he is able to help those who are being tempted" (Heb. 2:18). And as Peter wrote, "But if you suffer for doing good and you endure it, this is commendable before God. To this you were called, because Christ suffered for you, leaving you an example, that you should follow in his steps" (I Pet. 2:20b-21).

The martyrdoms of these Japanese Christians are similar in many ways to those of the Early Church, and had a similar effect upon those who watched these believers die with expressions of dignity and joy. "Faithfulness to death as martyrs became an article of faith among the Japanese believers, and bystanders marveled at the calm with which they accepted torture and death without resistance or recantation."[422] Even today in parts of Japan one can see memorials to the deaths of these innocents. While serving as a missionary in Japan, I was able to bring my church members to southern

Iwate prefecture in the Tohoku region, where there is a county that has set aside land for a park dedicated to the Christians who suffered martyrdom in that region. We encountered scale models depicting the checkpoints on the mountain roads and the forms of interrogation and torture that were used to push believers to the breaking point, resulting in either a recanting, or death. The museum guide spoke with pride about a spot above the museum grounds on top of a hill where there is a reconstruction of the hill of Golgotha, depicting the crucifixion of Jesus. This is not to say that a large percentage of the county is professing Christian—Iwate's population has a lower percentage of Christians than many other places in Japan. However, there is a deep admiration for the way these Christians endured their suffering.

Among Christians in Japan, there was a negative reaction to the book, *Silence*. Christians believed it too dark a depiction, and void of hope that Japan could ever be a fertile ground for the gospel. Endo then followed his novel, *Silence* with a play entitled, *The Golden Country*, in which the same period and persecution of the church is depicted, but with a very different mood. Whereas in *Silence*, Japan is spoken of as a mud-swamp in which nothing can survive, *The Golden Country* glorifies martyrs as truly noble believers, leaving one with the sense that Japan holds the potential to be a great Christian nation. Here are two fascinating accounts of the suffering Church in Japan, written by an award-winning Roman Catholic, who himself struggles with the sense of foreignness about his own faith.[423]

Following these severe persecutions, the agony of the church encountered a different kind of "silence," as the final anti-Christian edict closed Japan off from the rest of the world in 1639. This marked the end of the "Christian Century" in Japan. All commercial and religious ties with Portugal were cut off, and the country was declared off-limits to the Portuguese under penalty of death. Moffett quotes G. B. Sansom's comments on the contrast between the laudable aspects of the Japanese culture that missionaries praised, and the ruthless treatment of the Japanese church.

> One cannot wonder at the affection that the missionaries felt for the people of Japan, since nowhere else in Asia were Christian propagandists able to gain such a ready hearing for the gospel from all classes, and nowhere were they more kindly treated. Yet nowhere were they more savagely repressed. This paradox is to be explained by the dual character of Japanese society, which

combined a strong sense of social ethics with a great ruthlessness in the enforcement of the law.[424]

As we reflect back upon the history of Christianity's early entry into Japan, one can see many similarities with Buddhism, and in the work of the Church of the East. We have seen in all of these cases that the favor (or disfavor) of rulers played a large role in the acceptance of religion in Asia. Stephen Neill pointed this out clearly in his History of Christian Missions.[425] In addition, the roles of monasteries, educational institutions, hospitals, and care for the poor also played a part in the planting of the Church in Japan.

One fact that is a bit startling about the growth pattern in early-period Japan, is that the period under which Cabral was administrator—a man whose ideas seemed horribly ethnocentric and racist even for that day—saw significant growth in mission. While there were about three thousand Christians when Xavier left Japan, in the next twenty years Japan witnessed tenfold growth under Torres. Under Cabral, growth was still fourfold; and at the time of the 1614 edict, baptized membership had climbed to 300,000.[426]

Another amazing fact about the Jesuit movement in Japan is a startling negative—in contrast to the Buddhist missionary movement and the Nestorian movement in China—there was not a high emphasis upon the Scriptures being translated. Although the strategic genius of Valignano led him to bring in movable type to Japan and to produce and distribute literature, there is no mention by the missionaries of any printed translation of the Bible. Moffett picked up on this when he wrote, "Manuscripts of various portions of Scripture existed, including the first Japanese translations of the gospels as early as 1561, but the opportunity to publish and distribute even one full book of the gospels was apparently and unaccountably neglected."[427] With the reluctance to ordain Japanese leadership, and the neglect of Bible translation, it left the Japanese church in a precarious situation when the officials cracked down on the mission.

Japan also differed from China in that although a few daimyo converted and protected the church, the emperor and the shogun did not become the Asoka/Shotoku models that patronized and exported Buddhism. Although we cannot say that hinging one's successes on ruling powers is a good strategy, since royal favor can switch with dynasties, neither did Christianity demonstrate itself to be pro-Japan in the same way that Buddhism showed itself to be pro-China, pro-Korea, or pro-Japan. Christianity was perceived to be connected to foreign powers and thus pro-foreign and anti-Japan. Christianity has yet to show itself as "for" Japan. Not that the religion should become nationalistic in spirit, but it needs somehow to find a way to shake the image of the adversary while retaining the prophetic option to speak for justice.

When the Vistor, Valignano, turned the attention of the Jesuits back to China, he set himself to the study of the seventy years that Jesuits had worked in Asia, and came upon three emphases that would inform future work there. The first emphasis that caught his attention was the Jesuit connection to colonial trade expansion. He was able to see that such dependence upon Portuguese trade had worked against the mission. This was obvious when the Dutch moved in and Portuguese trade revenue shrank. He thus began to wean the mission from the Portuguese state.[428] Secondly, as we saw with Xavier's work in India, Xavier was preparing to call for the Roman Catholic Inquisition to become active in Goa. Valignano rightly saw that he must prohibit the mission from becoming entangled in such harsh policy. The third epiphany for Valignano is the one he is best known for, as he established as policy the principle of cultural accommodation or adaptation.[429] This principle would become the distinguishing mark of Jesuit missions, and the center of missiological debate for centuries to come.

In studying the situation in Macao (now Aomen), Valignano was dismayed to see that the Portuguese missionaries under his charge had given up any effort in learning Chinese, relying completely upon translators. To make matters worse, the missionaries were focusing the majority of their time on the 900 Portuguese living in Macao, and at that time there were five thousand Chinese Christians in the city. The missionaries were also insisting that the converts adopt Western dress and take European names. Valignano brought in Italian Michele Ruggieri to remedy the situation. His job was to reverse the trend of the mission so that all work would start with the Chinese cultural context, and continue to make the Chinese context foundational to all that would follow. Ruggieri learned that Portuguese traders were admitted to Guangzhou twice a year for trade fairs, and he latched on to one of the traders to gain entrance. His great respect for Chinese language and culture won him exemption from the rule that forbade foreigners from remaining overnight on Chinese soil. Therefore, the second visit he was given a residence next to the Siam (Thailand) embassy.

A timepiece he gave to the general of the army created a sensation; clocks would later become one of the keys to the entrance, and a pass to stay in China for the Jesuits. But first, a third Italian would join them.

Back in December of 1552, when Xavier lay ill on the island of Sancian with his gaze fixed on China, half a world away an Italian mother was nursing her newborn baby—one who would realize the dream of Xavier. Thirty years later, this same baby—now a young and promising Jesuit missionary—would join Valignano and Ruggieri in China. This young and extremely gifted recruit would become the most famous missionary in the history of Catholic missions in China.

After the initial reception of Ruggieri into China, the viceroy in charge denied him on four different occasions. Then, with an unexplained change of mind, he offered to not only allow Ruggieri and Ricci to live in the county seat, but offered to build them a chapel. However the Jesuits were taking a much more cautious approach after what they witnessed in Japan. They decided that for now they would not even baptize, even though they received baptismal requests. They wanted to allow the believers to grow in maturity, hoping to ward off defections, or as Ruggieri wrote, "in order not to give occasion to the Demon if some would then leave the faith in these beginning [times]."[430] This time there would be no seeking of mass baptisms.

The work was slow and tedious, and in time, Ricci concluded that the only way to make headway in China would be to obtain imperial favor. Ruggierez returned to Rome to ask for an official embassy to contact the emperor, feeling this would happen more quickly than two missionaries plodding to Beijing on their own. Ricci, however, grew impatient and set out to make the journey on foot, eventually reaching the capital. It was on that journey that Ricci came to the conclusion to switch from Buddhist garb to Confucian. Ruggieri had adopted the Buddhist robes, but Ricci determined that since Buddhist monks in China were considered superstitious and uneducated, the missionaries would be better off dressing like Confucian literati.[431] In China, the scholar was ranked at the pinnacle of value hierarchy, above the farmer, artisan, or merchant. This taking of such an identity would open more doors among the literati[432].

Ricci reached Beijing and received a permanent residence there in 1601. He was not able to reach the emperor, but from this time on the work began to turn for the better. Having made the emperor a present of clocks, he was able to stay in the capital for a number of years since the Chinese needed someone who understood clocks and could keep them wound.⁴³³ However, he found the southern dynastic capital of Nanjing more intellectually and culturally open than Beijing, and it was in Nanjing that they met the man who was to become their foremost convert, Paul Hsu (Xu Guangshi). For the next thirty years, his contribution to the work would "do more for the cause of Christianity in Ming dynasty China than any other Chinese of the century."⁴³⁴ Moffett describes Paul Xu as follows: (The reason Xu gives for his conversion is interesting in light of what we usually think about Jesuits using scientific learning as a means to reach the Chinese. Also included is his summary of the Christian faith.)

> Xu Guangshi (d. 1633) first met Ricci in 1600. Less than four years later, thoroughly converted not so much by the impressive scientific learning of the missionaries but by how far their moral teachings surpassed his Confucianism and how superior their religion was to Buddhism, he asked to be baptized. Later he phrased his position in an elegant Chinese motto: "[Christianity] Supplements Confucianism and Displaces Buddhism (*pu ru yi fo*)." One of his summaries of the Christian faith illustrates how he introduced Christianity to Confucianists: "According to [the Christians'] teachings, the service of Shangdi [God] is the fundamental principle; the protection of the body and the salvation of the soul are of utmost importance; loyalty, filial piety, compassion, and love are accomplishments; the reformation of errors and the practice of virtue are initial steps; repentance and the purification [of sin] are the prerequisites for personal improvement; the true felicity of celestial life is the glorious reward of doing good; and the eternal misery of hell is the recompense of doing evil."⁴³⁵

Paul Xu had come to understand the gospel through a book published by Ricci entitled *Tainzhu Shiyi (The True Idea of God)*. The Jesuits relied heavily on the concept of natural revelation, or "natural law philosophy" of Mencius, the most famous interpreter of Confucius. Ralph Covell refers to several important aspects of Mencius' thinking as outlined by Paul Sih in his work, *Chinese Culture and Christianity*.

1. Heaven (or, more personally, God) is the supreme ruler over the universe.

2. Heaven has given to all human beings equally the "law of nature."

3. In human nature may be found the embryonic virtues of "love, justice, propriety, and knowledge," which will develop naturally if not hindered by evil external conditions.

4. The norms by which human beings live, causing them to seek good and avoid evil, are not human creations but come from Heaven.

5. This theory may be applied morally, politically, and economically. Human beings may be exhorted to follow a high moral value system because this natural law is engraved in their hearts. The emperor, in order to rule over his kingdom, must be a moral man. His authority proceeds from his benevolence. Lacking reason, justice, and love, he will forfeit the blessing of Heaven, and it then becomes the responsibility of the people to overthrow him. "The recognition that the ultimate test of the validity of authority lies beyond authority itself is essentially a natural law proposition."

6. Finally, a truly benevolent ruler will concern himself for the economic welfare of his people. This will include, according to Mencius, equal distribution of land, the use of public granaries, a system of public schools, and a concern for all the needs of the people. It is according to reason that a ruler should care for his people in this "kingly way" (*wang dao*) and not mistreat the people (*ba dao*) as a tyrant might do."[436]

Of course, one does not have to take as positive a view of human nature as Mencius does to be Confucian. The Confucian scholar, Hsun Tzu (Xun Xi), of the Han dynasty, believed that human nature was basically evil and that society needed laws and the enforcement of laws to make humans do well. However, the point to be made is Ricci believed this tradition pointed to a supreme deity, and derived from ancient Jewish missions that had come to China after the flood. He wanted to encourage the Chinese to forsake the popular neo-Confucian thought of that day, which had incorporated much from Buddhism, and had led to a more secular worldview. Ricci wanted the Chinese to go back to traditional Confucianism, which had much more room for the Supreme Deity.

In his evangelism, Ricci did not go directly to the more important doctrines of salvation. This disturbed some of the other monastic orders, but it wasn't that Ricci had watered down the importance of these doctrines. He simply believed you had to lead the Chinese to those doctrines later, after you'd captured their interest with less controversial, and thus more easily accepted teachings. This would be similar to the pneumatological approach of Amos Yong today; he believes that rather than begin with the cross, we might see better results if we start people with the doctrine of the Holy Spirit, which is less of a foreign idea in most cultures.[437] It's essentially a discussion about what ought to be the entry path to belonging. Ricci was quite clear that once the Chinese became interested, the core teachings of Christianity would be introduced. The debate that ensued divided the Jesuits from the Franciscans and Dominicans. The latter took the approach that one dare not accommodate the gospel to Chinese culture. They believed that any similarities were pure coincidence, and insisted that Chinese converts abandon their ancient intellectual tradition and completely replace it with biblical revelation.[438] Referring back to our second chapter, many today on the far right of Bruce Fleming's chart would agree. To take such a position, one also has to hold that non-Christian religions have no value and cannot serve as a vehicle by which God might reveal even a little about Himself. Ricci and his team thought otherwise, and he argued this in *Tainzhu Shiyi*. The book is a dialogue between a Confucian scholar and a Western scholar. Through the dialogue, Ricci presents the argument that reason allows us to know something of God: through the order of the universe, the need for a Creator (in line with an Uncaused Cause), instincts of birds and animals, etc. With no reference to revelation, Ricci had to restrict himself to what is humanly knowable. The next question he dealt with is this—if one can recognize God, why have so many Chinese not done so? While maintaining the validity of natural revelation, Ricci also maintains that human religions lead one away from truth, and that the concept of emptiness in Buddhism and the nothingness of Daoism are not to be equated with the One True God. As the philosopher's dictum goes, "that which one does not have he cannot give to another as if he had it."[439] However, Ricci also displayed a give and take in the dialogue that attempted to show that to despise or belittle the Buddhist, as the Confucians did, is not the Christian way. Ricci's accommodation worked simultaneously to respect "the other," and to avoid compromising the truth of the Gospel. Although there were many accusations that the Jesuits were in fact compromising their message, documents from that era indicate that Ricci used a two-stage approach to his ministries: the pre-evangelism stage avoided the more controversial aspects of the gospel, while the teaching of the converted grounded the new believer in biblical essentials of salvation in Christ's death and resurrection. In fact, as mentioned in chapter 2, when opponents in the Chinese court brought accusations against a leading Jesuit in 1665, the first charge listed was the preaching of Christ crucified. Although Ricci was sensitive about preaching the crucifixion, because of the reaction of the emperor's eunuchs toward his crucifix (depicting a naked Christ on the cross), the truth of Christ's death and resurrection was not ignored.

A major shake-up in the Jesuit community came with the Rites Controversy; a conflict over accommodation that stayed with the Catholic Church for over one hundred and fifty years. The Jesuits had been choosing older Chinese men as candidates for the priesthood. Since the men had difficulty learning Latin, the Jesuits received permission to put the Catholic liturgy into Chinese which ultimately led to the question of terms, and what to use for the Chinese name for God. There was disagreement even among the Jesuits as to which Chinese term to use, one associated with the Confucian classics which had since picked up inappropriate connotations, or a more conservative choice that implied "Heavenly Lord," but communicated zero value to the average Chinese. The latter was the choice approved by the distant Vatican, and the Catholic Church in China is still known today as the Church of the Heavenly Lord.

The second issue in the Rites Controversy involved the issues surrounding ancestor rites. Ricci initially opposed ancestral ceremonies, but later came to see them as expressions of filial piety, with no religious significance. He felt that there was much to be found in ancestral rites that was acceptable to the Christian, and that believers should be allowed to engage in these rites, at least for the time being. On this issue the Jesuits were united, and went about "Christianizing" the ancestral name tablet used in the rites. A text on the right of the tablet explained that the tablet was only to serve as a reminder of the descendant's filial obligation. In the center of the tablet was inscribed the following: "Worship the true Lord, creator of heaven, earth and all things, and show filial piety to ancestors and parents."[440] There was also a list of prohibitions concerning ancestral rites that had to do with spirit worship. A similar issue that arose in the Rites Controversy related to the rites offered to Confucius, which had also become idolatrous in form. The Jesuits agreed that although the rites were originally civil ceremonies, they had "in the course of time become infected with erroneous preternatural or superstitious beliefs."[441]

So how much did the Rites Controversy affect the work on the whole? Again, taken alone they would likely appear insignificant, but in the larger context they were damaging. Much as in Japan, this related to the constant friction evidenced between Jesuits and the other orders. Covell takes the position that the animosity was for the most part national, and that a spirit of nationalism on the part of the Franciscans fueled the feud. Covell summarizes,

> In general, most of the Jesuits were aligned with the Chinese emperor against the pope and others of the Catholic missionary orders. At various times during this long period one side or the other seemed to be ascendant. Eventually a hard line was adopted: the Vatican took an inflexible stand against the Jesuit position. Christians went through many periods of intense persecution, until the faith finally was prohibited in China (1724), many priests deported, the Jesuits disbanded (1774), and irreparable harm done to the cause of Christianity in China.[442]

The whole history of the Jesuit mission in China will likely continue to generate controversy in the Church. Arnold Rowbotham joins K. S. Latourette in agreeing with the central authority of the church, saying that as with Nestorianism in China, where accommodation led to a degenerating into magic and charlatanry. The same would have happened with the Jesuit- planted church. Covell, on the other hand, draws a distinction between Ricci's work and that of later Jesuits who followed him.

What other factors contributed to the demise of the Catholic work in China? Covell lists five: (1) poor organization coupled with an ongoing disunity among the orders fed by a struggle for power. Covell points to the difference between early and later Jesuits, as the early Jesuits came humbly as "barbarian" learners. In this regard Covell writes, "Ricci had 'class' the others lacked."[443] (2) While the Jesuits initially sought to win officials and gentry, this emphasis waned, and following Ricci's death in 1610, was no longer consistently followed; (3) Unsettled times in the late Ming and early Qing dynasties with threats from foreign enemies intensified the atmosphere of xenophobia in China; (4) the antiforeign sentiment of Chinese officials led them to suspect all new religious sects as potential centers of revolt. This was less of a problem with Ricci than with his successors who were much less accommodating. (5) There were areas that even the Jesuits considered beyond accommodation: polygamy and overt idolatry, although these two points were not as controversial or problematic as Confucian and ancestral rites.[444]

Even if the Roman Catholic mission at this time was not a resounding success, the example of Ricci continues to provide insight into the need to communicate the gospel from within the context of the listener. Covell puts it well when he says that Ricci, "... saw clearly that before he could expect the Chinese to be changed, he must change in his approach and methods...He must go to the Chinese ideologically and not always expect them to come to him."[445] Another helpful lesson taken from Ricci is the wisdom of not looking for short-cut methods, but patiently laying a careful groundwork, and being patient if the process is long. Ricci's accommodations were not intended to be permanent solutions, but transitions allowing time for the Chinese church to grow and determine its own policies on controversial issues over time.[446] However, it must be said that the sooner a local church is invited to be involved in such decisions the better. Especially in more traditional societies, established precedents carry great weight and are not easily changed.

The other region touched by Jesuit Christianity is Korea, a spillover of the Jesuit mission in Japan. Moffett credits Gregorio De Cespedes, a Spanish Jesuit, with being the first Westerner known to set foot on Korean soil, in 1593. (The Dutch Lutheran, Karl F. A. Gützlaff would be the first Protestant to do so, in the 1830's.) However, this was not really a mission work in Korea, in fact, De Cespedes likely never spoke with a Korean. This was only a situation whereby a Jesuit was summoned to serve as an army chaplain for a Christian general who was attacking Korea, for purely imperialist reasons. As Moffett rightly observes in a later chapter, "It was the Koreans themselves, not foreign missionaries, who first brought the Christian faith to their own people from across its guarded borders. This was true of the planting of the church by Catholics, and then, almost a hundred years later, by Protestants. In both cases, the route of entry for the new faith was by way of China."[447] In 1783, a group of Confucian scholars, who had obtained books produced by Jesuits in China, became intensely interested in getting more. They saw their opportunity when a regular embassy visit was being arranged by Korean diplomats for a winter trip to the Chinese capital. They requested of a young scholar, who was to be a part of this embassy, that he bring back with him more of the Jesuit writings. By this time, the Jesuit mission in Beijing had dissolved, but a priest-mathematician was still working at the court. The young Korean scholar, Lee Seung-Hun, met the priest, was converted, and wasted no time in asking for baptism. "After a period of questioning, and with the permission of his father, he was baptized, the first baptized Korean in Korea. He was given the name Peter (Pierre), and was presented with Catholic books and devotional objects to take back to Korea, in the hope that he might be 'the first stone ["Peter"] of the Korean church.'"[448] Upon his return, "Peter" and his Confucian scholar friend Lee Pyok became zealous missionaries. Within months they saw a thousand followers asking for baptism. Untrained in the ways of the Catholic Church, they immediately began choosing leaders and ordaining them as priests. This awakening, however, was not to go unnoticed.

Within a year, as the movement spread, a Confucian reaction to this invasion of a foreign religion triggered an abrasive persecution. Ten Catholics were martyred. Shockingly, the two leaders, [Peter] Lee Seung-Hun and Lee Pyok, recanted under intense family pressure and withdrew from the community. But the example of the martyrs strengthened the little Catholic community and brought back to Christian leadership Lee Seung-Hun who, like the apostle Peter for whom he had been named, repented in anguish for his betrayal of his Lord. At great risk, Lee reestablished letter communication with Beijing, apologizing for the errors that, as he had discovered from further reading of the books, they had committed: the self-ordinations, the baptisms, and the masses. He pleaded forgiveness for his own apostasy, and concluded with a plaintive plea to the Beijing missionaries to find a way to bring the blessings of the sacraments to Korea: "the whole world is full of bishops and priests...Why should only this small corner of the earth which we occupy be excluded from the benefits of redemption?"[449]

The reaction in the Beijing missionary community was predictable: how could the faith be spreading this way without missionaries? At the same time, how could they not rejoice? The Franciscan bishop wrote to the new Korean Catholic community praising their zeal in the face of persecution, and for recognizing their baptisms as "lay baptisms," but they condemned the "uncanonical masses" and the ordination of priests without a bishop.[450] Church hierarchy lost no time in reigning in a people movement. This was followed by a strict prohibition of ancestral practices, which led to a second, and all-out persecution of the fledgling Korean church, which produced a second apostasy by "Peter." Nevertheless, in spite of all of this, "or because of the martyrdoms, in the next five years the number of converts quadrupled, from one thousand in 1790 to four thousand in 1795."[451]

Meanwhile, in Beijing, bishop de Gouvea set about searching for a way to get a missionary into "forbidden" Korea. The first Catholic missionary to Korea was a Chinese priest, Chou Wen-Mo (James Chou), who celebrated the first official Catholic mass in Korea. However, an informer posing as a convert betrayed him. He was a fugitive for five years, and then in 1801 he was captured and beheaded. Thus, he joined the ranks of the Korean church's early martyrs—all Asian. But again, the church kept growing, from four thousand when missionary Chou first arrived, to ten thousand when he was martyred five years later.[452]

The persecution did not stop here, however. It continued, wave after wave: in 1801, 1815, 1827, 1839, 1846, and the worst coming in 1866-1877. Just prior to this last outbreak, in 1863, it was reckoned that there were Roman Catholics in all of Korea's provinces, with the total number standing at twenty-three thousand. The persecution set off in 1866 appears to have been precipitated by a perceived threat of Russian encroachment into Korea. An offer for French missionaries to broker an alliance with France only furthered the suspicions of Christian ties with foreign powers. Taken with a false report that the Chinese were executing all foreigners in China, the momentum was sufficient to commence a mass slaughter of Christians. The response by the French, a naval attack on a port near the Korean capital, only fed the killing frenzy. The total number of Korean martyrs was estimated at eight thousand, about one-fourth of the total Catholic community. The budding Korean Catholic Church never recovered from the Great Persecution, but it did survive. Retirement of the nationalist regent, the Taewongung, and the accession to the throne by his son, led to more openness. The Confucians continued to protest foreign religions, but the new king, Kojong, showed himself to be more progressive. Treaties he made with Western nations led to edicts of religious tolerance. He believed that encouragement of Confucian manners and decency, not persecution, was best for the nation.[453]

The Protestants: Gospel of Power

The next movement we want to briefly examine is that of the Protestant missions in Northeast Asia. Again, in the brief amount of space we have, we can only hit the highlights. We will begin our survey, as we have before, in China. The beginnings of Protestant missions in China under the Jesuits, and the beginnings under the Protestants are starkly different in a number of ways. While the Jesuits had learned much in their Japanese experience, they came into China as humble "barbarians" eager to learn the culture. Moreover, they worked hard under Valignano's leadership to disassociate themselves from foreign powers (although Ruggieri's appeal for an embassy from Rome departed from this norm, with negative consequences). For nearly one hundred years prior to the arrival of the first Protestant missionary, Robert Morrison, in 1807, Chinese Catholics had endured severe persecution. Moffett cites figures of 800,000 Christians in China in 1700, dropping to only 187,000 in 1800.[454] They had counted the cost, and had been prepared to suffer. Jesuit missionaries before them, and with them, had done the same.

Ralph Covell has launched a blistering attack on Protestant missions of this period. According to him, Protestants were far less eager than their Catholic predecessors to risk martyrdom; they were ridiculously arrogant, belligerent, and obnoxious toward Chinese officials; and at times they proudly displayed their association with Western powers. A supreme example in Covell's account is the German Lutheran, Karl Gützlaff. But first, let us examine the early Protestant strategy.

The Englishman Robert Morrison holds the distinction of being the first Protestant missionary to China. Having prayed that he would be sent "where the difficulties were greatest, and most insurmountable," he arrived in Guangzhou (Canton) in 1807. Denied passage by the British East India Company, he took a roundabout journey through America, where he received a letter of introduction by Secretary of State James Madison to the American consulate in Canton. It was at this time that his famed conversation took place with the American ship's captain, who said to Morrison, "And so, Mr. Morrison, you really expect that you will make an impression on the idolatry of the great Chinese empire?" Morrison replied, "No, Sir. I expect God will."[455] Morrison adopted Chinese dress, at times even wearing a false queue and living in hiding much of the time. His language teachers carried poison with them at all times in case they were caught and tortured. Not seeing much result from this effort, Morrison had to make a choice: to preach and teach, or to pour all of his effort and time into Bible translation. He wisely chose the latter.

Morrison's work was plagued with difficulty. The East India Company that first refused him, later recognized his skill at language and provided him a job in translation. They gave him a legitimate reason to stay in China and supplied him with a livable wage. But the Company watched Morrison closely, forbidding him to evangelize. When they discovered he had translated the New Testament into Chinese they fired him but, recognizing his value to the company, never enforced their dismissal.

Morrison based his operations in the Canton region on China's east coast. Working in the interior was highly risky, so he concluded that missionaries would do better to restrict their work to the coastal region until times became more favorable. Protestant missionaries agreed with Morrison, arriving at a strategy whereby they could evangelize the Chinese, and even get literature into the nation, without going in themselves. They had decided to create what they called a "wall of light" around China's eastern perimeter. They located themselves in places such as Canton, Macao, Bangkok, Malacca, Penang and Singapore, with Singapore becoming their most important mission station. The idea was that when the old wall of resistance around China would finally crumble, the Christian "wall of light" from these places would brightly shine through every breach in the old wall, "and truth will win her way in even before her heralds."[456] Says Covell,

> Building a wall of light around China meant many things: learning the language for future use within the empire; acquainting churches in the West about needs and opportunities in China; encouraging the development of a better and expanded commercial relationship between China and the West; telling Chinese intellectuals in the border cities about the strange "barbarian" world of the west; producing literature such as the Bible, grammars, dictionaries, booklets, and tracts for use in China and among the Chinese diaspora; planning for and implementing model strategies for the future in evangelism, education, and medicine; establishing bases for limited forays around Canton, along the coast to the maritime provinces of China, and even up some rivers. This was an era of preparation as missionaries waited for China to "open to the gospel." They waited also for

God, and, despite some covert and clandestine low-profile efforts, they dared not throw their weight around in a situation that was always precarious and filled with potential danger.[457]

The missionaries of this time saw their activity as a "holding actions," as they awaited "wider doors." It was not their intention to continue this way indefinitely. In the meantime, schools, printing, medicine, and language study became a part of their temporary strategy. In time, they realized that much of their literature work was either not being read, or was not understandable, and very little of it was getting into China. As they thought about ways to pry the country open, they often discussed the way that early Buddhists used literature—perhaps broader distribution of literature and medicines was needed. But what really turned the tide for the Protestants was the obsession of the merchants for free-trade along China's coastal region. The missionaries began to see this as the opportunity they had been praying and waiting for; here is where Karl Gützlaff, of the Netherlands Missionary Society, comes into the picture. Neill paints Gützlaff in colorful terms, saying that he "may be variously judged as a saint, a crank, a visionary, a true pioneer, and a deluded fanatic."[458]

Gützlaff did not believe that missionaries should just wait for "doors to open." He was a doer, seeing himself as obedient to the Great Commission, and obligated to follow the zealous lead of the Jesuits, who "nourished by attachment to popery, found ways and means to penetrate into these regions..."[459] He was also one of the most skilled in the Chinese language, and was ready to face hardship. His first journey, on the *Sylph*, took place from June 18 - December 13, 1831. The crew was prepared to trade, and carried stocks of sugar, tin, sapan wood, pepper, European calico goods, and opium. Since this was to be a secret mission, Gützlaff and the captain changed the transliteration of their Chinese names and posed as officers of a merchant ship that had been blown off course. He was outspoken about his displeasure with Chinese laws that held foreigners at a distance, claiming that the missionaries had an innate right to walk where they pleased. Covell mentions that although Gützlaff did not openly advocate violent means, he noted that the fact that his boat, the *Lord Amherst*, carried "well-mounted long guns inspired the mandarins with respect."[460] Many of the Protestant missionaries apparently found it to their advantage to back Chinese officials down whenever they could. Covell points out that the captain of the *Lord*

Amherst went as far as to say, "...it would be no problem to stir up a war with China that would assure a firm basis for free trade."[461]

News of Gützlaff's journey was printed in missionary magazines around the globe, with his message that the doors of China were indeed not shut to those who were willing to push them open. This sparked a sharp rise in enthusiasm among mission agencies.

The London Missionary Society seemed less than convinced about the validity of Gützlaff's analysis, and determined that they would personally investigate the situation. They joined with the British and Foreign Bible Society to lead a strictly missionary voyage up the coast, with only Christian sponsorship. A vessel was chartered from an American company, the *Huron*, with no opium or articles for trade on board—only a few bags of rice and twenty thousand volumes of books including the Scriptures, a commentary on the Ten Commandments, a Life of Christ, theologies, etc. The chief missionary with the London Missionary Society, Walter Medhurst, gave three objectives for the journey: to discover the true situation along the coast; to enlighten the populace, and so the government, to their true intents by distributing the Scriptures; and to inspire their fellow missionaries to greater and more permanent efforts.[462] They were well received by the people, but opposed by the officials, who were obligated to enforce the emperor's exclusion edicts.

The missionaries generally took the stance that they had no choice but to conduct operations that were illegal—they had to "obey God rather than man." This the Jesuits also did. However, Covell maintains that the difference between Protestants and Jesuits was not in the illegality of their actions, but the attitudes with which they conducted those actions. Whenever Chinese officials were arrogant and impudent—which was generally the case—the missionaries felt obligated to reciprocate in kind. Says Covell,

> Declaring that Christian humility or prudence were not in question, they stated that they did not wish to be treated, even slightly, in a disrespectful manner. When Chinese officials wished them to stand in their presence, they deliberately sat down. Insults were exchanged for insults, disrespect for disrespect. If books they had distributed were burned by officials, then they did the same with gifts given to them in the name of the emperor.[463]

Missionaries believed that to do otherwise would only invite further ridicule from the officials and make things even more difficult for future missionaries. They did not want to appear ignorant and weak. The emperor responded to Medhurst's journey on the *Huron* by closing the literature work in Canton. Still, the missionaries showed determination. Other probes were made, which were also resisted by the officials, sometimes with a large show of force. The real problem, as the missionaries saw it, was not having enough workers to wear the Chinese down. Yet, some missionaries wondered if these efforts were accomplishing anything at all. Catholics working in the interior and sacrificing a great deal more looked upon the efforts of the Protestants with disdain. "They [the Protestants] have made their appearance on the coast only, like commercial travelers armed with a prospectus; they have done no more than toss Bibles from shipside upon the beach."[464]

As missionaries continued their work, and waited for God to act, political and commercial relations between China and Great Britain continued to decline. This resulted in the Opium War, and a humiliating defeat for China. While some missionaries saw this as morally reprehensible, some saw it as something that God was going to use to pry open the country for the propagation of the gospel to the Chinese. It did in fact open the country, but at what cost? Covell writes,

> The shame imposed upon China opened a door for the West. Several stipulations were written into the treaties drawn up from 1842 to 1844: the cession of Hong Kong; the opening of the five ports of Canton, Amoy, Fuzhou, Ningbo, and Shanghai to consuls, merchants and missionaries; a most-favored-nation clause; extraterritoriality; fixed tariffs; the right of Western warships to protect commerce and trade. Until this time relationships between the West and China had been based upon the ancient Chinese tribute system. The new conditions imposed upon China, euphemistically called "agreements," introduced an era of "unequal treaties" and power.[465]

While missionaries did not approve of opium trade or war, the war was still seen by some as the hand of God. As American missionary David Abeel commented, "It is true the spirit of war does not consort with the gospel of peace, but God is evidently employing the one in this country to prepare the way for the other."[466] Thus, the gospel of Jesus Christ was wrapped in the imperialist flags of commerce. Covell is strong in his assessment that missionaries could have done much more to awaken the conscience of the West on the moral issues of the opium trade, as was done earlier concerning the slave trade. They also could have been much less eager to assert their "rights" about things such as extraterritoriality, consular protection, "their right to rent whatever property met their fancy even if there might be neighborhood opposition...They could have campaigned for the elimination of obvious injustices in the treaty obligations. They could have avoided continued alignment with power by refusing to give time to the purely political duties—interpretation, service as government representatives, and the like—that they were over eager to perform for their governments."[467]

Moffett argues that some of the criticisms that people launch against the missionaries from this era are unfounded, since there was no other way to do some of these things, such as traveling with opium sellers. The opium vessels were often the only means of transportation up the rivers or along the coasts.[468] However, Covell's point is well taken. It was not so much the incidents themselves that caused harm, but the attitudes of the missionaries toward the Chinese officials, not to mention the hubris of the colonial powers, motivated by political and commercial interests, that caused damage that remains with us today. Columba Cary-Elwes sums up the damage as follows:

> Christ, so it seemed to the Chinese onlooker, was coming not with a Cross but with the sword, and the fateful prophecy must have been present to the minds of the more thoughtful, that those who take up the sword, perish by it. This question of the forcible defense of the rights of Christians to live as Christians is an age-old one, and will not be opened here. It is the fact that a historian must record, and the effects of its use. The Chinese responded in their inscrutable way, much as any subject people have always done. Resentment filled their hearts. In the long run the Portuguese protectorate had proved harmful; the same could be said of the French protectorate."[469]

Until 1842, Protestant missionaries were barred from living outside of Canton, and had not been able to organize a church until three years later. In all of China, they could only count three hundred and fifty-one Chinese Protestants. It did not look like the "Great Century" of Protestant missions in China.[470] Things were about to change, however.

The Wesleyan revivals of England supplied the theological foundations for a new wave of Protestant missions: "the lostness of the lost without Christ, and the good news of life eternal for as many as will believe in Him; the radical dehumanizing nature of sin, and the free gift of saving grace to those who repent and confess their sins; the authority of Scripture, and the importance of the experience of conversion. This was the missionary message."[471] In 1865, for China's two hundred and fifty to three hundred million people, there were only ninety-one Protestant missionaries. The following year, eighteen missionaries were on their way to China with veteran missionaries J. Hudson and Maria Taylor and their four children—the beginnings of the new China Inland Mission, the pacesetter of future faith missions.[472] In Taylor's lifetime, this force would grow to eight-hundred, and would keep growing after his death. After his frustrations with the Chinese Evangelization Society in his earlier years in China, he decided to headquarter the new CIM in China, to facilitate better response to missionaries on the field. Also, the missionaries received no set salary, but were to rely totally upon God for their support.

Early on, Taylor made an acquaintance with another missionary whose ideas would exert an influence not only on Taylor, but on the work of Presbyterians in the region, especially John Nevius. Nevius put a strong emphasis on expressing indigenization in a now famous three-fold form: self-supporting, self-propagating and self-governing.

The next Protestant example we will look at briefly is that of Protestant work in Korea. Amazingly, as in the case of Catholic mission in Korea a century earlier, Protestant work began not with a foreign missionary, but with a Korean. Sang-Yun Suh was a ginseng peddler who encountered some Presbyterian missionaries just across the border with China. These missionaries regularly recruited educated Koreans to assist them in the translation of the New Testament into Korean. Two years later, in 1878, Suh received baptism, and returned to his hometown with a translation of the Gospel of Luke. Later, in 1889, the first clergyman missionary, Horace Underwood, would come to that region and find thirty-three men who had received instruction from Suh and his brother, and were ready to receive baptism.[473]

In marked contrast to the example of the Portuguese traders in China, Korea's first contact with Protestant missionaries was couched in positive experiences with American diplomacy. Korea had long been a buffer state between China and its more northerly neighbors: Japan and Russia. As

China saw its neighbors gaining strength and putting pressure on Korea, she welcomed the growing relationship of Korea with the United States. While the American government did not have colonial ambitions, Americans were eager to get involved more extensively in global trade, and in the eighteenth century, American merchants were plying the waters of Asia. Diplomats followed the merchants, and at the urging of one Admiral Shufeldt, American Minister Lucius Foote boarded a ship for the harbor of Chemulpo. Everett N. Hunt, Jr. gives the following account of his arrival in Korea, in which he includes a quote from the New York Times.

> When Foote's ship arrived in the harbor at Chemulpo, and official party boarded to extend welcome in behalf of the king. Responding to the significance of the occasion, the ship's crew ran up a Korean flag they had made and gave it a twenty-one gun salute. After the salute its meaning was explained to the Koreans. "all agreed it was the first such international salute of courtesy Corea [sic] had ever received" (*New York Times* July 19, 1883).[474]

An embassy to the United States arrived the following September. High quality presidential appointees accompanied the group, including a translator who spoke Chinese, Japanese, and Korean. Eventually arriving in New York for a meeting with the president and the secretary of state, they also traveled the region for a tour of hospitals, farms, pharmaceutical firms, printing presses and the like, including a stop at West Point. These first contacts were very favorable, and dramatically helped to pave the way for future missionaries going to Korea.[475]

When the time came to recruit missionaries for long-term work in Korea, the Methodists were the first to help with the Reverend John F. Goucher leading the initiative. Goucher had been very instrumental in Methodist mission work in Japan and India, and had already raised a quarter of a million dollars for mission projects, including an Anglo-Japanese university in Tokyo. It was determined from the start to follow a pattern established in other missions in Asia, and to conduct mission work in cooperation with the diplomats. America did not seek to press for freedom to propagate Christianity; however, "it did press for religious toleration as well as an open door for the humanitarian aspects of nineteenth-century American Protestant mission endeavor."[476] The director of the Japan mission, Dr. R. S. Maclay, made the initial survey of possible sites in Korea—keenly attuned to the domestic and international climate there. He brought with him a letter addressed to the king, outlining the kinds of work they wanted to undertake, especially medical and school work, but taking care also to be up-front about the desire to evangelize. The king quickly responded with his permission to proceed. Maclay also approached the Japanese minister in Korea, who offered to do all in his power to assist the effort. Maclay returned to Japan overjoyed at the reception he had received, and at the king's permission, which removed all legal hindrances to opening work in Korea.[477]

The enthusiasm of the Methodists was soon picked up by the Presbyterians, who also had work in Japan. Yet, both the Methodist and Presbyterian boards expressed concern over reports regarding unstable political situations and the persecution of Catholics in Korea. However, enthusiastic insistence from missionaries in Japan, and a request from a medical doctor in China, Horace Allen, for a transfer to Korea, led to Allen becoming the first Protestant missionary to gain a career position in Korea. And yet, noting the unrest and the presence of anti-foreign sentiments, the home board continued calling for extreme caution. Korea was not yet permitting any preaching, and Allen limited his work to medical practice. Still, the forward-thinking king assured the Americans that education and medical work were essential to Korea's progress, and the progressive reformers continued to encourage the king in his efforts.

Allen quickly gained the favor of the court when the king's nephew was injured in an attempted coup between the reform-minded Progressives and his conservative pro-China group. The traditional court doctors wanted to treat the prince's wounds by inserting black wax, but Allen was able to convince them to let him try his methods, and much to the court's pleasure the prince recovered. Allen's position made a significant advance. His next move was to petition the king for a hospital funded by a "benevolent society in America." This calculated choice of wording permitted the king to avoid openly endorsing the mission. Allen also assured the court that such hospitals were furnished in China by Li Hung Chang, a move calculated to please the pro-Chinese faction that had succeeded in putting down the Progressive Party in Korea. Further, Allen stated that the hospital in Korea was to be named in honor of the king. Just seven months after Allen's arrival in Korea, the hospital opened. Medical mission work opened the way for other missionaries, and continued to be an important component to mission work in Korea.

In spite of these advances, preaching remained prohibited. The conservative pro-China faction had completely cut-off the efforts of progressives, severely restricting the glowing opportunities for open mission work. Even so, new recruits were already arriving in Japan, including Horace G. Underwood (Presbyterian) and the Henry Appenzellers (Methodist). The group met in Tokyo to plan and to pray for God's direction.[478]

Underwood, the bachelor Presbyterian, arrived in Korea with the Methodist Appenzellers on Easter Sunday 1885—Korea's first Protestant clergy-missionaries. However, the Appenzellers had to return to Japan temporarily, since Korea was not yet willing to accept foreign women outside the Western legations.[479] They were permitted to return to Korea, however, and in less than two years both Underwood and Appenzeller were baptizing their first converts. (This is remarkable, considering how Robert Morrison toiled in China for seven years without a convert.) Thus, the first churches were organized in Korea in 1887—one Methodist and one Presbyterian. These two groups would dominate the work of Protestants in Korea for the next hundred years.[480]

The Presbyterian mission seemed plagued with quarreling for the first several years, and after three years of mission work Dr. Allen resigned from the mission to take a post as a diplomat. He proved, however, to be a valuable friend to all of the Korean missions.

Hunt maintains one can trace the root of the problems to the original exploration of Korea by Maclay; though thoughtfully done, it did not allow enough time in the country for Maclay to get an adequate political sense of the uncertainties in Korea's relations with her neighbors. Nor did he pick up on the strongly conservative anti-foreign reactionary force that resisted any Western missionary prospects. "The progressives were assured of the support of the king, the Japanese, and the Americans. The conservatives were supported by China."[481] For the most part, the progressives ended up either killed or living in exile in Japan. Nevertheless, mission work continued, and although growth was slow, several things would follow this period that would encourage the strengthening of the young Korean church.

In 1890, the Presbyterian mission invited a veteran China missionary who would equip the work with principles of indigenization right from the start. John Nevius brought them what people came to refer to as the Nevius Plan, or the Three-Self Plan. Nevius counseled that it was never too early to begin applying the principles of self-government, self-support and self-propagation. In China, he said, missionaries had made the mistake of hanging on to the control of the churches for too long. Thus, he advised, missionaries should teach right from the start not only Bible study but also the practice of these three principles. Says Moffett, "Premature or not, the Nevius method proved to be one of the primary factors in the resulting numerical dominance of Presbyterianism in Korean Christianity..."[482] Historian Mark Noll agrees that the Nevius Plan provided the standard for missionary work. He comments, "With their emphasis on small group Bible study, the spiritual self-discipline of converts, and the missionary as itinerant facilitator, the Nevius principles formalized for mission purposes what was, in effect, the general shape of early Methodist practices in Britain and North America."[483]

However, both Moffett and Noll point to other factors in the growth of the church as well. As in many of the cases we have examined, the newly imported religion came into the country during a period of obvious social and cultural crisis.[484] There were great tensions manifesting between the king and fellow progressives on the one side, and the conservative pro-Chinese faction on the other. Also, China had long held Korea in a subject position, holding her at one time as a buffer on her borders, and at another time, as a battleground for her battles with other neighbors. Then, in 1894, the Japanese stormed into Korea to challenge China's dominance of the peninsula. China had to admit defeat in less than a year, the result being the independence of Korea, and the loss of Formosa (Taiwan). For the next fifty years, Japan all but controlled the nation. This produced an interesting response from the Koreans that was quite different from what we saw in other parts of Asia. Since Korea was not suffering at the hands of a Western power but an Asian one, Japanese dominance of Korea did not lead to an uprising against Western missionaries associated with colonial powers, but instead led to a resentment of Asian imperialism and culminated in the Koreans becoming friendlier in their relations with Western missionaries.[485] The Christian Church became a source of hope for Korea, and a source of establishing a national identity in the sort of incarnated indigenization that we see Lamin Sanneh writing about.[486] Noll comments as follows:

> Many historians of Korea have, thus, described Christianity as a religion offering a powerful message of hope for a desperately beleaguered people at an especially critical time. Also factoring into the rapid Christian expansion, however , was a critical

decision with Bible translation...Portions of the Scriptures were available in Korean from the late eighteenth century through the work of Catholic translators working out of China. As a result of protracted Catholic debate over the best Chinese word to use when translating the biblical "god" (the famous "term question"), Roman Catholics working in China at the end of the eighteenth century were following papal instruction by using the Chinese word *T'ien-Chu*. When Catholic translators adapted the Chinese usage for Korea, they transliterated the Chinese word into the Korean *Ch'onju*. When, however, the Protestant missionaries arrived, they agreed upon a missionary strategy (finalized at a meeting in 1893) aimed at the ordinary people, many of whom did not read the formal language that closely followed Chinese. A critical part of this strategy was to undertake a Bible translation that used ordinary Korean (*Hangul*) rather than a Chinese-based language. This determination led to the translation of "God" in Korean as *Hananim*, a word that was associated in time-honored Korean history with a more personal deity. Popular Korean resonance with the word *Hananim* was one of the reasons Christianity in Protestant dress appealed to the Koreans.[487]

This turning to Christian faith in the face of Asian imperialist oppression also led to the birth of the *Minjung* theology. In this Korean style of liberation theology, Jesus became a revolutionary figure who could identify with the *han* (unresolved suffering) of the *Minjung* (the people). During the Japanese occupation of Korea, David Kwang-sun Suh found the gospel of an experience of personal salvation alone to be insufficient, and opted for a socio-political savior where redemption from personal sin is not an issue.[488] In this scenario, we see two different kinds of distortions, where, in the words of Lesslie Newbigin, the Kingdom of God was separated from the Name of Jesus. On the one hand there was an experience of personal salvation without the cross of costly public action where Satan is challenging the rule of God. On the other was the action of the Church that did not go beyond an ideological crusade, leaving men and women with only the things of this world that ultimately do not satisfy.[489]

However, even though there was this expression within the Korean church, by and large the church functioned in forms as outlined above by

Mark Noll. Thus, it became a source of encouragement that the gospel truly can take root, make progress, and bear the fruit of the Kingdom of God in Asia.

Finally, we will turn our attention to Protestant work in Japan, which begins with the opening of the country after three-hundred years of self-imposed isolation, and extremely harsh persecution of the *Kirishitan* within her borders. But now, the Tokugawa shogunate that had destroyed all public evidence of the church in Japan was about to meet with its own demise. In 1853, the Tokugawa family was still in power, but suddenly, that summer a fleet of "black ships" took down Japan's wall of isolation. Says Moffett,

> Four black naval vessels intruded uninvited into Tokyo (then Edo) Bay. They were American ships led by the pride of the U.S. Navy, a smoke-belching sail-and-steam side-wheeler under the command of Commodore Matthew C. Perry. Perry carried a letter from President Fillmore to the emperor of Japan, asking for the opening of one or two Japanese ports on the sea route from San Francisco to Shanghai. Open Japan? The shock was felt throughout the close-guarded islands. It divided the shogunate council into two factions. One resisted any change; the other, impressed as much by new Western technology as by the size of the ships' guns, argued that change was inevitable. In the end, in little more than a decade the reformers had won, the shogunate withered away, and Japan had a ruling emperor again, the emperor Meiji (1868-1912).[490]

Naturally, as Catholic priests were able once again to enter the country, they wanted to know if any believers survived. A moving story recounts how in 1863 a priest by the name of Bernard Petijean arrived, and two years later built a new church in Nagasaki, which two hundred and fifty years earlier had been the center of Jesuit activity. Four weeks after the dedication (which had no Japanese in attendance), he noticed a dozen or so Japanese standing at the door in a silent and respectful fashion. As he opened the door and entered, the Japanese followed him in. As he knelt in the church to pray, a woman stood near him, and said, "All of us have the same heart as you." When the priest asked where they were from, she answered, "From Urakami...nearly everyone there has the same heart." They then asked to see the statue of Mary, and discussed with him about feast days, "We celebrate the Feast of our Lord on the 25th day of the Cold Month." Then learning that the priest was not married they were satisfied that he was a true Catholic priest. Upon further investigation, the priest discovered that there were hundreds, and then thousands of such Catholic believers. Some of them had accumulated superstitious practices, and their faith was so diluted that they were hardly recognizable as Christians. Eventually they determined there were likely thirty thousand or so of the *Kakure Kirishitan* (Hidden Christians). But only a third or so returned to the Catholic Church. After an initial wave of growth, however, persecution once again set in from enraged Buddhists, and this proved to be the last surge of growth experienced by the Catholics in Japan.

Some estimated that there may have been as many as ten times the number of reported believers that preferred to keep their mixed beliefs and practices as they were.[491] Such pockets of Japanese still exist today in some remote places, crossing themselves and performing rituals that are vestiges of a Christian past, but doing so without the remotest understanding of the true meaning behind them, and not knowing that the sign points to the Savior.

The very first Protestant service held in Japan actually took place aboard Commodore Perry's ship, July 11, 1853, in Tokyo Bay. One of the marines in that expedition, Jonathan Goble, would return to Japan as the first Baptist missionary, and accomplish the first translation of a book of the Bible (Matthew's Gospel) since the reopening of the nation.[492] The door to missions and evangelism did not open easily, however. The first American consul general, Townsend Harris, was told that the country would open to the outside world, but would not allow Christianity or opium to come in. Harris was persistent in pressing for freedom of religion, and was able to secure an agreement for American Christians to worship and to erect churches, but the ban on the "preaching" of the Christian faith to the Japanese was still not lifted.[493]

At last in July 1859, three ports opened to non-diplomatic foreigners: Nagasaki (south), Kanagawa (central), and Hakodate (north). The first Protestant missionaries to Japan included Dr. James Hepburn, M.D. (Presbyterian), and G. H. F. Verbeck (Dutch Reformed)—who would become president of the famed Imperial University. For the first ten years of Protestant mission work, the only groups involved would be Episcopalians, Presbyterians, American Dutch Reformed, and a small number of Free

Baptists. Historians have given high marks to this first wave of Protestant missionaries, complimenting them for the high degree of talent, breadth of experience, and achievement they brought with them.[494]

The work was hard and slow even with such talent. In 1872, after thirteen years of Protestant work, there were still only ten Japanese who had been baptized into the Protestant Church. The first organized church, although Presbyterian and Reformed in organization, was called non-denominational and given the name Church of Christ in Japan (*Nihon Kirisuto Kokai*).[495]

The fledgling church received a setback when a coup in 1868 deposed the shogun and enthroned the emperor as ruler. In April, an Imperial Rescript reaffirmed the Edict of 1614 against the "detestable sect of the Christians."[496] If that were not difficult enough, the government revived Shinto and proclaimed it the national faith. Torture and persecution of Christians followed. Buddhism also suffered restrictions with this turn of events.[497] This move, which included among other things the concept of the emperor's divinity, would be a source of great trouble for the future of the church in Japan. The nation had now moved from persecuting the church under the Tokugawas, to persecution under the emperor. The first article of the new Meiji constitution stated in its first article that the imperial family had ruled Japan for "ages eternal." Its third article declared that the emperor is "sacred and inviolable."[498] Persecution of Christians actually increased under the new system, and when the American minister protested their treatment in 1870, the answer he received declared, "this government rested on the Shinto faith, which taught the divinity of the Mikado [emperor], that the propagation of the Christian faith and religion tend to dispel that belief, and that consequently it was the resolve of this government to resist its propagation as they would resist the advance of an invading army."[499] However, by this time there was an international outcry against this persecution, and soon all the signs exhibiting the edicts prohibiting Christianity were taken down, although technically the law remained on the books. By 1880, missionaries were able to rent halls and hold meetings. But the problem of the "majesty of the national structure" which incorporated the doctrine of the divinity of the emperor, (together commonly referred to as *kokutai*), was far from over. The church would be faced with a strong emphasis on the unity of the Shinto religion and government.

In the first quarter of the twentieth century, both Protestants and

Catholics took the view that Shrine (State) Shinto rites were religious in nature, and they resisted them. However, by 1936, the National Christian Council of Japan did an about face, and declared, "We accept the definition of the government that the Shinto shrine is non-religious."[500] They gave their reasons at a 1949 gathering of the World Council of Churches gathering in Bangkok. "There seemed only two alternatives for the church to follow, either to clash with the militaristic regime at the expense of complete dissolution of the churches and even martyrdom, or to suffer together with their fellow countrymen in perseverance and sacrifice. The sense of national solidarity led our church people to choose the latter position."[501] How different this stance is from the example of the earlier Kirishitan over the centuries prior. Instead, for the most part, the church was taking the position that it was too dangerous to oppose what would in time be shown to be a great idolatrous evil. The Japanese proverb appeared to prevail, "*Nagai mono niwa makarero,*" or "One should not resist that which is more powerful." Sadly, the greater Power, against whom the "gates of hell shall not prevail," who has sustained the Church through millennia in spite of martyrdom, was considered by the Japanese church to be less than that of *kokutai*.

However, in these troubled times, there was one courageous Japanese believer who was not willing to compromise, no matter the cost. Kanzo Uchimura, a new Christian and a public school teacher, would get into deep trouble over his refusal to honor the Imperial Rescript by not bowing to a portrait of the emperor in a public school ceremony. His life will serve for us as an example of one way that a native Japanese believer gave expression to the gospel in the early days of the Protestant Church in Japan. Richard H. Drummond says that his life and work are considered by many to be" the most original single contribution as yet made by Japan to world Christianity."[502]

Kanzo Uchimura will forever stand out as a classic pioneer in regards to a "native" response to the gospel. A highly gifted and highly creative person, Uchimura found himself in his college years directly confronted by the opening of Japan to the West, as he chose to pursue an education in science in what was then called the Sapporo Agricultural College on the northern island of Hokkaido. The headmaster was an American, by the name of Clark, and he often utilized the school as a ground for Christian missionary work. Upon entering the school, Uchimura was confronted by the upperclassmen who had already converted to the Christian faith and had signed a covenant to spend the rest of their lives as Christ's ambassadors. Now these same men were bent on forcing the underclassmen to do the same.[503] Uchimura reluctantly and grudgingly complied. Though he strongly disagreed with their method, he never regretted signing the covenant and committing his life to the service of the Lord Jesus Christ. He was baptized by a Methodist missionary and began to attend his church. This marks a turning point in his Christian life. He and his friends very much disliked their church experience, perceiving that much had been imposed on the concept of "church" by western Christendom. Uchimura was convinced that the institutionalism, professionalism, and hierarchy that he saw there was nowhere near the model of the Early Church as depicted in the New Testament. Right from the start, he was formulating concepts for what would be known as the *Mukyokai*, commonly translated the "non-church" movement.[504]

Richard H. Drummond and Akio Dohi, both with extensive experience in the mission and church environment of Japan, see in this movement a rebellion not against forms *per se*, but against the traditional and institutional church. Dohi puts it in terms stronger than Drummond, seeing it as a "slap in the face" to the traditional church.[505] Although one can understand the sentiment, this is certainly an overreaction. Whereas Emil Brunner praised the movement as "unique in all of Christian history,"[506] this is also a bit overstated. More than likely, the *Mukyokai* was very much in harmony with the long history of the Church as one of many such reform or "resistance" movements. In fact, Drummond quotes an American Baptist, Raymond Jennings, as commenting that he saw Uchimura as "not too far from what I had long considered a more pure type of Baptist thinking than was prevalent for many Christians."[507]

Although Uchimura was indeed resisting the Western interpretation of Church and embracing what he viewed as a form more in keeping with the New Testament, his thoughts may well be reflected in Kosuke Koyama's explanation of what was happening here. Koyama looks at the Japanese word *Mukyokai* in a slightly different fashion from most who comment on Uchimura. The "*mu*" of *Mukyokai* is undeniably a prefix of negation. For example, the Japanese word for unlimited ("un" - limited) also employs the "mu" prefix (*mujoken*). However, this prefix can also mean "(one who) does not have." Koyama sees in Uchimura's term an invitation to those who do not find a home in the Western institutionalized form of church, and thus "do not have" a church home. The *Mukyokai* was an indigenous form of church for Japanese who did not fit the Western imported model. According to this view, it could be said that this was a "Church for those who have none." This may truly be the nuance that Uchimura had in mind.

There is no question, however, that in large part his action was borne out of a passion to resurrect a New Testament model of the church. Just as Luther had a problem with the *Kirche* of Germany, preferring the *Gemeinde* concept, Uchimura saw the rigid hierarchical institution that was being passed on to him as little more than a forgery of the genuine "holy flock" that was supposed to be his spiritual home.

Regrettably, part of his reaction to the Western and foreign forms was his decision to see the sacraments as non-essentials. Though he performed baptism on his dying daughter, and conducted communion at that time for his wife, his daughter, and himself, he did not encourage the *Mukyokai* to make the sacraments a part of their worship—a decision that brought much criticism from the established churches and foreign missionaries. Perhaps this reluctance to value the sacraments was also an expression of his rejection of perceived "foreignness," rather than any sharp disagreement with the concept itself.[508] Akio Dohi speaks of Uchimura's view as follows: "...sacraments (*sacramenta*), he says, are signs (*notae*) of holy things, and are visible expressions of the invisible grace of God."[509]

In the *Mukyokai's* formative years, Uchimura gathered around himself a number of like-minded students and developed a form of church in which everyone was a minister, with everyone taking their place in a Sunday rotation of preaching and leading in worship. They met on Sundays and on Wednesday evenings in Bible study. Uchimura also published a Bible study magazine, the format of which, basically, is still in use today. This Bible study emphasis would draw thousands in later years in Tokyo; and today, although they do not keep attendance records, estimates are that the *Mukyokai* accounts for 1/5 to 1/3 of Protestant Christianity in Japan.[510] This is a significant fact.

Who are the people associated with the *Mukyokai*? They tend to be the elite of Japan: college presidents and professors, corporate executives and highly trained citizens, though that was probably never Uchimura's intent. These people want to know the deeper meaning of life, and they commit themselves to a life study of the Word as Christ's disciples. For Uchimura, the Church is central to this, and consequently is a vehicle of God's revealing himself to the world in love.

Though conservative theologically, and a Pietist in many ways, Uchimura did not have a narrow view of the Christian life by any means. His Christian faith carried over into political and social activism. As a teacher in his early years, Uchimura was confronted, as were all educators in Japan at that time, with what is known as the Imperial Rescript on Education—a promulgation by the emperor on how the schools were to carry out education. Since the Rescript came from the emperor, the teachers were to gather and bow before the Rescript in worship. Uchimura publicly refused on the grounds that only the One True God was worthy of such worship. As a result, he was forced to resign his position.

This is but one example of how Uchimura took public stands on political and public issues from his Christian perspective. As a trained scientist, he also wrote many articles on topics like the environment and other popular issues of the day. His Christianity, though conservative by nature, was relevant. His faith was not a "private" matter; and since he had a reactionary personality he was not averse to applying his faith for the good of his country. Uchimura wanted to bring out what was good about Japan, not only for the immediate sake of the Japanese, but to let the world know that Japan had values other than blind loyalty and bloodthirsty aggression. His leadership is a good example of Christianity being *for* the people and the nation, and not an adversary.

An article he wrote entitled, "The Two J's" vividly depicts his emphasis. In it he says he loves two J's—Jesus and Japan—and he does not know which he loves more.[511] This statement got him into deep trouble with other church groups; however, it was not his intent to put Japan on an equal footing with Jesus Christ, rather, it was an acknowledgement that it was impossible for him not to be a "Japanese Christian." To attempt to renounce his nationality and Japanese character would be to make himself amorphous, resulting in a second loss also of his Christian identity. Luther, he said, did not stop being German when he was converted. The two identities of nationality and faith had to go hand in hand.

He also published articles on great figures of Japanese history, including Nichiren—the rebellious Buddhist monk who reacted against the denominationalism and corruption of Buddhism, instead making a Japanese Buddhism, which he claimed had been brought back to India to reform and purify Buddhism's source. Uchimura loved his nation, and sought to bring his Christian faith into integration with all facets of Japanese life.

For Uchimura, the "true Church" was the invisible Church above; he equated the Church with the Kingdom of God. This did not mean, however, that the visible manifestation of the Church had no connection to this world. He felt that it was the divine mission of the visible manifestation of Christ's Body, the Church, to reveal God to the world in Christ. The Church (*ecclesia Dei*) was to exemplify the presence of God in the world, and to manifest his reign (*regnum Dei*). Uchimura lived this out by loving his country. For him, this did not happen so much *via* a public institution, but rather in the gathering of "little flocks" for the study of Scripture and the personal penetration of society in everyday life. It was the living out of the Kingdom that was effective for him—to Uchimura, the gospel was manifested not in the institution, but in the following of Jesus in public life.

He also put a strong emphasis on proclamation of the simple gospel of Jesus Christ. He felt that it was wrong for missionaries to come to Japan and do things that a Japanese could easily do. Someone other than a missionary could do administration and even the teaching of theology. "We don't need missionaries to administer the YMCA," he said; others could do education, sports training, and the like.

For Uchimura, the gospel was to be applied to all of life, but evangelization was always central. He despised the modern forms of Christianity as practiced in the West that were all about social reform and politics, divorced from the foundational message that "Jesus Christ came into the world to save sinners." When the Exclusionist Bill was passed in the United States, he rejoiced, since Japan did not need what he saw as a Western diluting and corruption of the simple gospel message. At the same time, he called on the Christians of Japan to have compassion and pray for America so that we might be renewed and restored. In the same spirit though, he rejected the forms of the institutional model of the Church, aside from the question of ecclesiology, he was eager to cooperate with other church bodies and saw them as part of the universal Body of Christ.

Thus, for Uchimura, there is not a strong distinction between the Kingdom of God and the Church; nor between the practice of the Kingdom and the vocation of the Church; they go together. The reality of both is a heavenly reality which comes together in the expression of the Church on earth. Uchimura stood uncompromisingly for two things: a holy life in proclamation of the Good News that Jesus died to save sinners, and that the gospel is available to all. Though he did not take a hard position on issues like particularism or universalism, he saw comfort in believing that every individual would be won over by the reign of God through the gospel. (For him, this was only added assurance that he too would be with Christ forever.) Yet he never shied away from the urgency to call all to repentance and faith; and his was not only a verbal proclamation, it was a proclamation that included action borne out of a love for Japan and a love for justice in society. He taught that the one "J", Jesus, would make Japan better, and the other "J", Japan, would contribute to a more holistic and a more human Christianity in Japan. In his mind, one need not be pitted against the other.

Chapter Summary

In all of these examples of missionary work in Northeast Asia, one can see certain issues repeating, and also paralleling with the work of Buddhism in the region as well. One primary issue that confronts us is the issue of power. Power is a major problem for frail and sinful human beings who wish to represent the crucified and risen Christ to the world. This is an important concept that needs a great deal of consideration by the Church, in discovering what it means to be the representatives of Jesus Christ among the nations. In the case of the Jesuits, this meant not only connections with an imperial power from the home country, but also the added connection with the pope, even though the Jesuit missionaries at times stood against those powers. There was also the evident carry over of the culture of the Inquisition that added to the mix. This was more prominent in India and Japan, and thankfully was less so in China. Buddhism had the luxury of leaving behind the allegiances of home countries, although we saw in chapter 3 that they still brought their culture of religion and state with them, which posed an obstacle to their relations with the Chinese government.

This issue of power as far as the Protestants were concerned did not include the pope, of course, but there was nevertheless the problem of imperialism, unequal treaties, and extraterritoriality that stained their proclamation. Covell's account of the early Protestants in China depicts an extremely haughty attitude at times on the part of the missionary. Even with Moffett's qualification that missionaries had no other way to get to these places than to go with merchants and military, the early Jesuits were far better at coming as learners and servants (in contrast to some of the examples of Franciscans and Dominicans). They were much closer to the "crucified mind" of Christ that Koyama speaks of. At the same time, the sacrifices on the part of both Jesuits and Protestants is significant, compared to that of missionaries today, and must not be forgotten.

The means by which these pioneers shared the Good News of Christ also has some common elements. Education, preaching, Bible study, medicine, and at times the assumption of local dress and custom all served as means to contextualize the message. Some of these were more helpful at times than others, depending upon the needs of the culture.

A key component in all of these is something that was mentioned to Xavier by his Japanese friend, Yajiro. That is, that one's character and lifestyle must match the message. The heart of the missionary must reflect the heart of the One he or she serves, and not that of national policy, politics, or even the church that one represents.

Along these lines, there is also the issue of the goal of one's work: is it the Church (*ecclesia Dei*) or the Kingdom (*regnum Dei*)? Examples of each from history would be valuable to consider.

In our next chapter, it will be our task to lay out the issues above, and more, and to work with these in more depth in light of the theological and anthropological paradigms discussed in previous chapters. Hopefully, a paradigm will surface that will be consistent with *missio Dei*, and be informative as a tool to interpret our past and inform our future.

CHAPTER FIVE

Conclusion

In the first chapter of this book, we posed some salient questions that were to serve as the foci for writing this thesis. Let us now return to those questions: "Where does mission originate? What is its goal? What is God's intent for the Church in the realization of this goal? As God comes into the world in love, what does His coming look like? Where does one find God's presence and how does one discern and build upon that presence?" Those questions were asked in tandem with a question that was specifically directed to the region of Northeast Asia: "In spite of a great outlay of human and material resources over the centuries, why have we still not seen greater receptivity to the gospel in Northeast Asia? The other imported religion of major significance, *viz*, Buddhism, has created a home there, while Christianity, for the most part, is still the alien stranger standing outside the gate." We began with the assumption that we would be able to articulate some answers to the above questions once we laid a missiological foundation and surveyed Buddhist and Christian praxis in Northeast Asia. Having done that, this chapter will now summarize the arguments and findings of the previous four chapters, and offer some conclusions to the study. It is our prayer and our hope that this book and the following conclusions might serve Christ's Church as fuel for further missiological discussion and reflection. There is likely nothing in these pages that is new or novel. However, learning most often takes place not from encountering completely new concepts, but when something that has gone unnoticed finds itself under the spotlight and brought to center stage, or when something familiar is seen from a new and different perspective.[512] It is our expectation that new emphases and perspectives on the Church's role in *missio Dei* will emerge from this discussion.

Let us then begin by revisiting the missiological triad from our first chapter. The suggestion there was that the strongest evidence for the power of the gospel comes when the Church finds the ground and source of missions in *missio Dei*, with *regnum Dei* as the goal and focus. *Ecclesia Dei* finds its true meaning only as it is rooted back in *missio Dei*, and serves as a cruciform entry path to *regnum Dei*. In this manner, *ecclesia Dei* fulfills its role in service to God and the world He loves. However, that said, we must beware that we do not slip into thinking that the world shapes missions. While *ecclesia Dei* takes the role of the servant, *missio Dei* determines how the Church is to serve the world, and we find the character and goal of *missio Dei* defined in the revelation of God's will and heart for the world as recorded in the Scriptures. It is there that we learn that God has reached out to the world in Jesus Christ (through whose presence we see the Kingdom[513]), calling the world to repent and believe the gospel, offering reconciliation through Christ's sacrifice on the cross. When we speak of the Kingdom, we need to know that in part we are really speaking about the presence of Jesus. There is no Kingdom without Him. In Him, we also see that salvation from sin is a fruit of the Kingdom, along with all that Jesus brings to the world. As the world does a U-turn (*metanoia*), it turns from sin to God and begins to taste the fullness of the Kingdom in many and varied ways. This fullness will consist of justice for the poor, healing for the diseased, release for the oppressed, etc., but it will also include the joy of reconciliation with our Father through the gospel of Jesus Christ. "...Jesus declared, 'I tell you the truth, no one can see the Kingdom of God unless he is born again'" (Jn 3:3). We have seen in the history of the Church in early times and late, that when everything that is material and earthly is stripped away from believers so that all they have left is their relationship with the Father, they will give themselves to martyrdom before surrendering that relationship. The material and spiritual are complimentary in Jesus, not antithetical.

This is the holistic goal of mission; and *Missio Dei* begins and ends with, to use Kitamori's phrase, God's embracing *completely* those who should not be embraced.[514]

Thankfully, often there have been times when this cruciform perspective of missions has been prominent in the work of the Church. Sadly, often it also has been lacking. Some examples of the latter are the competition between the Jesuits and the Dominicans and Franciscans. It was also lacking in the Roman Catholic Church's display of imperial lust for empire that at times put the strict observance of religious traditions, like that of the historic episcopate, ahead of the work of the Spirit, as in the case of the seemingly spontaneous birth and growth of the Church of Jesus Christ in Korea. It was impossible for those missionaries in China to see that God could work ahead of the Church and apart from papal-inspired traditions. The preservation of *ecclesia Dei* as they understood it became the ground and source of all missions, and in essence swallowed up *missio Dei* and *regnum Dei*. Preservation of the ecclesiastical institution through tradition appeared to be paramount in their thinking.

The Protestants do not escape from the hold of ecclesio-centered missions either. Protestants openly despised Catholics, and placed themselves in direct competition with them. Protestants at times based their identity, in reverse, upon that of their perceived enemy.[515] They defined themselves by saying, "We are not like them." Thankfully, although Protestants publicly condemned some of the successful methods of the Jesuits, they quietly utilized them in their own missions work. And yet, while Catholics struggled with allegiance to an outside papal power in Rome, Protestants often flaunted the power of Western imperialism, and took shelter under its protective umbrella.

This raises the important issue of the gospel's connection to power. In chapter 4, we spoke of the work of Protestants in terms of the gospel of power. Ralph Covell presented us with repulsive images of missionaries responding to arrogant Chinese officials with equal or greater arrogance. Both Catholic and Protestant missions found themselves lumped together with imperial powers such as Portugal, Spain, and Great Britain. The Jesuits were the Catholic example of missionaries attempting to distance themselves from foreign powers, papal and colonial, as much as possible while in China. Simultaneously, however, they at times carried into their work attitudes that were rooted in the Inquisition. This was clear in Xavier as he left India, for example.

It is a long known fact that the foreign policies of the missionary's land of origin affect the missionary's work. The North American missionary, for example, cannot totally escape the fact of being North American. Moreover, scholars like Amin Maalouf have demonstrated how issues of identity can foster hostilities and violence. In light of this, it is imperative in this world of ours, which still operates according to tribal identities, that we do all that we can to minimize such affiliations with the gospel. We must remember that the gospel is the one Divine means given to us to overcome such divisive tendencies. Especially in areas where there are numerous identities living alongside of each other, it is important to show that while identities are indeed the things that separate us from others—"what prevents me from being identical to anyone else"[516]—identities can also serve to illumine the things we have in common with others. For example, in the Lutheran Brethren Seminary in Chad, one of the first tasks of the school each fall is to teach the students from various tribal backgrounds that the gospel frees and unites, that the gospel is greater than our tribal identities and consequent divisions; the gospel of Jesus provides commonality and unites them in our new and greater identity as the Body of Christ. Once the students bring their tribal identities to the foot of the cross of Jesus, then the work of unification, as well as their theological studies, can begin. The work of missions needs to take into sufficient account the identity issues that abound in our world, and cause those issues to be positive tools, rather than negative, for the work of *missio Dei*. There's a greater "identity" in Jesus Christ. The Church must be a catalyst and not a hindrance to this discovery.

Our identity in Christ carries abundant power for good. Lamin Sanneh has pointed out in *Translating the Message* and his later book *Whose Religion is Christianity?*, how missionaries often unwittingly equipped those whom they served with the knowledge and skills to rise up one day against their colonial oppressors. Also to their credit, missionaries often led the way in publicly opposing the colonial and merchant oppressors. When the missionaries understood that the power of mission was rooted in the gospel and was expressed in their humble service to God and people, they were worthy ambassadors of *missio Dei*. However, to the degree that their efforts flowed from a desire to increase the power and privilege of the sending Church, or from a desire to serve both the Church and their country of origin, the people among whom they hoped to plant a church tended to respond with hostility, seeing the missionaries as a threat to their continued existence. We also saw that when the work of the missionaries represented a desire to *serve the nation of their hosts* in Christlike ways, the response was often positive.

Much of this was true also with the Buddhist missions. Buddhist missionaries were not shackled to the ball and chain of a foreign home base to which they had to answer. And yet, as we saw in China, for quite some time the Buddhist missionaries resisted submitting themselves to the authorities of the Chinese government. Once they did, the hostility soon broke down. Nevertheless, this did not guarantee long-term government favor toward Buddhism. The relationship of government and religion is a quagmire of difficulty that deserves far more treatment than can be given here, and yet, to point out one example, we saw that when the Church in Japan acquiesced to Shinto-inspired government oppression, the gospel witness suffered severely. The question of under what conditions and to what extent religious groups should subject themselves to government authority is a worthy subject for further study.

An added problem with the Church's connections to colonial powers is the consequent lack of nerve on the part of missions when those same protective colonial structures collapsed in the twentieth century. Scherer discusses this problem at some length in *Gospel, Church, and Kingdom*. We talked about how Scherer wonders if this *loss of nerve* may conceal an even more serious *loss of faith*.[517] Thankfully, as Sanneh pointed out in *Whose Religion is Christianity?*, the Church did not suffer long from this problem, since today we are witnessing a resurgence of faith taking place in the two-thirds world. Will this two-thirds world church be God's instrument to bring future resurgence to the church in the West? Perhaps, but how He will do that remains to be seen.

Before we leave the topic of power and the gospel, we must point out that although the colonial era is history, this in no way implies that the problem of power and wealth influencing missions is over. We may not have colonialism as we once knew it, but all along, from the time of Columbus, we have had globalism running on a parallel track, and if anything, globalism has picked up momentum. How will the nations see the Church respond to the reductionist forces of what Benjamin Barber has termed MacWorld? Will the missional Church of today now ride the "gunboats" of globalism? Analysis of the problem has proved difficult, since, as with colonialism, missions have benefited from technology and innovation. However, as R. J. Schreiter has pointed out, "Technical rationality has the advantage of providing clear purpose and procedure, but it can become profoundly dehumanizing."[518] Samuel Escobar offers the following thoughts:

> The culture of globalization as it has been pointed out creates attitudes and a mental frame that may be the opposite of what the gospel teaches about human life under God's design.

If mission simply rides on the crest of the globalization wave, it might end by changing the very nature of the gospel. Coming from the experience of evangelistic movements that wanted to pattern their missionary activity according to biblical standards, in 1974 at Lausanne, René Padilla...criticized the total identification of modern Western values (the American way of life) and the gospel that was propagated in the name of Christian mission. He called it "culture Christianity" and commented: "In order to gain the greatest possible number of followers, it is not enough for 'culture Christianity' to turn the gospel into a product; it also has to distribute it among the greatest number of consumers of religion. For this the 20th century has provided it with the perfect tool—technology. The strategy for the evangelization of the world thus becomes a question of mathematical calculation."[519]

Escobar maintains that Padilla's criticism has not lost its validity, and he points out how American organizations have even turned prayer into "an industry in which teachings and methodologies are packaged and marketed." He continues,

The quantifying rationality of American technological culture has been uncritically applied even to the understanding of demonic activity. Nations that are at odds with the foreign policies of the United States have been represented in maps as "windows" in which we are told that through spiritual mapping it is possible to detect a more intense demonic activity than in other parts of the earth. Without any care for theological consistency, the warlike language of the Old Testament permeates liturgy and worship to an intolerable degree.[520]

At the same time, people like Escobar, Paul Pierson, and many others, including secular authorities have pointed out from time to time that the challenges of globalization will be overwhelming to local and national governments apart from the involvement of the Church and like minded voluntary organizations. As an example, Escobar points to Peter Drucker's article in the November 1994 issue of the *Atlantic Monthly*, where Drucker maintained that neither government nor the employing sector of America have the ability to cope with the effects of a shift from an industrial society to a knowledge-based society. Drucker called these effects, "social tasks of the knowledge society," such as "education and health care; the anomies of diseases of a developed and, especially, a rich society, such as alcohol and drug abuse; or the problems of incompetence and irresponsibility such as those of the underclass in the American city."[521] If we consider the inevitable spread of the effects of globalization, it becomes clear that for the growing social disparities confronting twenty-first century societies, the compassion of the Church of Jesus Christ will be the only hope for many. However, the world must see the Church as a part of the solution, not a part of the problem. "The challenge for missionaries will be how to avoid the pitfalls of missionary paternalism on the one hand and the failed secular welfare system on the other. Only the redemptive power of the gospel transforms people in such a way that it enables them to overcome the dire consequences of poverty."[522] Unlike the hostility toward the Church that was evident in the 1960's and 1970's, today we are seeing sociologists in far-flung places speaking of the Church as a source of hope for the urban poor.[523] However, to avoid another go at trendy human religion, we will need to develop a biblically-based ecclesiology that frees us to do missions in Christ's way—minus the sectarian or competitive spirit, paternalism, triumphalism and wasteful duplication of resources. Moreover, we will need to do it in a way that listens to the local church, and allows the local church to be the final arbiter of how we will best serve.

One example that we considered is that of Kanzo Uchimura and the *Mukyokai*. Although this example has elements that many will not consider orthodox in belief and practice, as is true of numerous indigenous movements today, Uchimura made a concerted effort to demonstrate that Western forms were not the only appropriate forms for the Church. In this scenario, we have the Jerusalem Council debate of the Early Church redivivus (Acts 15). The apostle Paul dealt with this issue again in the first chapters of his letter to the Galatians. What is important to Paul is not a cultural interpretation of how to do church, but that we are "acting in line with the truth of the gospel" (Gal 2:14). Uchimura's *Mukyokai* is an attempt at offering a truly Japanese expression of the Church in Japan that exercises freedom in all that is not necessary for salvation. This is also the spirit in which we find writers like C. S. Song and Aloysius Pieris expressing their desire for a truly Asian expression of the Church, free from Western forms. Such a process calls for more than an "Asian perfume" or Asian clothing, but an expression of biblical Christianity deeply rooted in what it means to be Asian.[524] Song refers to this as a need for a "more direct flight from Israel to Asia," without a large number of stopovers or a Western travel agent determining the itinerary.[525] Asian Christians will have to be the chief definers of what this means. We will likely face some tension over where the lines of gospel truth are drawn, but rather than responding like a reactionary foe, world partners in the work of world missions should come alongside these movements and encourage such expression through a contextualized approach that encourages freedom of form without the sacrifice of essential biblical content. One way to put this might be a call for a methodology that is conservative in orthodoxy and radical in orthopraxis. Indeed we cannot escape the necessity for such a process; it is already being forced upon the Church. In this regard, an exciting opportunity for a deeper experience of community lies before us.

Another aspect that we saw in both Buddhism and Christianity was the regard for translation. Buddhists placed a high value on translation work, especially in the southern sector of China where they concentrated their efforts on the intelligentsia. In chapter 4 we referred to the fact that some Protestant missions actually studied the Buddhist use of translation as a means for propagation. Protestants tended to give more attention to Bible translation than Catholics, and churches with the Scriptures have done a better job of preserving the faith under trials. The Nevius Plan of self-support, self-government, and self-propagation underscored the importance of the Church being equipped early on to work with the Scriptures.

A good literary base also heightens the possibility of a local church being able to add a fourth pillar to the Nevius structure: self-theologizing. It is a critical right and responsibility of the local church to theologize. Utililizing models of contextualization that emphasize such self-directed applications of Scripture, such as Hiebert's Critical Contextualization model, churches can apply the gospel early on as cultural insiders and they can also speak the gospel back to the missionary.

Carrying along the topic of translation, it is interesting to see how in the case of Buddhism and in the case of Ricci, there is the example of avoiding the translation of difficult doctrinal pieces at the outset. If we look at Buddhist practice in the Han period we do not see much in the way of Buddhist texts that deal with the fundamental doctrines such as The Four Noble Truths, Nirvana, *anatman*, etc. Instead, we see texts that exhibit similarities with Taoism—breathing techniques, concentration practices and the like. So also with Ricci, the pieces he used for early evangelism were much simpler than the catechetical texts constructed for the training of believers. He actually avoided some core doctrines in the material intended for evangelism. We mentioned how this might be somewhat similar to Amos Yong's suggestion to start with the doctrine of the Spirit in missions work, beginning with pneumatology rather than Christology, and to introduce the doctrines of Jesus Christ and the Trinity later on.[526] The argument that Yong advances for his method is that at the outset most cultures of the world will more readily relate to the doctrine of the Spirit. Considering also the fact that with religions such as Islam, the door to belonging is opened rather wide, perhaps Christians need to look again for ways whereby a sense of belonging can precede actual conversion and discipleship. It is true that Jesus taught "narrow is the way," and yet, it would appear that until He appeared to His disciples on the Emmaus Road, few if any understood that what He had been teaching for three years prior had anything to do with salvation from sin through the death and resurrection of a member of the Triune God. In our evangelism and missions efforts, the goal must certainly be to help people come to a fuller understanding of Jesus and to seek their conversion. However, recognizing the enormous paradigm shifts required, perhaps we could consider Ricci of old, and Amos Yong's suggestion that this may not be where we want to start. An approach that would be more akin to pre-evangelism may be in order in cultures far-removed from the gospel paradigm. It was my own experience in Japan, as well, that Japanese seekers were first attracted to the atmosphere of the church fellowship and the sense of belonging, long before they had an adequate understanding of how the gospel of Jesus Christ was applicable for them. Nevertheless, recalling the examples of mission that we have in the book of Acts, we dare not hold back from the "offense of the cross" for long. We must equally recognize that the Holy Spirit is the chief missionary, and in the final analysis, it is only the "offense of the cross" that saves.

Another challenge that Buddhism had to confront was that of ancestor veneration, which is still a controversial issue among Buddhists today, since in many ways it has reduced Buddhism to the status of a funeral religion. In this regard, it would seem highly probable that Buddhism accommodated too much in this area in the past. Christianity has tended to take a hard-line approach to ancestor worship, forbidding anything that has to do with its forms. Because of this stance, when Asians consider the possibility of becoming a follower of Jesus Christ, one of the first questions to surface will be this one—if I become a Christian, do I have to stop participating in all aspects of ancestor worship? And yet many pastors and leaders have asked the question, can the Church meet the Confucian, and biblical, admonition to honor the ancestors better and in more ways than indigenous religions? To address this question, the Asia Theological Association gathered ninety-eight theologians, pastors, and missionaries from nine countries in Asia in December of 1983 to discuss Christian alternatives to ancestor practices. According to the Korean missiologist Han Chul-Ha, the issue of ancestor veneration lies behind the persecution of so many Christians in Korea. The former president of Kobe Lutheran Seminary in Japan considered it a crucial issue in Japan, along with emperor worship and militarism. It is a primary obstacle to conversion in Taiwan as well.[527] However, since these practices rest upon the belief of an immaterial part of the human being that continues after death, we can easily find points of contact between the practices of the Church and the practices of non-Christians in Asia. Church historian Justo González, for example, gives an account of the Early Church practice of meeting in the catacombs different from the interpretation given by some,

> Some authors have dramatized the "church of the catacombs," depicting them as secret places where Christians gathered in defiance of the authorities. This is at best an exaggeration. The catacombs were cemeteries whose existence was well known to the authorities, for Christians were not the only ones with such subterranean burial arrangements. Although on occasion Christians did use the catacombs as hiding places, the reason they gathered there was not that they feared the authorities, but rather that many heroes of the faith were buried there, and Christians believed that communion joined them, not only among themselves and with Jesus Christ, but also with their ancestors in the faith.
>
> This was particularly true in the case of martyrs. As early as the middle of the second century, it was customary to gather at their tombs on the anniversary of their deaths, and there to celebrate communion. Once again, the idea was that they too were part of the church, and that communion joined the living and the dead in a single body. It was this practice that gave rise to saints' days; these usually celebrated, not their birthday, but the day of their martyrdom.[528]

The difficulty for Christians in Asia, however, is not so much the sense of any connectedness with deceased Christians, as it is how to respond to practices related to the death of non-Christians. Nevertheless, an established practice in the churches that communicates a high respect for the dead, and a spiritual connectedness to deceased Christians, like that spoken of by González, would go a long way toward sending a positive message to fellow Asians. Such a message would communicate that the problem for Christians does not relate to any lack of filial piety toward the dead, but rather the difficulty stems from a need to avoid specifically idolatrous aspects of non-Christian rites. To make such distinctions requires interpretation of the elements of non-Christian rites, and this has been part of the difficulty. In doing such analysis, we are immediately confronted with the additional fact that the meaning behind these rites differs according to generations—a religious meaning for older generations, while younger generations view them largely as social and cultural expressions. Such a difference in generational perception was illustrated when a mission executive traveled to Japan and asked a gathering of pastors the meaning of the Japanese bow—was there any religious meaning to it? The older pastors answered that the original meaning of the bow was in fact a gesture of respect to the "god" within the other. The younger pastors were unaware of any such tradition behind the bow, and saw it as a simple gesture of respect and greeting, comparable to a Western handshake.

In attempting to give a biblical response to the issues surrounding ancestor worship, the easiest answer one might choose would be total accommodation on the one hand, or outright rejection on the other. Thankfully, the more common response has been to steer a course between these two extremes, but this is also obviously the more complex and challenging choice. To find biblical answers to the challenges of ancestor veneration requires hard work, and I will present eight areas below that I believe constitute some of the main challenges that surround ancestral rites. I will use the context of Japan for the sake of illustration, but there will be carryover to other Asian societies as well.

First, there is the fact that the rites are tied into the *ie* (household) system. The household is perhaps the closest thing to an "eternal" part of Japanese existence. The tradition of the founders of the *ie* is passed down through the generations, and thus the measure of one's moral conduct is inextricably bound to how well one upholds the traditions of the forefathers. Regardless of any possible changes in legal obligation, loyalty to the *ie* remains one's ethic.[529] We must be careful to respect these ties. One partial solution is to communicate how being a better son or daughter, wife or husband, citizen or worker is a better way to demonstrate respect and loyalty to the *ie*. Our primary focus needs to shift from the dead to the living, while still showing respect for and honor to the dead.

The second challenge involves the fact that the ancestral rites serve a purpose of joining the living with the dead. A Japanese friend once told me that he often felt his deceased father's presence in his life and that he often turned to his father for advice and guidance in his business. Dr. Shuichi Kato, an outstanding literary critic, points out the example of how the survivors of the atomic blast at Hiroshima found peace of mind in literally talking to their family members who had died in the blast. Commenting on this same phenomenon, Chizuo Shibata wrote,

> This sense of being in unity with the dead fuels ancestor worship. Outwardly it is an act of the living talking to the dead in prayer for the repose of the souls of the latter. But on the contrary, often the living pray for the protection of the dead. Consequently, it is thought that ancestor worship should not be neglected by anyone. The dead watch over the living and offer aid and protection according to their needs.[530]

An oft-quoted survey by David L. Doerner, a Roman Catholic priest at a well-established church in Yokohama, was conducted in 1974 among 100 members. In reply to the question, "Where do you believe your ancestors are now?", only three responded with the answer, "Heaven." Sixty-one respondents, however, answered, "They are near," "They are around us," "They are always guarding and helping us." In this, it is evident that even in the Christian community there is near unanimity with the usual Japanese view of the dead.[531] The strength of this feeling is borne out in practices where the Catholic Church has encouraged a remembering of the departed on November 2nd, and in the process discovered that most Japanese Catholics continue to remember their departed on the traditional Japanese holidays set aside for doing so. It is not hard to imagine that from a Japanese perspective, if you want to give evidence that Christians can also demonstrate respect for the dead, you will want to do this when everyone else is doing so.

A third challenge we might look at may seem a truism, and yet it is an important aspect for Christians to consider, and that is that there is congruence between the form and the meaning of the rites. The *bosan* (rites at the grave) are miniaturized in the rites at the *butsudan* (household altar). Both communicate the joining of the living and the dead. Even if we were able to separate certain religious elements from non-religious elements, we must not mistakenly think that so-called "non-religious" elements can simply be transferred over into Christianity. We will still have to determine whether such borrowing will yield an integration of Christian doctrine and cultic practice, or agreement of form and content/meaning. As Jan-Martin Berentsen put it, "Forms are adopted and employed with the purpose of conveying a content."[532]

Fourthly, in ancestor rites, a person directs veneration or worship to the ancestors, not to God. Japanese look to their ancestors for aid. This conflicts with the biblical direction to worship God alone. If veneration is to happen, it must express only an honoring of the ancestors. The Church has a biblical obligation to fulfill the duty of helping believers to *honor* ancestors, and to do so in a better way, while *worshiping* God alone.

Fifthly, the rites communicate a caring for the departed, and ensure a type of assurance against offending the spirit, or polluting the ancestors or the family in some way. From the departed's final breath to the final anniversary, there are definite stages that one must pass through. Much of this seems totally arbitrary, and in this decades-long ritual process, undoubtedly there is a secondary assurance for the financial security of Buddhism. The expense of caring for the dead in Japan is a frequent topic in literature and cinema. In the funeral of one of our members, Taeko Kaneda, her family responded to us in shock and disbelief when we served them with six services (as is customary in Buddhism) over two days at no charge, simply because Taeko was a member of the church. Although there was a great deal of skepticism from this Buddhist family when her Buddhist husband first asked us to do the funeral in her honor, there was also a great deal of joy and comfort in their discovery that Taeko was already in the presence of *Kami-sama* (God) in heaven. They were also pleased to hear that her spirit would find final rest without being subjected to decades of dependence upon family survivors performing the various Buddhist rites. The Christian funeral offers a wonderful opportunity for a powerful witness to the hope of the gospel of Jesus Christ. We can address the needs of families in grief in powerful ways by adopting familiar cultural forms of service, by showing true caring during the funeral and by performing memorial services on anniversary dates that specifically honor the departed. When a proper grave site proves too expensive for one church to manage, groups of churches have cooperatively purchased a grave site, giving opportunity for their churches to show honor for their dead in ways beyond what would otherwise be possible.

After the funeral, the family remains tied to the ancestors through the *butsudan* (Buddhist altar), mentioned above. At the *butsudan*, one affirms one's identity, and ensures that he or she is still a member of *this* family. The altar serves as a symbol of the link one has with a specific group. This is illustrated in a conversation I had with the father of a woman who wanted to receive baptism. As we moved from discussing her baptism to the possibility of his own conversion, he informed me that he was the *chonan* in the family, the eldest son. To him fell the obligation to house the family *butsudan*. As the conversation progressed, he posed the possible solution of having a Christian form of the *butsudan*. Rather than utilizing it for the worship of ancestors, he suggested that one could hang a scroll with a Bible verse on it, and place a Bible on the altar in place of the normal Buddhist accoutrements. In this space he could have daily Bible readings and prayer—devotion to God in place of devotion to the ancestors. His next statement was revealing, "Then, when my relatives come to visit, I would still have an altar to show them." For him, having *any* kind of an altar would serve as symbol enough that he was still performing his duty as the *chonan*, a symbol that he was still maintaining the family ties. The challenge in such a solution would be the maintaining of proper congruity between form and content within the parameters of biblical teaching.

The most important expression of ancestral rites, however, is the rites at the grave site, of which the *butsudan* is a copy in miniature. My experience in Japan has led me to believe that younger pastors have a harder time than older pastors in grasping the importance of these rites. However, this issue is paramount to older Japanese; the fact that Buddhism has seen funerals and ancestral rites turn into an extremely profitable industry gives testimony to this. Churches must face the issue head on, and some churches are doing so cooperatively, even among churches of several denominations. Such collaboration between church groups is an ideal way to show respect for the dead on a scale not possible otherwise, and it has the added benefit of communicating the unity of the Church in spite of denominational differences. It returns ecumenism back into its historic missiological context.

Lastly, the *ihai*, or mortuary tablet, is considered by many to enshrine the spirit of the departed. This item is one form that is loaded with content specific to ancestral worship. The Jesuits in China developed an *ihai* that had Bible verses on it and a Christian symbol, and yet one can easily see how this would have sparked controversy. Donald McGavran suggested that an alternative, such as a display of the names of the ancestors along with some information about them might serve the intent of filial piety without the religious overtones.[533] Some churches have rooms where photographs of deceased members are hung, and thus remembered.

The Western Church has struggled for quite some time for a solution to this issue, and Asian Christians themselves have not found a satisfactory answer. Ultimately, we must let them come to a resolution on the problem. The solution must be an Asian solution for an Asian church. We can be encouraged that the Church has found a beachhead in Asia, and has endured in spite of long periods of persecution. In some parts of Asia, the period of persecution is in the past. Let us remember the hundreds of years that were required for Buddhism to be an equal player in many of these countries. Christianity is still relatively young in the region. The Church too must patiently progress through the steps that we observed were necessary for Buddhism. Major differences will have to be resolved in ways that do not compromise the Scriptural truths of the faith. Our methods will have to remain flexible in order to respond to the varying needs of Asian populations. Linguistic barriers are already largely overcome, and yet with the addressing of cultural barriers needs to be ongoing, with more and more responsibility resting with indigenous believers for indigenous solutions to the multiple challenges. The political and economic issues will vary from time to time, and although Christianity must seek to gain acceptance by all classes, it must avoid overt political ties, as history has shown us that while government can serve as a friend, it can just as easily turn foe.

One area that still needs a great deal work is the penetration of the gospel at all levels of society. In Buddhist history, this meant penetrating the arts, and the many-faceted cultural aspects of a people. In Japan, Christian influence has been out of proportion to its small numbers as far as producing many national leaders. Also, a couple of prominent authors arose in the twentieth century: Shusaku Endo and Ayako Miura. A Japanese print artist, Sadao Watanabe has also gained international recognition. Others are increasingly becoming known. Turning to the Chinese world, we have the outstanding example of He Qi, who is incorporating strong Chinese images into his biblically-themed prints and etchings. He also provides Internet links to sites of other Asian artists. In South Korea, there is a Campus Crusade for Christ dance troupe that does an excellent job of using traditional dance and costume to communicate the gospel. Much more needs to be done through cultural arts, perhaps in music and sculpture for example. The Church needs to communicate, as was often the case with Buddhism, that it is *for* the people, *for* the nation, and that it has more to offer than personal salvation. In demonstrations of the fullness of the Kingdom, we need to see the transformation of whole societies as part of our goal; and yet, the transformation of the individual is still the foundational building material of such a goal. The gospel contains the power to transform individuals and whole societies. Let us pray the Lord of the Harvest to raise up such people-movements in Asia, that will produce an Asian church with an Asian identity, which will in turn link arms with the Church world-wide in embracing all of humanity in Jesus Christ.

Such a goal must find its ground and source not in the Church, but in the world-embracing heart of God: *missio Dei*. Aside from being the only proper ground and source for mission, it is also the only overarching and universal norm, revealed to us in the Bible, that can unite the Church as a whole.[534] However, when the *ground and source* of the work of missions is located in the Church, the problem becomes "which church?" Is "the Church" the church that we see in Europe, in America, in Singapore or in South Africa? Who defines it? Who gets to be the model? Of course, there is no one single form and expression of the Church today, since people who live in many and various types of cultures make up the Church.

Moreover, when the Church is also the *goal* of the work of missions, the various expressions of the Church come into competition, and the focal point of the work becomes the growth and preservation of traditions and institutions of power, rather than serving the people that God wants to embrace. However, when instead the ground and source of missions is *missio Dei*, when the goal of missions is the increase of the fullness of the Kingdom of God, the Church then properly becomes the primary means by which God actively reveals His heart, opposes all forms of evil, and works healing in the world. The Church lives to be in relationship with God, and to invite the world into the Christ-won relationship with the One who has chosen to "embrace that which should not be embraced." As God has sent the Son and the Holy Spirit (the original meaning of *missio*), so today He sends the Body of Christ, the Church, into the world. The proper way of doing missions is the way of Christ, who came not to be served, but to serve, and to give His life a ransom for many.

Such a Church is a world-embracing Church that unites around the person of Jesus Christ who died and rose again that the world might have eternal life. It is Church that is truly ecumenical, that has taken the U-turn, and received the righteousness of Christ not simply for itself, but that it might also live to serve the other in Christ's Name. Such a Church may at times appear weak and vulnerable in the eyes of the world. Yet, it is in that very weakness that God will ultimately reveal His strength. The power of earthly kingdoms, or that of global enterprise, is powerless to transform, and is only temporal. The true Church goes beyond all of these, in the power of the gospel that "is the power of God for the salvation, of everyone who believes: first for the Jew, then for the Gentile" (Romans 1:16).

Works Cited

Allen, Roland. *Missionary Methods: St Paul's or Ours?* Grand Rapids, MI: Wm. B. Eerdmans Pub. Co., 1962.
Ambedkar, Ramji. *Writings and Speeches*, vol. 3. Edited by Vasant Moon. Bombay: Education Employment Department, 1987.
Amjad-Ali, Charles. *Passion for Change: Reflections on the Healing Miracles in St. Mark.* Rawalpindi, Pakistan: Christian Study Centre, 1989.
Anesaki, Masaharu. *History of Japanese Religion, with a Special Reference to the Social and Moral Life of the Nation.* Rutland, VT: Charles E. Tuttle Company, 1963.
Aram I. "The Incarnation of the Gospel in Cultures: A Missionary Event." In *New Directions in Mission and Evangelization 3: Faith and Culture*, ed. Stephen B. Bevans and James A. Scherer, 29-41. Maryknoll, NY: Orbis Books, 1999.
Atiya, Aziz. *A History of Eastern Christianity.* Notre Dame: University of Notre Dame Press, 1969.
Barrett, David. *Cosmos, Chaos, and Gospel: A Chronology of World Evangelization from Creation to New Creation.* Birmingham, AL: New Hope, 1987.
Barth, Karl. *Church and State.* Translated by G. Ronald Howe. Greenville, SC: Smyth & Helwys, 1991.
BBC. "Buddhism 'in decline,'" April 7, 1998. http://news.bbc.co.uk/2/hi/asia-pacific/75325.stm. Accessed Sept. 15, 2003.
Bechert, Heinz. "The Buddhist Community and Its Earlier History." In Hans Küng et al., *Christianity and the World Religions: Paths to Dialogue with Islam, Hinduism, and Buddhism.* Translated by Peter Heinegg, 329-339. Garden City, NY: Doubleday & Co., Inc., 1986.
Berentsen, Jan-Martin. "Ancestor Worship in Missiological Perspective." In *Christian Alternatives to Ancestor Practices*, ed. Bong Rin Ro, 261-285. Taichung, Taiwan, ROC: Asia Theological Association, 1985.
_____. "The Ancestral Rites—Barrier or Bridge." In *Christian Alternatives to Ancestor Practices*, ed. Bong Rin Ro, 287-301. Taichung, Taiwan, ROC: Asia Theological Association, 1985.
Beyerhaus, Peter. *Missions: Which Way? Humanization or Redemption.* Grand Rapids, MI: Zondervan, 1971.
Boniface VIII. *Unam Sanctum.* Papal Bull of Pope Boniface VIII, November 18, 1302. http://www.papalencyclicals.net/Bon08/B8unam.htm (ac2Response. Wilmore, KY: Bristol Books, 1987.
Bonino, José Miguez. *Doing Theology in a Revolutionary Situation.* Philadelphia: Fortress Press, 1975.
The Book of Concord: The Confessions of the Evangelical Lutheran Church. Edited by Robert Kolb and Timothy J. Wengert. Minneapolis, MN: Fortress Press, 2000.
Bosch, David. *Transforming Mission: Paradigm Shifts in Theology of Mission.* Maryknoll, NY: Orbis Books, 1991.
Bowers, Paul. "Church and Mission in Paul." *Journal for the Study of the New Testament* 44 (December 1991): 89-111.
Brock, Sebastian. *Perspectives on Late Antiquity.* Burlington, VT: Ashgate Pub. Co., 1984.
_____. *Studies in Syrian Christianity.* Brookfield, VT: Ashgate Pub. Co., 1992.

Buswell, Robert Evans, Jr. "Buddhism: Buddhism in Korea." In *The Encyclopedia of Religion*, ed. Mircea Eliade, 2:421-426. New York: Macmillan Pub. Co., 1987.

Cary-Elwes, Columba. *China and the Cross: A Survey of Missionary History*. New York: P. J. Kennedy & Sons, 1957.

Ch'en, Kenneth K. S. *Buddhism in China: A Historical Survey*. Princeton, NJ: Princeton University Press, 1964.

_____. *The Chinese Transformation of Buddhism*. Princeton, NJ: Princeton University Press, 1973.

Covell, Ralph R. *Confucius, the Buddha, and Christ: A History of the Gospel in Chinese*. Maryknoll, NY: Orbis, 1986.

DeSilva, Lynn A. "Theological Construction in a Buddhist Context." In *Asian Voices in Christian Theology*, ed. J. N. D. Anderson, 31-52. Maryknoll, NY: Orbis Books, 1976.Dohi, Akio. "The First Generation." In *A History of Japanese Theology*, ed. Yasuo Furuya, 11-42. Grand Rapids, MI: Wm. B. Eerdmans Pub. Co.,1997.

_____. "Historical Development of the Non-Church Movement in Japan." *Journal of Ecumenical Studies* 2, no. 3 (Fall 1965): 452-468.

Drummond, Richard H. "The Non-Church Movement in Japan," *Journal of Ecumenical Studies* 2, no. 3 (Fall 1965): 448-451.

DuBose, Francis M., ed. *Classics of Christian Missions*. Nashville, TN: Broadman Press, 1979.

Ehrman, Bart D. *After the New Testament: A Reader in Early Christianity*. New York: Oxford University Press, 1999.

Elwell, Walter A., ed. *Baker Encyclopedia of the Bible*. Grand Rapids, MI: Baker Books, 1988.

Endo, Shusaku. *The Golden Country*. Translated by Francis Mathy. Rutland, VT: Charles E. Tuttle Company, 1970.

_____. *Silence*. Translated by William Johnston. Rutland, VT: Charles E. Tuttle Company, 1969.

Engle, Paul E., and Gary L. McIntosh, ed. *Evaluating the Church Growth Movement*. Grand Rapids, MI: Zondervan, 2004.

Escobar, Samuel. "The Global Scenario at the Turn of the Century." In *Global Missiology for the 21st Century*, ed. William D. Taylor, 25-46. Grand Rapids, MI: Baker Academic, 2000.

Eusebius. *The History of the Church from Christ to Constantine*. Translated by G. A. Williamson. New York: Barnes and Noble Books, 1995.

Fleming, Bruce C. E. *Contextualization of Theology: An Evangelical Assessment*. Pasadena, CA: William Carey Library, 1980.

Gaede, S. D. *When Tolerance Is No Virtue: Political Correctness, Multiculturalism & the Future of Truth & Justice*. Downers Grove, IL: InterVarsity Press, 1993.

González, Justo L. *The Early Church to the Dawn of the Reformation*. Vol. 1 of *The Story of Christianity*. New York: Harper and Row, 1984.

Grayson, James Huntly. *Early Buddhism and Christianity in Korea: A Study in the Emplantation of Religion*. Leiden, Netherlands: E. J. Brill, 1985.

Gurukul Theological Research Group. *A Christian Theological Approach to Hinduism*. Madras, India: The Christian Literature Society, 1956.

Gutiérrez, Gustavo. *A Theology of Liberation: History, Politics, and Salvation*, 15th anniv. ed. Translated and edited by Caridad Inda and John Eagleson. Maryknoll, NY: Orbis Books, 1988.

Hage, Wolfgang. *Syriac Christianity in the East*. Kerala, India: St. Ephrem Ecumenical Research Institute, St. Joseph's Press, 1988.

Hanayama, Shinsho. *A History of Japanese Buddhism*. Translated by Kosho Yamamoto, Tokyo: CIIB Press, 1960.

Herrin, Judith. *The Formation of Christendom*. Princeton, NJ: Princeton University Press, 1987.

Hiebert, Paul. "Critical Contextualization." *International Bulletin of Missionary Research* 11 (July 1987): 104-112.

Hopfe, Lewis M., and Mark R. Woodward. *Religions of the World*, 9th ed. Upper Saddle River, NJ: Pearson Prentice Hall, 2004.

Hori, Ichirō. *Japanese Religion: A Survey by the Agency for Cultural Affairs*. Palo Alto, CA; Tokyo: Kodansha International Ltd., 1972.

Hughes, E. R., and K. Hughes. *Religion in China*. London: Hutchinson's University Library, 1950.

Hundley, Raymond C. *Radical Liberation Theology: An Evangelical Response*. Wilmore, KY: Bristol Books, 1987.

Hunt, Everett N., Jr. *Protestant Pioneers in Korea*. Maryknoll, NY: Orbis Books, 1980.

Jenkins, Philip. *The Next Christendom: The Coming of Global Christianity*. New York: Oxford University Press, 2002.

Kärkkäinen, Veli-Matti. *An Introduction to Ecclesiology*. Downers Grove, IL: InterVarsity Press, 2002.

Kitagawa, Joseph M. *The Christian Tradition: Beyond Its European Captivity*. Philadelphia: Trinity Press International, 1992.

_____. *On Understanding Japanese Religion*. Princeton, NJ: Princeton University Press, 1987.

_____. *Religions of the East*. Philadelphia: Westminster Press, 1960.

Kitamori, Kazoh. *Theology of the Pain of God*. Translated by M. E. Bratcher. Richmond, VA: John Knox Press, 1965.

Koyama, Kosuke. "Rejoice in Hope." In *Together on the Way: Official Report of the Eighth Assembly of the World Council of Churches*, ed. Diane Kessler. Geneva: World Council of Churches, 1999.

_____. *Waterbuffalo Theology*. Maryknoll, NY: Orbis Books, 1974.

_____. "What Makes a Missionary? Toward Crucified Mind, Not Crusading Mind." In *Mission Trends No. 1*, ed. Gerald H. Anderson and Thomas F. Stransky, 117-132. New York: Paulist Press, 1974.

Latourette, Kenneth Scott. *The Great Century: North Africa and Asia, A.D. 1800-A.D. 1914*. Vol. 6 of *A History of the Expansion of Christianity*. Grand Rapids, MI: Zondervan, 1970.

_____. *A History of Christianity, Volume 1: Beginnings to 1500*. San Francisco: HarperSanFrancisco, 1975.

Luther, Martin. "On the Bondage of the Will." In *Luther and Erasmus: Free Will and Salvation*, ed. Gordon E. Rupp and Philip S. Watson, 101-334. Philadelphia: The Westminster Press, 1969.

Maalouf, Amin. *In the Name of Identity: Violence and the Need to Belong*. New York: Arcade Publishing, 2001.

Malech, G. D. *History of the Syrian Nation and the Old Evangelical-Apostolic Church of the East*. Minneapolis, MN: private printing, 1910.

Mangalwadi, Vishal. *The Quest for Freedom and Dignity: Caste, Conversion and Cultural Revolution*. Mumbai, India: GLS Publishing, 2001.

Martinson, Paul Varo. Lecture in Christian Theology in Asia course, CM8499. Luther Seminary, Spring 1999.

Matsumoto, Shigeru. "Introduction." In *Japanese Religion: A Survey by the Agency for Cultural Affairs*, ed. Hori Ichiro et al., 11-27. Translated by Abe Yoshiya and David Reid. Palo Alto, CA; Tokyo: Kodansha International Ltd., 1972.

McDermott, Gerald R. *Can Evangelicals Learn From World Religions? Jesus, Revelation and Religious Traditions*. Downers Grove, IL: InterVarsity Press, 2000.

McGavran, Donald. *The Bridges of God: A Study in the Strategy of Missions*. New York: Friendship Press, 1955.

_____. "Honoring Ancestors in Japan." In *Christian Alternatives to Ancestor Practices*, ed. Bong Rin Ro, 303-318. Taichung, Taiwan, ROC: Asia Theological Association, 1985.

McGiffert, Arthur Cushman. *Early and Eastern: From Jesus to John of Damascus*. Vol. 1 of *A History of Christian Thought*. New York: Charles Scribner's Sons, 1950.

Miller, Allan L. "Religions of China, Japan, and India: Dynastic Change and the Three Traditions." In *Religions of the World*, 2d ed., ed. Niels C. Nielsen et al., 284-298. New York: St. Martin's Press, 1988.

Mingana, Alphonse. "The Early Spread of Christianity in Central Asia and the Far East: A New Document." *Bulletin of the John Rylands Library, Manchester* 9 (1925): 297-371.

"The Missionary Obligation of the Church." Proceedings of the International Missionary Council in Willingen, Germany, July 5-17, 1952. London: Edinburgh House Press, 1952.

Miyazaki, Kentaro. "Roman Catholic Mission in Pre-Modern Japan." In *Handbook of Christianity in Japan*, ed. Mark R. Mullins, 1-18. Leiden, Netherlands; Boston: Brill, 2003.

Moffett, Samuel. *A History of Christianity in Asia, Volume I: Beginnings to 1500*. Maryknoll, NY: Orbis Books, 2001.

_____. *A History of Christianity in Asia, Volume II: 1500-1900*. Maryknoll, NY: Orbis Books, 2005.

Moltmann, Jürgen. "Die Befreiung der Unterdruecker." *Evangelische Theologie* 38 (1978): 527-538.

_____. *The Church in the Power of the Spirit*. Translated by Margaret Kohl. Minneapolis, MN: Fortress Press, 1993.

_____. *The Experiment Hope*. Translated by M. Douglas Meeks. Philadelphia: Fortress Press, 1975.

_____. *History and the Triune God: Contributions to Trinitarian Theology*. Translated by John Bowden. New York: Crossroad, 1992.

_____. *Jesus Christ for Today's World*. Translated by Margaret Kohl. Minneapolis, MN: Fortress Press, 1994.

_____. "On Latin American Liberation Theology: An Open Letter to José Miguez Bonino." *Christianity and Crisis* 36, no. 5 (March 29, 1976): 57-63.

_____. "Perichoresis: An Old Magic Word for a New Trinitarian Theology." In *Trinity, Community, and Power: Mapping Trajectories in Wesleyan Theology*, ed. M. Douglas Meeks, 111-125. Nashville, TN: Kingswood Books, 2000.

_____. *Theology of Hope: On the Ground and the Implications of a Christian Eschatology*. Translated by James W. Leitch. New York: Harper and Row, 1967.

Moreau, A. Scott, Gary R. Corwin, and Gary B. McGee. *Introducing World Missions: A Biblical, Historical, and Practical Survey*. Grand Rapids, MI: Baker Academic, 2004.

Nakamura, Hajime. *Ways of Thinking of Eastern Peoples: India, China, Tibet and Japan*, rev. English trans. Edited by Philip P. Wiener. Honolulu: East-West Center, 1964.

Neill, Stephen. *A History of Christian Missions*. New York: Penguin Books, 1986.

Nelson, Richard D. *First and Second Kings*. Atlanta: John Knox Press, 1987.

Nestorius. *The Bazaar of Heracleides*. Edited and translated by G. R. Driver and L. Hodgson. Oxford: Oxford University Press, 1925.

Newbigin, Lesslie. *Mission in Christ's Way: A Gift, a Command, an Assurance*. New York: Friendship Press, 1987.

Niebuhr, H. Richard. *Christ and Culture*. New York: Harper and Row, 1951.

Noll, Mark. "Evangelical Identity, Power, and Culture in the 'Great' Nineteenth Century." In *Christianity Reborn: The Global Expansion of Evangelicalism in the Twentieth Century*, ed. Donald M. Lewis, 31-51. Grand Rapids, MI: Wm. B. Eerdmans Pub. Co., 2004.

Nùñez C., Emilio A. *Liberation Theology*. Translated by Paul E. Sywulka. Chicago: Moody Press, 1985.

O'Brien, P. T. *Gospel and Mission in the Writings of Paul: An Exegetical and Theological Analysis*. Grand Rapids, MI: Baker Books, 1995.

Peters, George W. *A Biblical Theology of Missions*. Chicago: Moody, 1972.

Pieris, Aloysius. *Fire and Water: Basic Issues in Asian Buddhism and Christianity*. Maryknoll, NY: Orbis Books, 1996.

Rad, Gerhard von. *God at Work in Israel*. Translated by John H. Marks. Nashville, TN: Abingdon, 1980.

Reischauer, E. O., and J. K. Fairbank. *East Asia the Great Tradition*. Tokyo: Charles E. Tuttle Company, 1926.

Reynolds, Frank E. "Buddhism: Buddhism as a World Religion." In *Religions of the World*, 2d ed., ed. Niels Nielsen et al., 233-259. New York: St. Martin's Press, 1988.

_____. "Buddhism: The Three Main Traditions." In *Religions of the World*, 2d ed., ed. Niels Nielsen et al., 214-232. New York: St. Martin's Press, 1988.

Richardson, Don. *Eternity in Their Hearts*, rev. ed. Ventura, CA: Regal Books, 1984.

Ro, Bong Rin, ed. *Christian Alternatives to Ancestor Practices*. Taichung, Taiwan, ROC: Asia Theological Association, 1985.

Roberts, Alexander, and James Donaldson, eds. *The Ante-Nicene Fathers: Translations of the Writings of the Fathers down to A.D. 325*. Vol. 1, *The Apostolic Fathers with Justin Martyr and Irenaeus*. Grand Rapids, MI: Wm. B. Eerdmans Pub. Co., 1950.

Robinson, Charles Henry. *History of Christian Missions*. New York: Charles Scribner's Sons, 1915.

Ross, Andrew C. *A Vision Betrayed: The Jesuits in Japan and China, 1542-1742*. Maryknoll, NY: Orbis Books, 1994.

Sanneh, Lamin. *Translating the Message: The Missionary Impact on Culture*. Maryknoll, NY: Orbis Books, 1997.

_____. *Whose Religion Is Christianity?: The Gospel Beyond the West*. Grand Rapids, MI: Wm. B. Eerdmans Pub. Co., 2003.

Scherer, James A. *Gospel, Church, and Kingdom: Comparative Studies in World Mission Theology*. Minneapolis, MN: Augsburg Publishing House, 1987.

_____. "Lutheran Mission." In *Evangelical Dictionary of World Missions*, ed. A. Scott Moreau, 586. Grand Rapids, MI: Baker Books, 2000.

Scherer, James A., and Stephen B. Bevans, ed. *New Directions in Mission & Evangelization 1*. Maryknoll, NY: Orbis Books, 1992.

Schillebeeckx, Edward. *Christ: The Experience of Jesus as Lord*. Translated by Hubert Hoskins. New York: Seabury Press, 1979.

_____. *Jesus: An Experiment in Christology*. Translated by John Bowden. New York: Seabury, Press, 1979.

Schineller, Peter. "Inculturation: A Difficult and Delicate Task." *International Bulletin of Missionary Research* 20, no. 3 (July 1996): 109-10, 112.

Scholasticus, Socrates. "The Ecclesiastical History of Socrates Scholasticus." In *Nicene and Post-Nicene Fathers of the Christian Church*, 2d series, Vol. II, ed. Philip Schaff and Henry Wace, 1-178. Grand Rapids, MI: Wm. B. Eerdmans Pub. Co., 1952.

Schreiter, Robert J. "Changes in Roman Catholic Attitudes toward Proselytism and Mission." In *New Directions in Mission & Evangelization 2: Theological Foundations*, ed. by James A. Scherer and Stephen B. Bevans, 113-125. Maryknoll, NY: Orbis Books, 1994.

_____. "Contextualization from a World Perspective." In *Ministry & Theology in Global Perspective: Contemporary Challenges for the Church*, ed. Don A. Pittman, Ruben L. F. Habito, and Terry C. Muck, 315-327. Grand Rapids, MI: Wm. B. Eerdmans Pub. Co., 1996.

_____. *The New Catholicity: Theology Between the Global and the Local*. Maryknoll, NY: Orbis Books, 1997.

Shi (Shih), Hu. "The Indianization of China: A Case Study in Cultural Borrowing." In *Independence, Convergence, and Borrowing*, ed. Charles H. Dodd, 219-247. Cambridge, MA: Harvard University Press, 1937.

Shibata, Chizuo. "Some Problematic Aspects of Ancestor Worship." In *Christian Alternatives to Ancestor Practices*, ed. Bong Rin Ro, 247-260. Taichung, Taiwan, ROC: Asia Theological Association, 1985.

Shorter, Aylward. *Toward a Theology of Inculturation*. Maryknoll, NY: Orbis Books, 1988.

Smith, Huston. *The World's Religions: Our Great Wisdom Tradition*. New York: HarperSanFrancisco, 1991.

Song, Choan-Seng. *The Compassionate God*. Maryknoll, NY: Orbis Books, 1982.

_____. *Third Eye Theology*. Maryknoll, NY: Orbis Books, 1979.

Stewart, John. *Nestorian Missionary Enterprise*. Edinburgh: T. & T. Clark, 1928.

Sugden, Christopher. "Placing Critical Issues in Relief." In *Mission in Bold Humility: David Bosch's Work Considered*, ed. Willem Saayman and Klippies Kritzinger, 139-150. Maryknoll, NY: Orbis Books, 1996.

Suh, David Kwang-sun. *The Korean Minjung in Christ*. Hong Kong: The Christian Conference of Asia, 1991.

Tamaru, Noriyoshi. "Buddhism." In *Japanese Religion: A Survey by the Agency for Cultural Affairs*, ed. Hori Ichiro et al. Translated by Abe Yoshiya and David Reid, 43-62. Palo Alto, CA; Tokyo: Kodansha International Ltd., 1972.

Tippet, Alan. *Introduction to Missiology*. Pasadena, CA: William Carey Library, 1987.

Tucker, Ruth. *From Jerusalem to Irian Jaya: A Biographical History of Christian Missions*, 2d ed. Grand Rapids, MI: Zondervan, 1983.

Uchimura, Kanzo. *How I Became a Christian*. Vol. 15, *The Works of Uchimura*. Tokyo: Kyobunkwan, 1895.

Upkong, Justin. "What is Contextualization?" *Neue Zeitschrift für Missionswissenschaft* 43 (1987): 161-168.

Van Engen, Charles. *God's Missionary People: Rethinking the Purpose of the Local Church*. Grand Rapids, MI: Baker Books, 1995.

_____. *Mission on the Way: Issues in Mission Theology*. Grand Rapids, MI: Baker Books, 1996.

Van Gelder, Craig. "Gospel and Our Culture View." In *Evaluating the Church Growth Movement*, ed. Paul E. Engle and Gary L. McIntosh, 73-120. Grand Rapids, MI: Zondervan, 2004.

Verkuyl, Johannes. *Contemporary Missiology: An Introduction*. Translated by Dale Cooper. Grand Rapids, MI: Wm. B. Eerdmans Pub. Co., 1978.

Vicedom, Georg F. *The Mission of God: An Introduction to a Theology of Mission*. Translated by Gilbert A. Thiele and Dennis Hilgendorf. St. Louis: Concordia Publishing House, 1965.

Vööbus, Arthur. *History of Asceticism in the Syrian Orient: A Contribution to the History of Culture in the Near East*, vol. 1. Louvain, Belgium: Secretariat du CorpusSCO, 1960.

Wigram, W. A. *An Introduction to the History of the Assyrian Church of the Sassanid Persian Empire 100-640 A.D.* London: S.P.C.K., 1910.

Winter, Ralph D. "The Task Remaining: All Humanity in Mission Perspective." In *Perspectives on the World Christian Movement: A Reader*, rev. ed., ed. Ralph D. Winter and Steven C. Hawthorne, B:176-B:183. Pasadena, CA: William Carey Library, 1992.

"The World Mission of the Church: Findings and Recommendations of the International Missionary Council." Proceedings of the International Missionary Council, Tambaram, Madras, India, December 12th-29th, 1938. New York: International Missionary Council, 1939.

Yamamoto, Kosho. *A History of Japanese Buddhism*. Tokyo: CIIB Press, 1960.

Yong, Amos. "Discerning the Spirit(s) in the World of Religions: Toward a Pneumatological Theology of Religions." In *No Other Gods Before Me?*, ed. John G. Stackhouse, Jr., 37-61. Grand Rapids, MI: Baker Academic, 2001.

Young, John M. L. *By Foot to China*. Tokyo: Radiopress, 1984.

_____. *The Two Empires in Japan*. Philadelphia: The Presbyterian and Reformed Publishing Co., 1961.

Young, William A. *The World's Religions: World Views and Contemporary Issues*, 2d ed. Upper Saddle River, NJ: Pearson Education, Inc., 2005.

Zürcher, Erik. *The Buddhist Conquest of China: The Spread and Adaptation of Buddhism in Early Medieval China*. Leiden, Netherlands: E. J. Brill, 1959.

Endnotes

[1]"The Missionary Obligation of the Church," Proceedings of the International Missionary Council in Willingen, Germany, July 5-17, 1952 (London: Edinburgh House Press, 1952), 2.

[2]South Korea would, of course, be a notable exception.

[3]Although the word "mission" often denotes all the Church does to point toward the Kingdom of God, in this thesis it will appear as a synonym of *missio Dei*, unless otherwise designated. It will refer to the saving activity of God in mission, while implying that the Church is a God-ordained, and therefore essential, partner and participant in this activity. A primary goal of this saving activity is conversion to Jesus Christ. Consequently, this activity is not synonymous with the Kingdom of God, which refers more broadly to God's reign and the manifestations of that reign over all of creation. Thus, while the terms are inseparable, they do not refer to the same thing. For example, following the Ghana meeting of the IMC (1957-1958), Eric W. Nielsen wrote, "We have not said that everything the Church does is Mission, but we have said that in the very existence of the Church, and therefore in everything that the Church says and is and does, there must be a 'missionary perspective.'" Cited in James A. Scherer, *Gospel, Church, and Kingdom: Comparative Studies in World Mission Theology* (Minneapolis, MN: Augsburg Publishing House, 1987), 101.

[4]Chapter 4 will present some of the details of this phenomenon. Although recognized as one of the greatest, if not the greatest mission movement of all time, this important legacy of the work of the Spirit through the Church of the East has not received proportionate treatment in our history texts. It is even more interesting when one considers the fact that this work took place through a so-called heretical movement, and during the time of rapid Islamic expansion. Further, if this kind of phenomenon was true of the East, how much more might this be true in the regions south of the Mediterranean? This area of missio-historical research has been largely neglected because of our preoccupation with the Western regions, but another reason for neglect is that much of the data from these movements has been lost, posing immense challenges for those wanting to understand more of these periods of mission history. For example, most of our knowledge of the Nestorian movement in China is taken from one source—the Nestorian monument. The above citation is from John M. L. Young, *By Foot to China* (Tokyo: Radiopress, 1984), 2.

[5]Alphonse Mingana, "The Early Spread of Christianity in Central Asia and the Far East: A New Document," *Bulletin of the John Rylands Library, Manchester* 9 (1925): 318.

[6]Ruth Tucker, *From Jerusalem to Irian Jaya: A Biographical History of Christian Missions*, 2d ed. (Grand Rapids, MI: Zondervan, 1983), 45.

[7]David Barrett, *Cosmos, Chaos, and Gospel: A Chronology of World Evangelization from Creation to New Creation* (Birmingham, AL: New Hope, 1987), 29, 96.

[8]Without getting into all of the technical discussion that has come out of the work of C. H. Dodd and others, suffice it to say that the word kerygma is used here in a specific sense, *viz.*, the gospel and

the preaching of the gospel. "In simplest outline the kerygma is made up of : (1) a proclamation of the death, resurrection, and exaltation of Jesus, seen as the fulfillment of prophecy and involving human responsibility; (2) the resultant evaluation of Jesus as both Lord and Christ; and (3) a summons to repent and receive forgiveness of sins." Walter A. Elwell, ed., *Baker Encyclopedia of the Bible*, s.v. "Kerygma."

[9] Scherer, *Gospel, Church, and Kingdom*, 61. Hereafter, GCK.

[10] Karl Barth, *Church and State*, trans. G. Ronald Howe (Greenville, SC: Smyth & Helwys, 1991), 61.

[11] Charles Van Engen, *Mission on the Way: Issues in Mission Theology* (Grand Rapids, MI: Baker Books, 1996), 22-26.

[12] Ibid., 22.

[13] See Jürgen Moltmann's discussion of the Trinity in "Perichoresis: An Old Magic Word for a New Trinitarian Theology," in *Trinity, Community, and Power: Mapping Trajectories in Wesleyan Theology*, ed. M. Douglas Meeks (Nashville, TN: Kingswood Books, 2000), 111-125. The perichoretic doctrine of the Trinity appears with some frequency in writings on a "missional" understanding of the Church. It lends itself well to the discussion of the role of Christian community in evangelization.

[14] Some examples of this are: Georg F. Vicedom, *The Mission of God: An Introduction to a Theology of Mission*, trans. Gilbert A. Thiele and Dennis Hilgendorf (St. Louis: Concordia Publishing House, 1965); Lesslie Newbigin, *Mission in Christ's Way: A Gift, a Command, an Assurance* (New York: Friendship Press, 1987); and James A. Scherer, GCK.

[15] Vicedom, *The Mission of God*, 4.

[16] David Bosch, *Transforming Mission: Paradigm Shifts in Theology of Mission*, (Maryknoll, NY: Orbis Books, 1991), 15, 16.

[17] Aram I, "The Incarnation of the Gospel in Cultures: A Missionary Event," in *New Directions in Mission and Evangelization 3: Faith and Culture*, ed. Stephen B. Bevans and James A. Scherer (Maryknoll, NY: Orbis Books, 1999), 38-39.

[18] Rooting the activities of the Church in the *missio Dei* brings to mind the oft-quoted statement by Stephen Neill that "If everything is mission, nothing is mission." See Charles Van Engen, *God's Missionary People: Rethinking the Purpose of the Local Church* (Grand Rapids: MI, Baker Books, 1991), 30. Charles Van Engen sees this statement as a reaction against the activism of the 1960s which defined the Church in terms of its contribution to social change. However, in Neill's missiology, there is a separation of Church and mission which works against the concept of mission defining the essence of the Church. While Van Engen rightly argues that the "essential nature of the local congregation is, in and of itself, mission" (Van Engen, *God's Missionary People*, 70), his insertion of Neill's view tends to bring more confusion than clarity to the discussion of the missional church. Neill was fighting against a secularization of mission, which rendered the Church irrelevant. However, defining the essence of the Church in terms of the larger framework of the *missio Dei* will serve to enhance the value of evangelism and mission because the Trinity, not the world, will set the agenda, and the activities of the Church will be carried out with the intent of impacting the world outside of itself for Christ. This paper argues that since the Church is the creation of the Holy Spirit for participation in God's mission, the essence and activities of the Church must find their *ground and source in* and be *informed by* the overarching theme and movement of the *missio Dei*.

[19] George W. Peters, *A Biblical Theology of Missions* (Chicago: Moody, 1972), 83-86.

[20] Bosch, *Transforming Mission*, 107. Hereafter, TM.

[21] There is a paradox in this receiving of the gracious and merciful gifts of God. In the receiving of the gift, there is certainly a sense in which one "owns" the gift that is freely received. And yet the Divine intent of the giving is not our hoarding or selfish enjoyment of the gift. One multiplies the gift in sharing it. Consider the parable of the talents in Matthew 25, or the distribution of the five loaves and two fishes to the crowds of thousands in Matthew 14 and 15. Private ownership is not to exclude sharing, and yet the act of sharing does not result in less, but in more for the owner. "And the disciples picked up twelve basketfuls of broken pieces that were left over" (Matt. 14:20).

[22] Choan-Seng Song, *The Compassionate God* (Maryknoll, NY: Orbis Books, 1982), 32-34.

[23] Gerhard von Rad, *God at Work in Israel*, trans. John H. Marks (Nashville, TN: Abingdon, 1980), 52.

[24] Richard D. Nelson, *First and Second Kings* (Atlanta: John Knox Press, 1987), 179.

[25] Ibid., 180.

[26] Jesus stopped short of reading further of the vengeance of God—something He curiously does in the gospels more than once. In so doing, He delivers a powerful statement: this is not the time for vengeance, but for mercy. See Bosch, TM, 110.

[27] Newbigin, *Mission in Christ's Way*, 18.

[28] Charles Amjad-Ali comments on this passage and others from Mark's Gospel in his *Passion for Change: Reflections on the Healing Miracles in St. Mark* (Rawalpindi, Pakistan: Christian Study Centre, 1989), 43-50.

[29] Kosuke Koyama, "Rejoice in Hope," in *Together on the Way: Official Report of the Eighth Assembly of the World Council of Churches*, ed. Diane Kessler (Geneva: World Council of Churches, 1999), 40.

[30] Kosuke Koyama, "What Makes a Missionary? Toward Crucified Mind, Not Crusading Mind," in *Mission Trends No. 1*, ed. Gerald H. Anderson and Thomas F. Stransky (New York: Paulist Press, 1974), 117-132.

[31] Ralph Winter uses these categories of E-1, E-2 and E-3 to illustrate the boundaries the gospel must cross at varying levels of culture. The primary meaning of this text is certainly the intended rippling effect of the gospel as it moves out from Jerusalem/Judea and makes its way around the world. At the same time, it is obvious that as the gospel ripples outward, the cultural/linguistic challenges will increase. Winter refers to this factor. See Ralph D. Winter, "The Task Remaining: All Humanity in Mission Perspective," in *Perspectives on the World Christian Movement: A Reader*, rev. ed., ed. Ralph D. Winter and Steven C. Hawthorne (Pasadena, CA: William Carey Library, 1992), B:176-B:183.

[32] Bosch, TM, 16-17.

[33] Ibid., 19.

[34] Christopher Sugden, "Placing Critical Issues in Relief," in *Mission in Bold Humility: David Bosch's Work Considered*, ed. Willem Saayman and Klippies Kritzinger (Maryknoll, NY: Orbis Books, 1996), 141-142.

[35] Roland Allen, *Missionary Methods: St Paul's or Ours?* (Grand Rapids, MI: Wm. B. Eerdmans Pub. Co, 1962), 62.

[36] Paul Bowers, "Church and Mission in Paul," *Journal for the Study of the New Testament* 44 (December 1991): 89-111.

[37] The idea of the atonement being definite, or limited to the elect, which is generally attributed to Calvin, has colored Reformed teaching and has continued to crop up as a stumbling block to mission activity over the centuries. For example, when William Carey presented his argument that the church was obligated to do mission work, his clerical colleagues replied that if it so pleased God to save the heathen, He could do so without our help. Charles Henry Robinson quotes Calvin as

[38] having written, "we are taught that the kingdom of Christ is neither to be advanced nor maintained by the industry of men, but this is the work of God alone." See Charles Henry Robinson, *History of Christian Missions* (New York: Charles Scribner's Sons, 1915), 43.

[38] Bosch, *TM*, 137-138.

[39] P. T. O'Brien, *Gospel and Mission in the Writings of Paul: An Exegetical and Theological Analysis* (Grand Rapids, MI: Baker Books, 1995), 83-91.

[40] Ibid., 94-97.

[41] Ibid., 113-114.

[42] Jürgen Moltmann, *Theology of Hope: On the Ground and the Implications of a Christian Eschatology*, trans. James W. Leitch (New York: Harper and Row, 1967), 193.

[43] Bosch, *TM*, 41.

[44] Ibid., 41.

[45] Bart D. Ehrman, *After the New Testament: A Reader in Early Christianity* (New York: Oxford University Press, 1999), 28-30.

[46] This "already/not yet" concept can be found in Bultmann, Barth, G. E. Ladd, Charles Van Engen and others, including Bosch in his treatment of *regnum Dei*.

[47] Charles Van Engen, *God's Missionary People: Rethinking the Purpose of the Local Church* (Grand Rapids, MI: Baker Books, 1995), 26-27.

[48] Barth, *Church and State*, 40.

[49] Arthur Cushman McGiffert, *Early and Eastern: From Jesus to John of Damascus*, vol. 1 of *A History of Christian Thought* (New York: Charles Scribner's Sons, 1950), 97.

[50] Missiologists still visit and revisit this concept today in debates over contextualization and syncretism. The next chapter will argue that alarm over syncretism to the extent that it excludes contextualization (in other words, the *tabula rasa* approach) will actually *produce* the kind of syncretism the missionary wishes to avoid. One must avoid the two extremes of elevating culture to the exclusion of biblical authority on the one hand, and the elevation of biblical authority to the exclusion of culture on the other. See chapter 2 for further discussion on contextualization concepts.

[51] Kenneth Scott Latourette, *A History of Christianity, Volume 1: Beginnings to 1500* (San Francisco: HarperSanFrancisco, 1975), 142-143.

[52] A major debate along this line continues today between varying positions of exclusivists (also called particularists) such as Harold Lindsell, Donald McGavran and J. Herbert Kane; inclusivists working off of Karl Rahner, and pluralists in the tradition of John Hick. A fundamental quest in these writings is to wrestle with the tension in Scripture between God's judgment of the damned on the one hand, and God's will that none should perish, and that "all" should come to a saving knowledge of the truth. The first two positions claim a basis in the Bible, the third (pluralism) considers both of the first two positions to be too restrictive since they both insist on a Christocentric soteriology. The ultimate question of all of these positions is certainly an eschatological/soteriological problem: in the *telos*, ultimately, who are the elect, who are the inheritors of God's salvation?

[53] James A. Scherer, "Lutheran Mission," in *Evangelical Dictionary of World Missions*, ed. A. Scott Moreau (Grand Rapids, MI: Baker Books, 2000), 586.

[54] James A. Scherer, *GCK*, 59-60.

[55] Johannes Verkuyl, *Contemporary Missiology: An Introduction*, trans. Dale Cooper (Grand Rapids, MI: Wm. B. Eerdmans Pub. Co, 1978), 5.

[56] Bosch, *TM*, 256-257.

⁵⁷Ruth Tucker, *From Jerusalem to Irian Jaya*, 68.

⁵⁸Scherer, *GCK*, 66.

⁵⁹Ibid., 67.

⁶⁰Ibid., 66-72. See also Stephen Neill, *A History of Christian Missions* (New York: Penguin Books, 1986), 188-189.

⁶¹Scherer, *GCK*, 71-72.

⁶²Tucker, *From Jerusalem to Irian Jaya*, 69.

⁶³Bosch, *TM*, 254.

⁶⁴Scherer, *GCK*, 73.

⁶⁵Neill, *A History of Christian Missions*, 188-189. Hereafter, *HCM*.

⁶⁶Bosch, *TM*, 254.

⁶⁷Ibid., 255.

⁶⁸S. D. Gaede, *When Tolerance Is No Virtue: Political Correctness, Multiculturalism & the Future of Truth & Justice* (Downers Grove, IL: InterVarsity Press, 1993), 81-82.

⁶⁹Scherer, *GCK*, 15.

⁷⁰Ibid., 33-35.

⁷¹Ibid., 35.

⁷²Bosch, *TM*, 16.

⁷³Boniface VIII, *Unam Sanctum*, Papal Bull of Pope Boniface VIII, November 18, 1302, http://www.papalencyclicals.net/Bon08/B8unam.htm (Accessed December 31, 2004).

⁷⁴Latourette, *A History of Christianity*, 350.

⁷⁵Veli-Matti Kärkkäinen, *An Introduction to Ecclesiology* (Downers Grove, IL: InterVarsity Press, 2002), 39.

⁷⁶SA 3, 12:2-3, in *BC*, trans. Robert Kolb and Timothy J. Wengert (Minneapolis, MN: Fortress Press, 2000), 324-5.

⁷⁷AC, Ger. 7:1 in *BC*, 42. Having said this, the Apology acknowledged that "many hypocrites and evil men" who "belong to the kingdom and body of the devil," would mingle with the saints and share the outward marks of the Church. See *Ap*, 7 and 8:17-29, in *BC*, 176-9.

⁷⁸Craig Van Gelder points out that the ecclesiology/missiology of the nineteenth century is much the same as that which has been driving the Church Growth movement of the twentieth century. "This ecclesiology, with its emphasis on the functioning of the church, is related to the missiology of the Great Commission theology, with its emphasis on obedience. The church is defined by what it is supposed to do. Historically, ecclesiology has first focused on the nature of the church and its attributes (what God has done) and then discussed the functionality of the church in relation to its attributes (what we do in light of what the church is). One of the implications of taking a primarily functional approach to ecclesiology is the tendency to conceive of the church in malleable terms as an instrument that we are responsible to build...A clear pragmatism pervades Church Growth thinking and practice. This stems from exercising a hermeneutical approach to Scripture that looks for biblical principles and identifies biblical practices as the basis for shaping Church Growth principles." (82) See Craig Van Gelder, "Gospel and Our Culture View," in *Evaluating the Church Growth Movement*, ed. Paul E. Engle and Gary L. McIntosh (Grand Rapids, MI: Zondervan, 2004), 81-82.

⁷⁹Scherer, *GCK*, 19.

⁸⁰Lamin Sanneh, *Whose Religion Is Christianity?: The Gospel Beyond the West* (Grand Rapids, MI: Wm. B. Eerdmans Pub. Co., 2003), 17, 24. Also, Scherer, *GCK*, 22-26.

[81] Scherer, GCK, 14-19.

[82] Ibid., 15-19.

[83] Francis M. DuBose, ed., *Classics of Christian Missions* (Nashville, TN: Broadman Press, 1979), 342.

[84] A. J. Appasamy, V. Chakkarai and P. Chenchiah were prominent in this attempt. Their views appear in a series of articles in *The Guardian*, 1938, and in the book, *Rethinking Christianity in India*, quoted at length by the Gurukul Theological Research Group of the Tamilnad Christian Council in *A Christian Theological Approach to Hinduism* (Madras, India: The Christian Literature Society, 1956).

[85] Gurukul Theological Research Group, *A Christian Theological Approach to Hinduism*, 51.

[86] DuBose, *Classics of Christian Missions*, 352.

[87] Scherer, GCK, 21, 33.

[88] Van Engen, *Mission on the Way*, 127-144.

[89] For example, the Joint Working Group established by the Vatican Secretariat for Christian Unity and the WCC Commission on World Mission and Evangelism in 1980 produced a document entitled "Common Witness and Proselytism." The Lausanne Covenant, along with the 1974 Nairobi Assembly document, "Confessing Christ Today," and the *Evangelii Nuntiandi* of 1975, were taken into account in preparation for the Joint Working Group's resulting document, "Christian Witness—Common Witness." Similarly, the WCC Central Committee's 1982 "Ecumenical Affirmation: Mission and Evangelism" cites the Lausanne Covenant in its discussion of a temporary moratorium on mission (6:38). Also, M. M. Thomas referred to the Covenant at the WCC Nairobi Assembly in 1975, stating that he saw a striking theological convergence "between the work of the 1973 Bangkok Assembly (CWME) and the 1974 Lausanne Congress, the Roman Bishop's Synod and the Orthodox Consultation." Cited in Scherer, GCK, 127. See also James A. Scherer and Stephen B. Bevans, ed., *New Directions in Mission & Evangelization 1* (Maryknoll, NY: Orbis Books, 1992), 18, 48.

[90] Scherer, GCK, 94.

[91] Craig Van Gelder writes of one of the successors of the Church Growth movement that emerged in the 1980's, a movement termed "Gospel and Our Culture" (GOC), and its relationship to *missio Dei*. "The primary missiology that undergirds the GOC conversation is the *missio Dei*, which is understood as the triune God being in mission within all the world. This GOC understanding of mission theology is about the church as a called community of the triune God being sent into the world to participate fully in God's mission. The social reality of the Godhead in three persons is understood as the foundation of the church's being missionary by nature as the creation of God. Just as the Father sent the Son to accomplish salvation, so also the Father and the Son continue to send the Spirit into the world to guide and teach the church to participate fully in God's redemptive reign in Christ." Van Gelder, "Gospel and Our Culture View," 86-87.

[92] A. Scott Moreau, Gary R. Corwin, and Gary B. McGee, *Introducing World Missions: A Biblical, Historical, and Practical Survey* (Grand Rapids, MI: Baker Academic, 2004), 81.

[93] Van Engen, *Mission on the Way*, 28. Hereafter, MW.

[94] Bosch, TM, 35.

[95] Ibid., 11.

[96] This idea was first clarified for me in an article by Moltmann published in 1978. The concept is still appearing some 15 years later in Moltmann's work. In spite of theological/political changes in his thinking over the years, he does not seem to have done away with this particular concept in his writing. Compare his early article, "Die Befreiung der Unterdruecker," *Evangelische Theologie*

38 (1978): 527-538, and the chapter "Justice for Victims and Perpetrators" in his later work, *History and the Triune God: Contributions to Trinitarian Theology*, trans. John Bowden (New York: Crossroad, 1992), 44-56.

[97]Jürgen Moltmann, *The Experiment Hope*, trans. M. Douglas Meeks (Philadelphia: Fortress Press, 1975), 3.

[98]David Kwang-sun Suh, *The Korean Minjung in Christ* (Hong Kong: The Christian Conference of Asia, 1991).

[99]Paul Varo Martinson, Lecture in Christian Theology in Asia course, CM8499 (Luther Seminary, Spring 1999).

[100]Jürgen Moltmann, *The Church in the Power of the Spirit*, trans. Margaret Kohl (Minneapolis, MN: Fortress Press, 1993), 96-97.

[101]Ibid., 97, italics mine.

[102]Kazoh Kitamori, *Theology of the Pain of God*, trans. M. E. Bratcher (Richmond, VA: John Knox Press, 1965), 12.

[103]Ibid., 45.

[104]Ibid., 45.

[105]Choan-Seng Song, *Third Eye Theology* (Maryknoll, NY: Orbis Books, 1979), 78.

[106]Ibid., 78.

[107]This is equally true of Moltmann's view. In discussing the act of God suffering in Christ, he addresses the question of why God took the suffering of Christ upon Himself. "What is the meaning of that terrible happening on Golgotha? There are two answers to this question. First, so that God could be *beside us* in our suffering and with us in our pain. That means *God's solidarity* with us. Second, so that he could be there *for us* in our guilt, freeing us from its burden. That means: God's *atoning intervention* for us." Jürgen Moltmann, *Jesus Christ for Today's World*, trans. Margaret Kohl (Minneapolis, MN: Fortress Press, 1994), 38.

[108]Kitamori, *Theology of the Pain of God*, 24. Hereafter, *TPG*.

[109]Kitamori, *TPG*, 23.

[110]Song, *Third Eye Theology*, 78.

[111]Martinson, lecture.

[112]This is Kitamori's definition of God's pain. Kitamori, *TPG*, 12.

[113]Scherer, GCK, 236.

[114]Neill, HCM, 22.

[115]*LC* 2, 49-58, in *BC*, 426-428.

[116]Scherer is here quoting Lesslie Newbigin's "Mission to Six Continents," in *The Ecumenical Advance*, 2:175. See Scherer, GCK, 33.

[117]Martin Luther, "On the Bondage of the Will," in *Luther and Erasmus: Free Will and Salvation*, ed. Gordon E. Rupp and Philip S. Watson (Philadelphia: The Westminster Press, 1969), 180.

[118]*tsedeq* is used to speak of just balances (Lev 19:36), just judgment (Deut 16:18), the kind of person who walks in integrity (Isa 26:7) and so on. *mishpat* is also sometimes used to indicate just balances (Prov 16:11) and, in its abstract sense, to indicate right or privilege (Deut 21:17).

[119]Bosch, TM, 16.

[120]Paul Hiebert, "Critical Contextualization," *IBMR* 11 (July 1987): 104.

[121] We might also insert the name of Francis Xavier here, since he is another giant of Jesuit mission work in the region, and yet his name does not appear as often in the discussions of the accommodation controversy. However, we will take up his example when we discuss more specifically the history of mission work in Japan.

[122] Andrew C. Ross, *A Vision Betrayed: The Jesuits in Japan and China, 1542-1742* (Maryknoll, NY: Orbis Books, 1994), 178.

[123] Ibid., 179.

[124] Ibid., xiv.

[125] Ibid., 179-181.

[126] Bosch, *TM*, 449.

[127] H. Richard Niebuhr, *Christ and Culture* (New York: Harper and Row, 1951), 45-82.

[128] Columba Cary-Elwes, *China and the Cross: A Survey of Missionary History* (New York: P. J. Kennedy & Sons, 1957), 109.

[129] Ralph R. Covell, *Confucius, the Buddha, and Christ: A History of the Gospel in Chinese* (Maryknoll, NY: Orbis Books, 1986), 64.

[130] Ibid., 56.

[131] Hiebert, "Critical Contextualization," 104.

[132] Ibid., 104-105.

[133] Bruce C. E. Fleming, *Contextualization of Theology: An Evangelical Assessment* (Pasadena, CA: William Carey Library, 1980), 4-5.

[134] Ibid., 4-5.

[135] Ibid., 7.

[136] It soon becomes clear that under this system, any synthesis of these two elements (theology and context) will likely favor the context over theology. Theology will find its grounding and source in the context.

[137] Bosch, *TM*, 421. See Justin Upkong, "What is Contextualization?" *Neue Zeitschrift für Missionswissenschaft* 43 (1987): 161-168. We must remember here that there are many different kinds of Liberation Theology and that although Bosch lumps Latin American Theology with black theology and feminist theology, in reality, Latin American, African, and some black American theology is much more radical than other types, and will often view violence as the only solution to their problems. But most of feminist theology, for example, will not resort so quickly to violence. Many Latin American Liberation Theologians, such as José Miguez Bonino, feel that theologians in the West have tried to tame their movement for their own purposes, turning it into what Bonino calls a "theological consumer product." (A response by Moltmann on this issue will follow.) See also Raymond C. Hundley, *Radical Liberation Theology: An Evangelical Response* (Wilmore, KY: Bristol Books, 1987).

[138] Jürgen Moltmann, "On Latin American Liberation Theology: An Open Letter to José Miguez Bonino," *Christianity and Crisis* 36, no. 5 (March 29, 1976), 60.

[139] Emilio A. Nùñez C., *Liberation Theology*, trans. Paul E. Sywulka (Chicago: Moody Press, 1985), 44.

[140] Bosch, *TM*, 424.

[141] Moltmann, *Theology of Hope*, 84.

[142] See Gustavo Gutiérrez, *A Theology of Liberation: History, Politics, and Salvation*, 15th anniv. ed., trans. and ed. Caridad Inda and John Eagleson (Maryknoll, NY: Orbis Books, 1988).

[143] Gutiérrez, *A Theology of Liberation*, 40.

[144] Ibid., 240. For example, Avante-garde Roman Catholic Liberation Theologian Edward Schillebeeckx was a major source of inspiration for Moltmann. See Schillebeeckx's works, *Christ: The Experience of Jesus as Lord*, trans. Hubert Hoskins (New York: Seabury Press, 1979), and his *Jesus: An Experiment in Christology*, trans. John Bowden (New York: Seabury Press, 1979).

[145] José Míguez Bonino, *Doing Theology in a Revolutionary Situation* (Philadelphia: Fortress Press, 1975), 145-146.

[146] Bosch, *TM*, 420-425.

[147] Moltmann, "On Latin American Liberation Theology," 57.

[148] Peter Schineller, "Inculturation: A Difficult and Delicate Task," *IBMR* 20, no. 3 (July 1996): 109.

[149] Aylward Shorter, *Toward a Theology of Inculturation* (Maryknoll, NY: Orbis Books, 1988), 5.

[150] Bosch, *TM*, 422.

[151] Aram I, "The Incarnation of the Gospel in Cultures: A Missionary Event," 30.

[152] Ibid., 33.

[153] This was a frequent theme at the 1938 Tambaram-Madras meeting of the International Missionary Council. See "The World Mission of the Church: Findings and Recommendations of the International Missionary Council," Proceedings of the International Missionary Council, Tambaram, Madras, India, December 12th-29th, 1938 (New York: International Missionary Council, 1939).

[154] Fleming, *Contextualization of Theology*, 49. Hereafter, *CT*.

[155] Kosuke Koyama, *Waterbuffalo Theology* (Maryknoll, NY: Orbis Books, 1974).

[156] Ibid., 20.

[157] Fleming, *CT*, 49. See Koyama, *Waterbuffalo Theology*, 40.

[158] Fleming, *CT*, 50.

[159] Ibid., 50. See Koyama, *Waterbuffalo Theology*, 40.

[160] Fleming, *CT*, 128. Lynn A. DeSilva's comments are from "Theological Construction in a Buddhist Context," in *Asian Voices in Christian Theology*, ed. J. N. D. Anderson (Maryknoll, NY: Orbis Books, 1976), 40.

[161] It is recognized in this statement that there are also inevitable and healthy forms of syncretism. God does not enforce uniformity upon those to whom the gospel comes. We do not lose our personhood, nor do we lose all forms of cultural expression. The gospel does, however, recognize that cultures are not inherently pure. Evil exists within cultures, as well as good, and the gospel sits in judgment upon evil wherever it is found.

[162] It is maintained here that the Bible, though not being God, is never the less divinely inspired revelation that holds the unique position of being an "absolute," and consequently is supracultural. Any other norm will, by necessity, be cultural and relativistic. It is only natural, then, that the Bible can serve as the sole norm for cultures.

[163] Barth, *Church and State*, 1-12. This argument is not to be confused with Barth's discussion of *analogia fidei*, whereby any communication between the Creator and the creature is totally dependant upon God's self-revelation. Nor are we referring to *analogia entis*, associated with Aquinas, that something can be known of the Creator from known objects and the natural order of creation. The argument above is instead referring to the need to base true reconciliation among humans and the hope of a new and restored world not on human effort alone, but on the finished work of the cross of Jesus Christ which has reconciled us to God.

[164] See Peter Beyerhaus' discussion of this debate in *Missions: Which Way? Humanization or Redemption* (Grand Rapids, MI: Zondervan, 1971). The book is his reaction to the statements coming out of the 1968 General Assembly of the World Council of Churches in Uppsala, Sweden.

[165] Moltmann, *The Experiment Hope*, 3.

[166] Hiebert, "Critical Contextualization," 104-112.

[167] Ibid., 109-112.

[168] Robert J. Schreiter, "Contextualization from a World Perspective," in *Ministry & Theology in Global Perspective: Contemporary Challenges for the Church*, ed. Don A. Pittman, Ruben L. F. Habito, and Terry C. Muck (Grand Rapids, MI: Wm. B. Eerdmans Pub. Co, 1996), 320.

[169] Ibid., 320.

[170] Ibid., 321.

[171] Robert J. Schreiter, "Changes in Roman Catholic Attitudes toward Proselytism and Mission," in *New Directions in Mission & Evangelization 2: Theological Foundations*, ed. James A. Scherer and Stephen B. Bevans (Maryknoll, NY: Orbis Books, 1994), 118.

[172] Ibid., 118.

[173] Joseph M. Kitagawa, *Religions of the East* (Philadelphia: Westminster Press, 1960), 188.

[174] Kenneth K. S. Ch'en, *The Chinese Transformation of Buddhism* (Princeton, NJ: Princeton University Press, 1973), 3.

[175] Ibid., 3.

[176] Ibid., 3.

[177] Ibid., 4.

[178] Ibid., 5.

[179] Ibid., 5.

[180] Koyama uses this terminology concerning the mission of the gospel in a Japanese context, as he explains, "Theological re-rooting is a thoughtful attempt to translate the inner meaning of the message of Jesus Christ from one historical and cultural milieu and root it into another... But theological re-rooting is something more than the accommodation of the text. It is highly *interpretative* work. It has to do with the inner meaning (interpreted meaning) of the message concerning Jesus Christ." See Koyama, *Waterbuffalo Theology*, 121.

[181] Ch'en, *The Chinese Transformation of Buddhism*, 4. Hereafter, *CTB*.

[182] Ibid., 4.

[183] Kitagawa, *Religions of the East*, 189.

[184] E. R. Hughes and K. Hughes, *Religion in China* (London: Hutchinson's University Library, 1950), 65.

[185] Ch'en, *CTB*, 4-5. Notice here how Ch'en speaks of "Indian" as synonymous with Hindu, as though all Indians are Hindus. Although this may not be Ch'en's intent, such wording invalidates the Buddhist, Muslim and Christian elements of India, which is precisely what radical Hindu political parties are promoting today.

[186] The Buddha never asked that his teachings be written down, and until the first century B.C., the majority of the texts were passed on orally. The oldest collection of these texts consisted only of the Vinaya (texts on monastic discipline) and the Sutra (doctrinal texts). See Heinz Bechert, "The Buddhist Community and Its Earlier History," in Hans Küng et al., *Christianity and the World's Religions: Paths to Dialogue with Islam, Hinduism, and Buddhism*, trans. by Peter Heinegg (Garden City, NY: Doubleday & Co., Inc., 1986), 333.

[187] Hughes and Hughes, *Religion in China*, 67. Hereafter, *RIC*.

[188] Later expressions of Buddhism, such as Nichiren, reject this canon altogether, substituting other texts, such as the Lotus Sutra.

[189] In a reputed deathbed pronouncement, Siddhartha Gautama expressed his will that no one person or institution should lead his movement into the future. This opened the door to a very

pluralistic approach in the dissemination of Buddhism.

[190] Lewis M. Hopfe and Mark R. Woodward, *Religions of the World*, 9th ed. (Upper Saddle River, NJ: Pearson Prentice Hall, 2004), 134.

[191] The second century A.D. marks the beginning of the development of Mahayana. At this time, Buddhism would have already spread southward to Sri Lanka and Southeast Asia, a region which today is still representative of Theravada, the more conservative expression of Buddhism. Later frontiers would become home to Mahayana. With each missionary advance, the type of Buddhism that took hold in the new frontiers would be the kind of contemporary Buddhism that was in vogue at that time.

[192] Mahayanists applied the term "Hinayana" to this group as a pejorative expression. However, over time, the word has lost its pejorative impact, and Theravadins will even employ the term in reference to themselves. Today, Hinayana and Theravada, for the most part, are interchangeable names for this branch of Buddhism.

[193] Hopfe and Woodward, *Religions of the World*, 136. Hereafter, *RW*.

[194] Ibid., 136.

[195] In a footnote in *Religions of the World*, the authors Lewis Hopfe and Mark Woodward point out that the belief in more than one Buddha was not unique to the Mahayana tradition—Theravada Buddhists also held to a belief in the existence of multiple Buddhas. The difference in these positions would be that the while Mahayanists teach the existence of many Buddhas located throughout the cosmos, Theravadins, "maintain that like other humans they are mortal, and that there can be only one at a time. According to Theravada teachings, long periods of time exist during which there is no Buddha in the world." Hopfe and Woodward, *RW*, 137.

[196] Ibid., 136-137.

[197] Ibid., 137.

[198] Ibid., 137. In the innovation of the Bodhisattva, we can discern a similarity with Plato's cave analogy, where the "coming back to tell others" is a moral imperative. There is also an obvious analogy here to the Philippians 2 reference to Jesus emptying Himself on our behalf, to show us the Father.

[199] Kenneth K. S. Ch'en, *Buddhism in China: A Historical Survey* (Princeton, NJ: Princeton University Press, 1964), 13.

[200] Sanskrit: Avaloketasvara; Kanon in Japanese.

[201] Ch'en attributes this transformation to the influence of Tantric Buddhism, which became prominent in China during the eighth century. See Ch'en, *CTB*, 6-7. See also Covell, *CBC*, 145.

[202] See Ramji Ambedkar's interesting essay entitled "Buddha or Karl Marx," *Writings and Speeches*, vol. 3, ed. Vasant Moon (Bombay: Education Employment Department, 1987), 441-450. In this essay, he compares the Buddha and Karl Marx, seeing the Buddha not as a religious leader, but as a social liberator, whose aim for society was the same as that of Marx, but without the violence element.

[203] This is not to say there are no examples of Buddhism succumbing to nationalistic or racist sentiment. There are, although such cases are rare. See Aloysius Pieris, *Fire and Water: Basic Issues in Asian Buddhism and Christianity* (Maryknoll, NY: Orbis Books, 1996), 108-109.

[204] Vishal Mangalwadi writes on this topic from personal experience in India. In a recent publication of his, Ram Raj gives his perspective in the introduction to the book. Vishal Mangalwadi, *The Quest for Freedom and Dignity: Caste, Conversion and Cultural Revolution* (Mumbai, India: GLS Publishing, 2001).

[205] Hopfe and Woodward, *RW*, 135.

[206] Ch'en, *Buddhism in China*, 16-20. Hereafter, *BIC*.

[207] Ibid., 17.

[208] Kitagawa, *Religions of the East*, 198.

[209] Frank E. Reynolds, "Buddhism: The Three Main Traditions," in *Religions of the World*, 2d ed., ed. Niels Nielsen et al. (New York: St. Martin's Press, 1988), 215.

[210] Ch'en points out that early records depict a Central Asia much more inhabited than we see today. "All accounts spoke of flourishing towns and cities with a high level of civilization." He argues that monks would have used the Central Asiatic highway rather than routes through Assam or Nepal and Tibet. Ch'en, *BIC*, 19.

[211] Ibid., 15-16. In this same passage in his book, Ch'en also argues that there was a strong influence of Iranian thought on Mahayana Buddhism.

[212] Ibid., 48-49.

[213] Hu Shi (Shih), "The Indianization of China: A Case Study in Cultural Borrowing," in *Independence, Convergence, and Borrowing*, ed. Charles H. Dodd (Cambridge, MA: Harvard University Press, 1937), 225.

[214] James Huntly Grayson, *Early Buddhism and Christianity in Korea: A Study in the Emplantation of Religion* (Leiden, Netherlands: E. J. Brill, 1985), 3.

[215] Ibid., 12-15.

[216] Covell, *CBC*, 135.

[217] This is to say that for Confucius, the "world" consisted of a network of social relationships. A truly great society would consist of people knowing, and keeping, their places in this network. For example, the nobleman knew his place as loyal servant before the emperor, and the emperor knew that he was to be a benevolent ruler over his subjects. The younger brother served the elder brother who in turn did not lord it over the younger. Confucius taught that relationships, and the appropriate rituals that accompanied them, were the building blocks of society. One worked hard to execute one's place in society appropriately. To be a public servant, one learned the classics, and sought wisdom in the ways of the glorious feudal past. Taoism, however, was at the opposite end of the spectrum. Theoretically, relationships did not really matter to the Taoist. An ideal Taoist might live in a small village all his life and never meet anyone outside the village. For that matter, living alone in a cave might be the ideal. One looked to nature as the model for the "world." A stream never struggles up a mountain to gain great heights; it is instead content to follow gravity down the mountainside, taking the path of least resistance. Things as they naturally are, not striving to improve or advance, are the goal for this counter-cultural way of life. Thus, for the Confucian, relationships, and striving to be the noble person, this is the "world" to which he relates. For the Taoist, the "natural way" is his guide and the "world" he relates to; "active non-activity," an intentional avoidance of striving after achievement, is the Taoist key to life.

[218] This is certainly not to say, however, that there was no religious element in Confucianism—there was. For example, Confucius taught that nothing could happen to him that "Heaven" did not allow. Among his interpreters, Confucius would stand between Mencius, who emphasized the role of Heaven, and Hsun Tzu (Xun-zi) who was skeptical about any spiritual existence, and felt that rites had only social benefits. On the religiosity of Confucianism, Hopfe and Woodward point out the following: "Some scholars have suggested that the Chinese during this period were very close to developing an ethical monotheism similar to that enunciated by the Hebrew prophets in the eighth century B.C.E. However, the emphasis on morality as a means of satisfying the High God remained in the hands of the rulers, and prophets never arose in this period of Chinese history. Nevertheless, the emperors of China held their thrones with one eye upon the heavens and a concern for personal morality and good government." Hopfe and Woodward, *RW*, 173. That

said, we must recognize that Confucius worked to shift Chinese thinking from Heaven to Earth, placing the higher value on human relationships. See also Huston Smith, *The World's Religions: Our Great Wisdom Tradition* (New York: HarperSanFrancisco, 1991), 183-187.

[219] Erik Zürcher, *The Buddhist Conquest of China: The Spread and Adaptation of Buddhism in Early Medieval China* (Leiden, Netherlands: E. J. Brill, 1959), 11.

[220] According to Ch'en, "By the end of the Han Dynasty a new spirit of independence was developing within Buddhism; it no longer accepted the close connection with Taoism. Probably the first step toward independence was the appearance of the work *Mou-tzu*, which took a definite stand against Taoist doctrines and occultism, and asserted that Buddhism was ready to stand on its own feet in China. On the part of the Taoist, the renunciation of relations did not occur so early. For a long time the Taoists insisted that Lao-tzu went west to convert the barbarians and to become the Buddha. [This is the doctrine of *hua-hu*.] This insistence was to lead to a series of Buddhist-Taoist debates lasting over a thousand years, to be settled finally by the Mongol emperors in favor of Buddhism." See Ch'en, *BIC*, 53.

[221] Tippet uses this phrase to speak of the experience of conversion, especially the kind of experience when Christ enters an Animistic culture and encounters the spirits of that culture. According to Tippet, this is when people experience the *exousia* over the *dunamis*, as the Apostle Luke records it. See Alan Tippet, *Introduction to Missiology* (Pasadena, CA: William Carey Library, 1987), 75.

[222] Grayson, *Early Buddhism and Christianity in Korea*, 9. Shamanism has been an ever-present undercurrent in any number of societies worldwide, and many expressions of religion have shamanistic elements in them. In practice, it fulfills the need for healing and for favor from the spirits of the climate and the harvests. The shaman does not personally have the power to heal or to curse or do whatever the situation calls for; rather, they serve as a channel for the spirit world to do this. Strong elements of shamanism remain today throughout northeast Asia. Though this form of religion has never achieved a dominant political stature, it has had a deep and lasting influence on the psyche of the people, and has had a strong syncretistic effect upon major religions in these areas. Like animism, shamanism seems to be a kind of religion to which human nature naturally gravitates.

[223] Grayson, *Early Buddhism and Christianity in Korea*, 9-13. Hereafter, *EBCK*.

[224] Ibid., 12-15.

[225] Richardson used these words to speak of an analogy found in a non-Christian culture by which one might illustrate an aspect of the gospel. See Don Richardson, *Eternity in Their Hearts*, rev. ed. (Ventura, CA: Regal Books, 1984).

[226] Covell, *CBC*, 140-141.

[227] However, many in Buddhist clergy have protested the practice of ancestor veneration, and Buddhism's consequent major role in funerary rites. The argument in this instance has been that for most Buddhists, Buddhism has become simply a funeral religion, and the core elements of Buddhist teaching are lost in the process.

[228] Here it is interesting to compare our own contemporary North American culture that prefers the "new." Our culture often denigrates traditional ways of thinking and acting, while often unquestioningly embracing new ways, simply for their *avant-garde* qualities and their usefulness for challenging the conventional.

[229] Ch'en sees the salvation factor in Buddhism and Taoism as having the following points of similarity: "The Buddhist taught the indestructibility of the soul and rebirth in the Brahman heavens; the Taoists believed in the land of the immortals in the Eastern Seas, or sought immortality in the Heaven of Grand Purity. Because of these numerous elements of apparent similarity between the

two, the Buddhists and the Taoists joined forces." Ch'en, BIC, 49. According to Erik Zurcher, "Buddhism is not and has never pretended to be a 'theory', an explanation of the universe; it is a way to salvation, a way of life." Zürcher, *The Buddhist Conquest of China*, 1. Hereafter, BCC.

[230]This connection of the religious with the seats of power had its times that were greatly beneficial to Buddhism's widespread acceptance and growth, but there also came times of political disfavor, and a resulting long-term instability for Buddhism in the region. In this overall sense, we view the marriage of governing power with Buddhism, and the consequent utilitarian emphasis, as a harmful alliance.

[231]The struggle of Buddhism with the vacillating climates of power is not totally unlike that experienced by Taoism or Confucianism. When Confucius was an itinerant teacher at an earlier time of decline in China (sixth century B.C.), he, like many others, had to compete for the ears of the local and regional rulers. Moreover, while Confucius apparently held office in the state of Lu, he never did realize his own personal goal of achieving a permanent state position (something the legendary Lao-Tzu is purported to have spurned).

[232]See Zürcher, BCC, 3, 4. The phrase, "Dark Learning" is from the Chinese, *hsuan-hsue*. The term, *hsuan*, refers to "dark" or "mysterious." According Alan L. Miller, "Scholars, poets, and painters who disdained official positions would meet to discuss their respective pursuits and to enjoy one another's company. Taoism provided them with a sense of participation in the mysterious and dark life of the cosmos, and no doubt it helped compensate them for the loss of their influence in the political world." Allan L. Miller, "Religions of China, Japan, and India: Dynastic Change and the Three Traditions," in *Religions of the World*, 2d ed., ed. Niels C. Nielsen et al. (New York: St. Martin's Press, 1988), 289.

[233]Buddhism's continued struggle for influence in the region was evidenced in a conference held in Kyoto, Japan in 1998, where the Dalai Lama and other Buddhist leaders from across Asia gathered to discuss the declining popularity of Buddhism. See an online BBC article entitled, "Buddhism 'in decline,'" April 7, 1998, http://news.bbc.co.uk/2/hi/asia-pacific/75325.stm (accessed Sept. 15, 2003).

[234]Ch'en has a helpful chapter on the issues of translation of the Tripitaka into Chinese. The translation appears to have been from the Sanskrit, rather than the earlier Pali texts, and there was considerable debate concerning whether to go with a free style translation or a more literal. In either case, the concern was to make the doctrines of Buddhism understandable to the Chinese. At least initially, the emphasis appears to have been on a translation that served both the *lingua franca* and the *lingua religioso*. See Ch'en, BIC, 365-386. According to Frank Reynolds, it also seems that this did not detract from Theravadins' insistence on maintaining the canonical authority of the Pali version, coupled with a strong interest in preserving purity of doctrine. "Nevertheless, it is clear from their commentaries and manuals that the later Theravadins introduced innovations from their own reflections and meditative experience and also absorbed and reacted to influences from various Sanskrit forms of Buddhism." See Frank E. Reynolds, "Buddhism: Buddhism as a World Religion," in *Religions of the World*, 2d ed., ed. Niels Nielsen et al. (New York: St. Martin's Press, 1988), 236.

[235]Grayson, EBCK, 13.

[236]Ibid., 14-15.

[237]Ibid., 15. Grayson uses the word "emplantation" to mean, "to root firmly in the social order of an alien culture ideas, beliefs and practices which had their origin in another culture." See Grayson, EBCK, 1.

²³⁸Covell, *CBC*, 137. The reference here is not to any doctrinal compromise, but to compatibility at the level of occult practice. Reynolds also discusses the magical powers of Theravadin monks and the role of magic in relation to Taoist practice. See Reynolds, "Buddhism: Buddhism as a World Religion," 238.

²³⁹Ch'en, *BIC*, 53.

²⁴⁰Covell, *CBC*, 147.

²⁴¹Ibid., 147. Points three and four may seem incompatible; however, the "sect of Daoism" approach was an early approach that missionaries would later abandon, once Buddhism gained strength. Covell's reference to a "people movement" refers to a coming together of Chinese peoples of the more intellectual "gentry" Buddhism, with people won in the north through a "power encounter" style, a movement that happened much later.

²⁴²Ibid., 137.

²⁴³More about this will follow in the next two chapters.

²⁴⁴Covell, *CBC*, 144.

²⁴⁵Ibid., 144.

²⁴⁶*Li* refers to proper moral actions based in heaven and patterned on earth, dealing with spirit worship, funerals, family, diplomatic visits, etc. It includes the rule: Don't do to others what you would not want others to do to you. It is doing the right thing at the appropriate time. *Li* is indispensable to the five relationships: emperor to subject; father to son; eldest brother to younger; husband to wife; and elder to junior.

²⁴⁷Covell, *CBC*, 143.

²⁴⁸Ch'en, *CTB*, 124.

²⁴⁹William A. Young, *The World's Religions: World Views and Contemporary Issues*, 2d ed. (Upper Saddle River, NJ: Pearson Education, Inc., 2005), 135.

²⁵⁰Grayson, *EBCK*, 19-20.

²⁵¹Ibid., 21.

²⁵²Ibid., 24, 38.

²⁵³Ibid., 25.

²⁵⁴Robert Evans Buswell, Jr., "Buddhism: Buddhism in Korea," in *The Encyclopedia of Religion*, ed. Mircea Eliade (New York: Macmillan Pub. Co., 1987), 2:421.

²⁵⁵Grayson, *EBCK*, 25.

²⁵⁶Ibid., 26.

²⁵⁷Ibid., 26.

²⁵⁸Buswell, "Buddhism: Buddhism in Korea," 2:421.

²⁵⁹Grayson, *EBCK*, 27.

²⁶⁰Buswell, "Buddhism: Buddhism in Korea," 2:421-422.

²⁶¹Grayson, *EBCK*, 27. See also Joseph M. Kitagawa, *On Understanding Japanese Religion* (Princeton, NJ: Princeton University Press, 1987), 243.

²⁶²Masaharu Anesaki, *History of Japanese Religion, with a Special Reference to the Social and Moral Life of the Nation* (Rutland, VT: Charles E. Tuttle Company, 1963), 52.

²⁶³Kitagawa, *On Understanding Japanese Religion*, 102. Hereafter, *OUJR*.

²⁶⁴Grayson, *ECBK*, 29.

²⁶⁵Ibid., 29-30.

²⁶⁶Buswell, "Buddhism: Buddhism in Korea," 2:421.

[267] Grayson, *EBCK*, 30.

[268] Ibid., 31.

[269] Ibid., 30.

[270] Ibid., 32.

[271] Ibid., 33.

[272] Ibid., 33.

[273] Ibid., 34.

[274] Ibid., 39.

[275] Ibid., 39.

[276] Ibid., 39.

[277] Ibid., 61.

[278] With this sentence, I have taken the liberty to apply a corrective to Grayson's analysis of his six stages. He appears to lump this activity in with the second stage, and mistakenly refers to Penetration as the third stage, leaving out any reference in his analysis to the actual third stage: Growth and Evangelism. It seems to fit his categories, and dates, however, to put the increased educational activity of the monks, and mission outreach to Japan, into the Growth and Evangelism stage. In doing this, I trust that I have been faithful to his intent. (These activities, of course, followed into later stages as well, as when the seventh century monk, Sūng-jōn, brought a large number of commentaries back from T'ang and presented them to the legendary monk Ūi-sang, who used them for evangelism. See Grayson, *EBCK*, 47.) Grayson's book also references the fifth period as the fourth, but correctly sums up the sixth stage as the "final" one.

[279] Grayson, *EBCK*, 61.

[280] Ibid., 61.

[281] Ibid., 61-62.

[282] Buswell, "Buddhism: Buddhism in Korea," 2:421.

[283] Kitagawa, *Religions of the East*, 205.

[284] References to Yamato, the early name for Japan, indicate a loose confederation of power located in central Japan, the Yamato plain (now called Nara prefecture). This early historic period, what archeologists refer to as the Kofun (tumulus) period spans roughly from 250 to 600 A.D. Myth credits the founding of the "Yamato kingdom" to the legendary first emperor, Jimmu Tenno. More reliable records credit its founding to a fourth-century chieftain of the imperial clan, probably Ījin, the fifteenth emperor mentioned in official chronicles. See Kitagawa, *OUJR*, 50-51, 84.

[285] Anesaki, *History of Japanese Religion*, 21.

[286] Kitagawa, *OUJR*, 45-46.

[287] Ibid., 45.

[288] Ibid., 45.

[289] Ibid., 37, 44.

[290] Shigeru Matsumoto, "Introduction," in *Japanese Religion: A Survey by the Agency for Cultural Affairs*, ed. Hori Ichiro et al., trans. Abe Yoshiya and David Reid (Palo Alto, CA; Tokyo: Kodansha International Ltd., 1972), 13.

[291] Kitagawa, *OUJR*, 48.

[292] Ibid., 44.

[293] Ibid., 53.

²⁹⁴Ibid., 52-53. Kitagawa says that Christians, as well as Buddhists and Confucians, participated in this way of thinking, but cites no examples.

²⁹⁵Ibid., 55-56.

²⁹⁶Ibid., 56-57. The final sentence in this block quote is from Hajime Nakamura's *Ways of Thinking of Eastern Peoples: India, China, Tibet and Japan*, rev. English trans., ed. Philip P. Wiener (Honolulu: East-West Center, 1964), 437.

²⁹⁷Kitagawa, OUJR, 57.

²⁹⁸Ibid., 72.

²⁹⁹The *Nihonshoki* is an early chronology of Japanese history, written in Classical Chinese in 720 A.D. (Nara Period: 710-794), by order of the Japanese government approximately two centuries after the entry of Buddhism. See Shinsho Hanayama, *A History of Japanese Buddhism*, trans. Kosho Yamamoto (Tokyo: CIIB Press, 1960), 3. For a discussion of the earlier dates for the entrance of Buddhism to Japan, see the previous section of this chapter.

³⁰⁰Hanayama, *A History of Japanese Buddhism*, 4-5. Hereafter, *HJB*. According to Maseharu Anesaki, the Mononobes stood for high-handed measures toward foreign countries, and the Nakatomis stood with them, although the Nakatomis would later become ardent Buddhists. See Anesaki, *History of Japanese Religion*, 54-55.

³⁰¹Hanayama, *HJB*, 5-6. Hanayama says nearly forty years, Anesaki says about fifty.

³⁰²Ibid., 5-6.

³⁰³Anesaki, *History of Japanese Religion*, 55.

³⁰⁴Ibid., 59.

³⁰⁵Ibid., 60.

³⁰⁶Here too, we should perhaps exercise some caution, as to how much embellishment has fed the legends surrounding such an individual. Nevertheless, he remains a remarkable individual who did much to promote Buddhism in Japan.

³⁰⁷Anesaki, *History of Japanese Religion*, 57-58.

³⁰⁸Hanayama, *HJB*, 9-10.

³⁰⁹Ibid., 10.

³¹⁰Ibid., 15.

³¹¹Tamaru, "Buddhism," 58.

³¹²Hanayama, *HJB*, 91-92.

³¹³Tamaru, "Buddhism," 59.

³¹⁴Ibid., 60.

³¹⁵Ibid., 59-60.

³¹⁶The earlier shogun, Nobunaga, does not appear in this list, since his stance was largely anti-Buddhist—due to his displeasure with militant monks. Instead, he favored the Kirishitan (Roman Catholic) missions, for motives that are obscure. Hideyoshi seemed to also favor the Kirishitan missions briefly, but turned on them when he became irritated with their allegiance to the Pope—an allegiance he found difficult to understand. There may have also been some private irritations toward the missions as well. See Anesaki, *History of Japanese Religion*, 244-245.

³¹⁷Also called the *gonin gumi*, this was a neighborhood system based upon units of five families. Kentaro Miyazaki writes that leaders formed these groups to foster group responsibility and mutual assistance from within the group. "The systems of remunerating denouncers and of five-family groups were combined in 1642 making the apprehension of Kirishitan [the word used for early Roman Catholic Christians in Japan] an obligation of group responsibility. If a member of one's

five-family group accused someone to be a Kirishitan the remaining four households were not censured, but if a member was accused by someone of another group all members of a five-family group were executed." Kentaro Miyazaki, "Roman Catholic Mission in Pre-Modern Japan," in *Handbook of Christianity in Japan*, ed. Mark R. Mullins (Leiden, Netherlands; Boston: Brill, 2003), 14.

[318] Japanese typically refer to their emperors by the name of their era. For example, the emperor of the World War II era, known in the West as Hirohito, the Japanese know as Emperor Showa. His name, Hirohito, is for the most part, unknown in Japan.

[319] Kitagawa, *OUJR*, 207.

[320] Ibid., 208.

[321] See Shusaku Endo, *Silence*, trans. William Johnston (Tokyo; Rutland, VT: Charles E. Tuttle Company, 1969). This novel will be referenced again in chapter 4.

[322] In saying this, it is with the recognition that total avoidance of syncretism is not possible, neither is it desirable. This is because God Himself has become incarnate in human flesh, and thus became "contaminated" in our world, even to the extent of becoming sin on our behalf. In like manner, the gospel of Jesus Christ needs to become "incarnated" in cultures through the Church—it must become "human" in all cultures. "As the Father has sent me, I am sending you" (Jn 20:21). That said, it is equally recognized that there is indeed a kind of syncretism that God's messengers must avoid: that which allows conflicting non-biblical teachings and practices to remain side by side with biblical ones. As was said in chapter 2, the local believers should, in large part, determine this for themselves through the application of biblical truths to their cultural practices.

[323] Justo L. González, *The Early Church to the Dawn of the Reformation*, vol. 1 of *The Story of Christianity* (New York: Harper and Row, 1984), 180.

[324] Young, *By Foot to China*, 2.

[325] Philip Jenkins, *The Next Christendom: The Coming of Global Christianity* (New York: Oxford University Press, 2002), 22-23.

[326] Ibid., 23.

[327] Mingana, "The Early Spread of Christianity in Central Asia and the Far East: A New Document," 347.

[328] Samuel Moffett puts the figure of martyrs at possibly 190,000 from 340-401 A.D. See Samuel Moffett, *A History of Christianity in Asia, Volume I: Beginnings to 1500* (Maryknoll, NY: Orbis Books, 2001), 137-145.

[329] In referring to Tatian's *Diatessaron*, Sebastian Brock maintains that it is quite certain that Tatian changed the wording about the diet of John the Baptist to show John eating "milk" and honey instead of locusts and honey, as the ascetics would have considered locusts as meat. Brock also makes the interesting case that "if one sees the ascetics of the fourth century onwards as heirs to the martyrs, it helps one to realise why they regarded their way of life as simply carrying on the norm of Christian life in pre-Constantian times...when to be a Christian was usually a matter of real seriousness." Sebastian Brock, *Syrian Perspectives on Late Antiquity* (Burlington, VT: Ashgate Pub. Co., 1984), 2-5.

[330] Moffett, *A History of Christianity in Asia, Volume I*, 75. Moffett also explains on page 75 that the word Encratite means "self control," but that Western theologians employed the word to refer to abnormal self-denial stemming from a conviction that matter is evil.

[331] Ibid., 75.

[332] See Judith Herrin, *The Formation of Christendom* (Princeton, NJ: Princeton University Press, 1987), 109, for a discussion of the Syrian stylites.

[333] Moffett, *A History of Christianity in Asia, Volume I*, 78. Hereafter, HCA I.

[334] Ibid., 78.

[335] Ibid., 79. Moffett referenced the text from Quasten, *Patrology*, 1:172.

[336] John Stewart, *Nestorian Missionary Enterprise* (Edinburgh: T. & T. Clark, 1928), 36.

[337] W. A. Wigram, *An Introduction to the History of the Assyrian Church of the Sassanid Persian Empire 100-640 A.D.* (London: S.P.C.K., 1910), 238-240.

[338] G. D. Malech, *History of the Syrian Nation and the Old Evangelical-Apostolic Church of the East* (Minneapolis, MN: private printing, 1910), 242.

[339] Stewart, *Nestorian Missionary Enterprise*, 37.

[340] Ibid., 37.

[341] Ibid., 44.

[342] The year Alaric the Goth burned Rome.

[343] According to Sebastian Brock, "The West Syrian recension concludes with the statement that 'we are in agreement with the faith of the 318 bishops in the city of Nicaea; this is our confession and our faith, which we have received from our holy fathers.'" See Chapter XII in Sebastian Brock, *Studies in Syrian Christianity*, Brookfield, VT: Ashgate Pub. Co., 1992), 126. The chapter is also given in this citation because the page numbers in the book are not sequential, but instead are page numbers of the journals from which these articles are reprinted.

[344] Young, *By Foot to China*, 5.

[345] Wigram, *An Introduction to the History of the Assyrian Church*, 124.

[346] Ibid., 124.

[347] Wolfgang Hage, *Syriac Christianity in the East* (Kerala, India: St. Ephrem Ecumenical Research Institute, St. Joseph's Press, 1988), 11.

[348] Latourette, *A History of Christianity, Volume 1: Beginnings to 1500*, 164-170.

[349] Ibid., 169.

[350] These terms are used here in place of "monophysitism" and "Nestorianism," both of which are used polemically and pejoratively by their respective opponents. These issues were debated more explicitly at Chalcedon in 451.

[351] Moffett, HCA I, 175.

[352] Ibid., 175.

[353] Aziz Atiya, *A History of Eastern Christianity* (Notre Dame: University of Notre Dame Press, 1969), 251-252.

[354] Ibid., 260.

[355] Ibid., 260.

[356] Ibid., 260. There is debate as to whether or not the legendary "Prester John" is a Western invention. Some connect him with a Christian Kerait chief, an uncle of Genghis Kahn. Stephen Neill cites several possible sources for the legend. There seemed to be a wish on the part of the Western Church to find the kingdom of and ally with Prester John, finally to bring the Muslims to their knees. See Neill, HCM, 120-121. Was "Prester John" simply a fictional wish of the Church in the West for a protector like Constantine to appear in the East? There seems to be no solid answer available to us at this time.

[357] The story of this monument is available in many sources, including P. Y. Saeki, S. Moffett, S. Neill et al. Moffett includes Saeki's translation of the theological introduction to the monument, with notes, in an Appendix. See Moffett, HCA I, 514-517.

[358] Neill, HCM, 82.

[359] E. O. Reischauer and J. K. Fairbank, *East Asia the Great Tradition* (Tokyo: Charles E. Tuttle Company, 1926),175.

[360] Neill, *HCM*, 83.

[361] Cary-Elwes, *China and the Cross*, 35-37.

[362] Latourette, *A History of Christianity*, 402.

[363] Neill, *HCM*, 113-115.

[364] Bosch, *TM*, 122.

[365] Stephen Neill, however, takes the position that "some Eastern Christians were in part technically heretical, having followed the Monophysite or Nestorian way..." We would not take issue with such a statement, except to say that Nestorius himself was probably not "Nestorian" in doctrine. See Neill, *HCM*, 55. See also Sebastian Brock, who strongly argues that Nestorius never had anything like the position of authority of Theodore Mopsuestia, and to say that there was a "nestorianization" of the Persian church over the century and a half following the synods of the 480s is "to be beguiled by the rhetorical hyperbole of the theological opponents of the Church of the East, who regularly labeled anything to do with Theodore as, by implication, Nestorian." Chapter XII in Brock, *Studies in Syrian Christianity*, 130.

[366] Nestorius would likely have interpreted the *communicatio idiomatum* as an Apollinarian fusing of the two natures together, or the two substances becoming one. To ascribe human attributes to "God" would have been ascribing humanity to the "Godhead." Thus, he could not say that "God" could be "two and three months old." See Socrates Scholasticus "The Ecclesiastical History of Socrates Scholasticus," in *Nicene and Post-Nicene Fathers of the Christian Church*, 2d series, Vol. II, ed. Philip Schaff and Henry Wace (Grand Rapids, MI: Wm. B. Eerdmans Pub. Co., 1952), 170-171. At the same time, in his opposition to Arianism, he resisted calling the Word of God a creature. Nestorius' response to his opponents' charges appears in the work attributed to him. See Nestorius, *The Bazaar of Heracleides*, ed. and trans. G. R. Driver and L. Hodgson (Oxford: Oxford University Press, 1925).

[367] Theodore told him to be careful, to be moderate, and to respect the opinions of others. All of which he appears to have ignored. See Moffett, *HCA I*, 173.

[368] The Nestorians were noted linguists, who translated Greek science and philosophy first into Syriac, then into Arabic. For this reason many Nestorian scholars were favored in Muslim courts. See Joseph M. Kitagawa, *The Christian Tradition: Beyond Its European Captivity* (Philadelphia: Trinity Press International, 1992), 13.

[369] Moffett, *HCA I*, 300-301.

[370] Ibid., 306.

[371] Walter Sundberg, from a December 16, 1999 e-mail correspondence.

[372] This is likely the reason that the Portuguese came to know them as "Syrians." See Neil, *HCM*, 123.

[373] Neill, *HCM*, 122-123.

[374] Cary-Elwes, *China and the Cross*, 39.

[375] There are times where those who were identified as Nestorian, simply because they had some knowledge of Christian things, may have in fact been Manicheans, who also had a presence in China.

[376] Cary-Elwes, *China and the Cross*, 42.

[377] Neill, *HCM*, 126.

[378] Ibid., 127.

[379] Ibid., 127.

[380] Ibid., 127.

³⁸¹Ibid., 127.

³⁸²Gonzáles, *The Early Church*, 404.

³⁸³Kitagawa, *The Christian Tradition*, 12. The Portuguese also understood that although the Pope apportioned to them the vast territory of Africa, the entire Orient covered too much area to conquer. It made better sense to forsake the idea of conquest and pursue a policy of trade. See González, *The Early Church*, 403.

³⁸⁴González, *The Early Church*, 402.

³⁸⁵Samuel Moffett, *A History of Christianity in Asia, Volume II: 1500–1900* (Maryknoll, NY: Orbis Books, 2005), 11.

³⁸⁶Neill, *HCM*, 128.

³⁸⁷Gonzáles, *The Early Church*, 404.

³⁸⁸Neill, *HCM*, 129.

³⁸⁹Gonzáles, *The Early Church*, 405.

³⁹⁰Japanese refer to their country as either Nihon or Nippon, which means the place where the sun rises, written with the Chinese characters for "sun" and "source."

³⁹¹Neill, *HCM*, 132.

³⁹²Those who would follow him—Toyotomi Hideyoshi, and the Tokugawa rulers—would reverse this policy by supporting Buddhism and severely persecuting Christianity.

³⁹³Neill, *HCM*, 133.

³⁹⁴Ibid., 134.

³⁹⁵Ibid., 134-135.

³⁹⁶Cary-Elwes, *China and the Cross*, 79.

³⁹⁷Neill, *HCM*, 135.

³⁹⁸Ibid., 135.

³⁹⁹Ibid., 135.

⁴⁰⁰Ibid., 135-136.

⁴⁰¹Lamin Sanneh, *Translating the Message: The Missionary Impact on Culture* (Maryknoll, NY: Orbis Books, 1997), 93.

⁸⁰Ibid., 94.

⁴⁰²Ibid., 94-95.

⁴⁰³Ibid., 95.

⁴⁰⁴Ibid., 95.

⁴⁰⁵Ibid., 96.

⁴⁰⁶Ross, *A Vision Betrayed*, 47.

⁴⁰⁷Anesaki, *History of Japanese Religion*, 242-243.

⁴⁰⁸Ibid., 243. On this same page, 243, Anesaki praises Ukon Takayama's life, as a "happy union of the valour [sic] of a Japanese warrior and the fidelity of an ardent Catholic. His brilliant military achievements, his moral integrity and deliberateness in critical moments, his dauntless spirit combined with meek soul, his earnest zeal in piety expressed in his generosity and charity, all this should be noted as a fruit of Kirishitan missions." Moffett gives information, in his second volume of *A History of Christianity in Asia*, on the career of Takayama Ukon, also noting his strong faith in adversity. See Moffett, *A History of Christianity in Asia, Volume II*, 80-81. Hereafter, *HCA II*.

⁴⁰⁹Anesaki, *History of Japanese Religion*, 244.

⁴¹⁰Hideyoshi sent five questions to Coelho. Among them were the following: why the Jesuits induced their disciples and secretaries to overthrow the Buddhist temples, why they persecuted the *bonzes*

(priests), and why they allowed the merchants of their nation to buy Japanese as slaves for the Indies. Kosaku Tamura cites a quotation from the archives of the Academy of History in Spain describing this heinous traffic. "Even the very lascars and scullions of the Portuguese purchase and carry slaves away. Here it happens that many of them die on the voyage, because they are heaped up upon each other...it even often happens that the Kaffirs cannot procure the necessary food for them. These scullions give a scandalous example by living in debauchery with the girls they have bought, and whom some of them introduce into their cabins on the passage to Macao. I here omit the excesses committed on the lands of the pagans, where the Portuguese spread themselves to recruit youths and girls, and where they live in such a fashion that the pagans themselves are stupefied at it." See John M. L. Young, *The Two Empires in Japan* (Philadelphia: The Presbyterian and Reformed Publishing Co., 1961), 14-15.

[411] Ross, *A Vision Betrayed*, 84.

[412] Moffett, HCA II, 81. Then, for what appears to have been a fear of Christianity becoming a political threat, another wave of persecution broke out once again. The government promulgated edicts in 1606 and again in 1614 forbidding Christianity. They posted public signposts around the country with the following details: Christianity is forbidden; heresy is strictly forbidden; an informant against a padre will be given 200 pieces of silver; 100 pieces will be given to an informant against an Irmao (brother); 50 pieces of silver to an informant against a Christian. If the informant is a Christian and forsakes the faith, they will be forgiven and awarded as outlined above. Under the Tokugawas, the gains made under Nobunaga were lost. Reports from 1634 showed that there were no priests in Japan; by 1672, reports said that there were no Christians in Japan. The reality is that the church went underground. According to Latourette, "Several thousand Christians, most of them in the hills back of Nagasaki, held to their faith. Outwardly they were Buddhists, but they kept up baptism and Christian prayers, transmitting them to their children and the latter in turn to theirs. It was not until the second half of the nineteenth century that they were revealed to a startled Europe and to hostile political authorities." See Latourette, *A History of Christianity*, 938.

[413] Moffett, HCA II, 84-85.

[414] Ibid., 85.

[415] Ibid., 85.

[416] Ibid., 85.

[417] Ibid., 87.

[418] Ibid., 88.

[419] Ibid., 88.

[420] Ibid., 90.

[421] Ibid., 89-90.

[422] See Endo, *Silence*, and Shusaku Endo, *The Golden Country*, trans. Francis Mathy (Rutland, VT: Charles E. Tuttle Company, 1970).

[423] Moffett, HCA II, 92.

[424] Neill, HCM, 160.

[425] Moffett, HCA II, 89.

[426] Ibid., 83.

[427] Ibid., 107.

[428] Ibid., 107.

[429] Ibid., 108. Brackets are Moffett's.

[430] Ibid., 109-110.

⁴³¹Covell, *CBC*, 41.

⁴³²Neill, *HCM*, 139.

⁴³³Moffett, *HCA II*, 111.

⁴³⁴Ibid., 111.

⁴³⁵Covell, *CBC*, 46.

⁴³⁶Amos Yong, "Discerning the Spirit(s) in the World of Religions: Toward a Pneumatological Theology of Religions," in *No Other Gods Before Me?*, ed. John G. Stackhouse (Grand Rapids, MI: Baker Academic, 2001), 37-61. Although there is validity in considering the aspect pre-evangelism in such cultures, one cannot ignore the pattern of the apostles and others in the book of Acts, who used aspects of culture for the purpose of analogy. Nevertheless, at the same time, the death and resurrection of Jesus remained central in their preaching of the gospel, even if it meant martyrdom.

⁴³⁷Covell, *CBC*, 47-48.

⁴³⁸Ibid., 48-49. It is interesting to compare the *kenosis* of Jesus and the "nothingness" of Buddhism, as Koyama has done. Although there are similarities, such as a repudiation of selfish desires, there are also great differences that affect the outcome of each, and make an eternity of difference in the disciple of each. In Buddhism, the goal is to escape suffering through renunciation of the "I," or the extinction of the self, which is the way of *apatheia*. In Christianity, suffering is resolved in Jesus who is full of *pathos* and who took suffering unto Himself on our behalf. See Koyama's chapter, "Cool *Arahant* and Hot God," in *Waterbuffalo Theology*, 133-160.

⁴³⁹Covell, *CBC*, 62-63.

⁴⁴⁰Ibid., 64.

⁴⁴¹Ibid., 64.

⁴⁴²Ibid., 65.

⁴⁴³Ibid., 65-66.

⁴⁴⁴Ibid., 66.

⁴⁴⁵Ibid., 66.

⁴⁴⁶Moffett, *HCA II*, 309.

⁴⁴⁷Ibid., 309. Brackets are Moffett's.

⁴⁴⁸Ibid., 310.

⁴⁴⁹Ibid., 310.

⁴⁵⁰Ibid., 311.

⁴⁵¹Ibid., 312-313. Moffett's chapter fourteen, from which this information is taken, appears to have an earlier draft form inserted into it, since from page 311-313, the information of the first paragraphs is repeated in a second section with different wording. Then his last thought from the first section picks up in a third section on page 313.

⁴⁵²Ibid., 316-317.

⁴⁵³Ibid., 286.

⁴⁵⁴Ibid., 287.

⁴⁵⁵Covell, *CBC*, 69-70.

⁴⁵⁶Ibid., 70.

⁴⁵⁷Neill, *HCM*, 242.

⁴⁵⁸Covell, *CBC*, 76.

⁴⁵⁹Ibid., 75.

⁴⁶⁰Ibid., 75.

⁴⁶¹Ibid., 76-77.

⁴⁶²Ibid., 78.

⁴⁶³Covell, *CBC*, 81. Brackets are Covell's.

⁴⁶⁴Ibid., 82.

⁴⁶⁵Ibid., 82.

⁴⁶⁶Ibid., 84.

⁴⁶⁷Moffett, *HCA II*, 297.

⁴⁶⁸Cary-Elwes, *China and the Cross*, 200-201.

⁴⁶⁹Moffett, *HCA II*, 463-464.

⁴⁷⁰Ibid., 466.

⁴⁷¹Hudson Taylor first landed in Shanghai in 1854, under the Chinese Evangelization Society. Neill referred to the CES as "a curiously incompetent body which almost wholly failed to meet its obligations, and after an inglorious career went into dissolution." See Neill, *HCM*, 282. It was during this period that Taylor adopted Chinese dress and style and found it to his liking.

⁴⁷²Moffett, *HCA II*, 531.

⁴⁷³Everett N. Hunt, Jr., *Protestant Pioneers in Korea* (Maryknoll, NY: Orbis Books, 1980), 7-8.

⁴⁷⁴Ibid., 10-11.

⁴⁷⁵Ibid., 12.

⁴⁷⁶Ibid., 13.

⁴⁷⁷Ibid., 22.

⁴⁷⁸Moffett, *HCA II*, 532.

⁴⁷⁹Ibid., 532-533.

⁴⁸⁰Hunt, *Protestant Pioneers in Korea*, 30. Hereafter, *PPK*.

⁴⁸¹Moffett, *HCA II*, 536.

⁴⁸²Mark Noll, "Evangelical Identity, Power, and Culture in the 'Great' Nineteenth Century," in *Christianity Reborn: The Global Expansion of Evangelicalism in the Twentieth Century*, ed. Donald M. Lewis (Grand Rapids, MI: Wm. B. Eerdmans Pub. Co., 2004), 49.

⁴⁸³Ibid., 49.

⁴⁸⁴Moffett, *HCA II*, 533.

⁴⁸⁵See Sanneh, *Translating the Message*.

⁴⁸⁶Noll, "Evangelical Identity, Power, and Culture in the 'Great' Nineteenth Century," 49-50.

⁴⁸⁷See Suh, *The Korean Minjung in Christ*.

⁴⁸⁸Newbigin, *Mission in Christ's Way*, 9.

⁴⁸⁹Moffett, *HCA II*, 502.

⁴⁹⁰Ibid., 503-504.

⁴⁹¹Ibid., 504.

⁴⁹²Ibid., 505.

⁴⁹³Ibid., 505.

⁴⁹⁴About a year later (1861), a Russian Orthodox missionary arrived on the northern island of Hokkaido. It would be seven years before he saw his first two converts baptized. The Russian Orthodox Church managed to keep itself free from Russian politics, and emphasized the inclusion of Japanese leaders into the supervision of the church along with European missionaries. In 1875, at the first Great Synod of the Japanese Orthodox Mission, the first two

Japanese priests were ordained, and they saw a total membership of 25,700. See Moffett, *HCA II*, 506-507.

⁴⁹⁵Ibid., 507.

⁴⁹⁶ Ibid., 507.

⁴⁹⁷Young, *The Two Empires in Japan*, 31-32.

⁴⁹⁸Ibid., 32.

⁴⁹⁹Ibid., 69.

⁵⁰⁰Ibid., 69.

⁵⁰¹Richard H. Drummond, "The Non-Church Movement in Japan," *Journal of Ecumenical Studies* 2, no. 3 (Fall 1965): 448-450.

⁵⁰²Akio Dohi, "The First Generation," in *A History of Japanese Theology*, ed. Yasuo Furuya (Grand Rapids, MI: Wm. B. Eerdmans Pub. Co.,1997), 18-19. See also Uchimura's autobiography, in Kanzo Uchimura, *How I Became a Christian*, vol. 15 of *The Works of Uchimura* (Tokyo: Kyobunkwan, 1895), 19.

⁵⁰³Drummond, "The Non-Church Movement in Japan," 449.

⁵⁰⁴Akio Dohi, "Historical Development of the Non-Church Movement in Japan," *Journal of Ecumenical Studies* 2, no. 3 (Fall 1965): 453.

⁵⁰⁵Drummond, "The Non-Church Movement in Japan," 449.

⁵⁰⁶Ibid., 451.

⁵⁰⁷Ibid., 450.

⁵⁰⁸Dohi, "The First Generation," 38.

⁵⁰⁹Drummond, "The Non-Church Movement in Japan," 448.

⁵¹⁰Kanzo Uchimura, *How I Became a Christian*, vol. 15 of *The Works of Uchimura* (Tokyo: Kyobunkwan, 1895), 19.

⁵¹¹See Gerald R. McDermott, *Can Evangelicals Learn From World Religions? Jesus, Revelation and Religious Traditions* (Downers Grove, IL: InterVarsity Press, 2000), 13-14.

⁵¹²Newbigin, *Mission in Christ's Way*, 7.

⁵¹³Kitamori, *Theology of the Pain of God*, 12, 22. Italics added.

⁵¹⁴Amin Maalouf, *In the Name of Identity: Violence and the Need to Belong* (New York: Arcade Publishing, 2001), 14. Maalouf explores the issue of identity, especially in light of human violence. It is another voice in the conversation enjoined by scholars such as Samuel Huntington and Benjamin Barber. Since identity has become an important topic, especially with the end of the cold war, we may find here yet another perspective that lends itself to important thinking and discussion about missions and evangelization.

⁵¹⁵Maalouf, *In the Name of Identity*, 10.

⁵¹⁶Scherer, *GCK*, 35.

⁵¹⁷Robert J. Schreiter, *The New Catholicity: Theology Between the Global and the Local* (Maryknoll, NY: Orbis Books, 1997), 9.

⁵¹⁸Samuel Escobar, "The Global Scenario at the Turn of the Century," in *Global Missiology for the 21st Century*, ed. William D. Taylor (Grand Rapids, MI: Baker Academic, 2000), 30-31.

⁵¹⁹Ibid., 31.

⁵²⁰Ibid., 32.

⁵²¹Ibid., 33.

⁵²²Ibid., 33. Escobar cites reports on Philadelphia, PA, Brazil, South Korea and South Africa.

[523] Song, *Third-Eye Theology*, 9.

[524] Song, *The Compassionate God*, 7.

[525] See Yong, "Discerning the Spirit(s) in the World of Religions," 37-61.

[526] See the report, Bong Rin Ro, ed. *Christian Alternatives to Ancestor Practices* (Taichung, Taiwan, ROC: Asia Theological Association, 1985).

[527] González, *The Early Church to the Dawn of the Reformation*, 95.

[528] Jan-Martin Berentsen, "Ancestor Worship in Missiological Perspective," in *Christian Alternatives to Ancestor Practices*, ed. Bong Rin Ro (Taichung, Taiwan, ROC: Asia Theological Association, 1985), 265.

[529] Chizuo Shibata, "Some Problematic Aspects of Ancestor Worship," in *Christian Alternatives to Ancestor Practices*, ed. Bong Rin Ro (Taichung, Taiwan, ROC: Asia Theological Association, 1985), 252.

[530] Jan-Martin Berentsen, "The Ancestral Rites—Barrier or Bridge," in *Christian Alternatives to Ancestor Practices*, ed. Bong Rin Ro (Taichung, Taiwan, ROC: Asia Theological Association, 1985), 290-292.

[531] Berentsen, "The Ancestral Rites—Barrier or Bridge," 294.

[532] Donald McGavran, "Honoring Ancestors in Japan," in *Christian Alternatives to Ancestor Practices*, ed. Bong Rin Ro (Taichung, Taiwan, ROC: Asia Theological Association, 1985), 312.

[533] For this reason, if for no other, we must take the Bible seriously as God's revealed Word and the only revealed source and norm for faith. While Barth held that the action of God alone is revelation, Jesus also held to the authority of the Word, "It is written..." Although this Word must not negate human culture, as has sometimes been the case with Fundamentalism, it must nevertheless speak prophetically to culture, and serve as the final arbiter of Truth for all cultures.

Acknowledgments

First, I thank God for the opportunity to know Him and to serve Him through the love and grace of our Lord Jesus Christ, and for His sustaining grace throughout this process. I am also thankful for the many people He has placed in my path over the years who have encouraged me to grow in the knowledge of His Truth, and to serve Him with my life. I wish to thank the many professors, pastors, colleagues and friends in the Church of the Lutheran Brethren, and at Northwestern College, St. Paul, who have had a hand in providing a Godly and biblical foundation for the vocation to which God has called me. I am also grateful for my students at Northwestern College for giving me the opportunity to put into practice and to share with others what I have received.

My appreciation also goes to the capable faculty and staff of Luther Seminary for their dedication to equipping and enabling their students to become what God has called us to be. I wish to express particular thanks to Dr. Mark Swanson and Dr. Frieder Ludwig for serving as my thesis readers, and to Dr. Lois Malcolm, Dr. Lee Snook, and Dr. Kosuke Koyama who graciously helped me through my exams and dissertation proposal.

I praise the Lord especially for my family—my wife Joy, and my children Tim, Michelle and Joel, who encouraged me throughout the process of studying and writing. I also thank the Lord for my extended family—those associated with both the Mathiesens and the Larsens—who stood alongside of us and cheered us on.

Finally, I wish to express my deepest gratitude to my doctoral advisor, Dr. Charles Amjad-Ali, who proved to be a dear brother and friend as well as a very capable mentor. I am deeply thankful to him for the achievement of this milestone.